Routledge Revivals

A Siberian Journey

A Siberian Journey

The Journal of Hans Jakob Fries,
1774-1776

Walther Kirchner

First published in 1974 by Frank Cass and Company Limited

This edition first published in 2018 by Routledge
2 Park Square, Milton Park, Abingdon, Oxon, OX14 4RN
and by Routledge
52 Vanderbilt Avenue, New York, NY 10017, USA

Routledge is an imprint of the Taylor & Francis Group, an informa business

© 1974 Walther Kirchner

All rights reserved. No part of this book may be reprinted or reproduced or utilised in any form or by any electronic, mechanical, or other means, now known or hereafter invented, including photocopying and recording, or in any information storage or retrieval system, without permission in writing from the publishers.

Publisher's Note
The publisher has gone to great lengths to ensure the quality of this reprint but points out that some imperfections in the original copies may be apparent.

Disclaimer
The publisher has made every effort to trace copyright holders and welcomes correspondence from those they have been unable to contact.
A Library of Congress record exists under ISBN:

ISBN 13: 978-0-367-02265-5 (hbk)
ISBN 13: 978-0-367-02268-6 (pbk)
ISBN 13: 978-0-429-40049-0 (ebk)

Printed in the United Kingdom
by Henry Ling Limited

RUSSIA THROUGH EUROPEAN EYES No. 20

General Editor:

Dr. A. G. CROSS, University of East Anglia

A Siberian Journey

A Siberian Journey

The Journal of Hans Jakob Fries, 1774-1776

Translated from the German and edited
with a bibliographical introduction by

Walther Kirchner

FRANK CASS: LONDON

First published 1974 in Great Britain by
FRANK CASS AND COMPANY LIMITED
67 Great Russell Street, London WC1B 3BT, England

and in United States of America by
FRANK CASS AND COMPANY LIMITED
c/o International Scholarly Book Services, Inc.
P.O. Box 4347, Portland, Oregon 97208

Introduction Copyright © 1974 Walther Kirchner

First German Edition 1955
First English Edition 1974

ISBN 0 7146 2964 2

Library of Congress Catalog Card No. 72-92962

All rights Reserved. No part of this publication may be reproduced in any form or by any means, electronic, mechanical, photocopying, recording or other, without the prior permission of Frank Cass and Company Limited in writing.

Printed in Great Britain by Netherton & Worth Ltd., London and Truro.

Contents

Preface to the First English Edition ix
A Note on the Translation x
Preface to the Original German Edition xi

PART I TRAVEL ACCOUNTS OF SIBERIA, 1725-1825

1 Bibliographies and Guides to Sources 3
2 Travel Accounts before 1775 11

John Bell (1719-21); Georg Johann Unverzagt (1719-21); Lorenz Lange (1719-21); Daniel Amadeus Messerschmidt (1720-6); Philipp Johann von Strahlenberg (1720-2); The Swedes: C. F. von Wreech, J. B. Müller, H. Fick, H. Busch, J. Ch. Schnitscher, J. G. Renat, G. Schober (1711-43); Johann Unkowski (1722-3); Vitus Bering (1725-30, 1733-41); Sven Waxell (1733-49); Johann Georg Gmelin (1733-42); Louis de l'Isle de la Croyère (1733-41); Gerhard Friedrich Müller (1733-41); Johann Eberhard Fischer (1740-1); Stepan Petrovich Krasheninnikov (1733-41); Georg Wilhelm Steller (1738-46); Jakob Lindenau (1733-46); Chappe d'Auteroche (1761); Johann Ludwig Wagner (1759-63); Peter Ivanovich Rychkov (1762); Erik Laxmann (1763-9, 1786-90); Mauritius Augustus de Benyowski (1770); Peter Simon Pallas (1768-74); Johann Peter Falck (1771-3); Johann Gottlieb Georgi (1771-3); Ivan Lepekhin (1770); N. P. Rychkov and D. S. Gmelin (1769-71).

3 Travel Accounts after 1775 33

Regnier (1774-5); A. M. Patrin (1781-2); Samuel Bentham (1781-2); Peter Ivanovich Shangin (1785); Joseph Billings (1785-6); John Ledyard (1786-7); Gavriil Andreevich Sarychev (1785-6); Jean Baptiste de Lesseps (1788); Johann Sievers (1790-4); Abbé de Fabry (1798-1800); Augustus von Kotzebue (1801); Gavrilo Ivanovich Davydov (1802-3); Georg von Langsdorff (1807-8); John D'Wolf (1807); Julius Heinrich von Klaproth (1805-7); Peter Dobell (1812); Andrei Efimovich Martynov (1812);

Johann Friedrich Erdmann (1816); John D. Cochrane (1820-2); James Holman (1820-4); F. P. Vrangel (1820-4); Alexander von Humboldt and M. Hedenström (1829); Adolph Erman (1828-9); Christoph Hansteen (1828-9).

4 Hans Jakob Fries   48
His Life; His Travel Descriptions; His Routes.

PART II   HANS JAKOB FRIES'S JOURNEY THROUGH SIBERIA, 1774-1776

Introduction; Campaign against the Turks; Winter Quarters in Poland; Expedition against the Zaporogian Cossacks; Winter Quarters on the Volga; Preparations for the Siberian Trip; From Kazan to Orenburg; From Orenburg to Omsk; From Omsk to Irkutsk; In Irkutsk; Across Lake Baikal; To the Chinese Border; In Kiakhta and Maimachen; Back to Omsk; Across the Urals; In Orenburg and on the Volga; To St. Petersburg; Conclusion; Postscript.

Notes and References   155
Bibliography   168
Index   175

Maps

		Page
1	Fries's journey from Moscow to Wallachia and back to the Volga, 1773-1775	80
2	Fries's journey through Western Siberia from Kazan to Kainsk and his way back to Samara, 1776	97
3	Fries's journey through Central Siberia from Kainsk to the Chinese border at Kiakhta and back to Kainsk, 1776	128

List of Illustrations

		Facing Page
1	Russian sledges used for travelling and for conveying baggage, provisions, etc. in winter	68
2	View of Tobolsk	69
3	View of Tomsk	69
4	View of Irkutsk	84
5	View of Chinese frontier town, Maimatschin, with the brook Kiakhta, taken from the West	84
6	Interior of a Russian dwelling at night	85

Preface to the first English edition

Twenty years have passed since the publication of the original German version of the Fries manuscript and of the extensive introduction serving to give a survey of eighteenth-century Western travellers who visited Siberia and published accounts of their experiences. During these years, interest in Russia's Eastern possessions has steadily increased. Soviet scholars, in particular, have taken a new look at the early history of that vast area, and in East and West, substantial bibliographical and descriptive works have been published. When the need for republishing the Fries account of 1779—in an English translation—arose, I was, therefore, faced with the question whether or not to make additions to the original publication. I am particularly grateful to the publishers, Frank Cass, and to Dr. Anthony Cross of East Anglia University, for having not only agreed to a change but for having encouraged me in my intention to review the whole and enlarge its scope. Dr. Cross, in particular, has made valuable suggestion as to materials previously not included. Thus, the new edition extends to some aspects at the beginning of the period here under investigation and to some geographical areas, especially in the Far East, which had not been considered in the earlier edition. In connection with these changes, the bibliography has also been enlarged.

Finally, my thanks go to the Osteuropa Institut in München, to its former director, Professor G. Stadtmüller, and to Dr. G. Robel for kind permission to publish the Fries book in a new form—and in English.

Princeton, N.J. WALTHER KIRCHNER
April 1974

A Note on the Translation

Transliteration follows the rules applied by the Library of Congress, as modified by leading journals, but for names or words in common use, the customary and conventional spelling has been preferred. In the text of the published manuscript, the original spelling of names of persons and places has been preserved and, wherever necessary, an English spelling has been added in parenthesis.

Preface to the Original German Edition

In the summer of 1948, when visiting Swiss archives and libraries in order to study early Russian-Western relations, my path led me also to Zürich. The director of the Zentralbibliothek there kindly called my attention to the manuscript which I here submit to the reader.

I want to express my thanks to him and his assistants for the interest which they have taken in my studies. Likewise, I wish to thank the Committee of Research of the University of Delaware for a grant given me to assist with my study of Swiss materials. My special thanks go, moreover, to the numerous librarians, archivists and library assistants who, owing to their interest, knowledge, and understanding, have done so much to further the progress of my investigations. Without their help, many an important document which contributed to the successful conclusion of my study would have escaped my attention.

Last not least, my thanks go to the Deutsche Forschungsgemeinschaft in Bad Godesberg for making possible the publication; to Professor Hans Koch for accepting this travel account for the historical series of the Osteuropa Institut in München, and to his co-workers for the scholarship and care shown when getting the manuscript ready for the printer.

University of Delaware, Newark WALTHER KIRCHNER
December 1955

PART I

Travel Accounts of Siberia, 1725-1825

1 Bibliographies and Guides to Sources

Our knowledge of eighteenth-century Siberia is both considerable and unsatisfactory. Significantly enough there is ample material available dealing with administrative measures, economic conditions, social structure, and institutional problems. Everything that reaches the world and, ultimately, the historian through official channels, through statistics, orders, and government reports, is well provided for. Two studies in the English language, such as George Lantzeff's *Siberia in the seventeenth century*[1] and Raymond H. Fisher's *The Russian Fur Trade, 1550–1700*[2] have shown how clear a picture—for the seventeenth century—can be gained of conditions prevailing in Russia's eastern dominions. Yet these very studies also indicate the limitations of our knowledge and make us wish for more sources on the natural history of Siberia and for additional, more intimate and direct personal observations that are able to give life to governmental institutions and blood and passion to men at work.

If such is the case for the seventeenth century, it is still more so for the following one. For, peculiarly enough, our information for the seventeenth century compares in many respects favourably with that for the eighteenth, possibly because in the early stages of the penetration of Siberia the scope of the country's history is limited; it is largely concerned with discoveries and the setting up of an administrative machinery, while in the eighteenth century Siberia became a large, expanding and complex organism, an understanding of which asks for a far greater amount of historical sources. Soviet scholars have done considerable research, but first-hand information is by no means available in proportion to the increase in Siberia's importance, and particularly personal observations preserved for us in sober, discriminating travel accounts, which have proved so valuable for the writing of American, German, and French history, remain disappointing. Visitors to Russian Asia, to be sure, were rapidly increasing in numbers, but most of them were officials who either lacked the time, opportunity, or interest to observe, or the ability to write, or—if they were possessed of both—the courage to report fully and frankly. Indeed, the Russian government in many respects imposed strict secrecy upon them, an obligation that most visitors respected. Therefore, those accounts which we do possess, while generally more detailed, scientific and satisfactory than earlier ones, are by no means numerous. No comprehensive study, list, or collection of them is available, even though a number of discussions of travel accounts, encompassing much of Siberia's history, exist. There is, for instance, the compilation by M. P. Alekseev, who in his *Sibir: V isvestiakh zapadno-evropeiskikh puteshestvennikov i pisatelei*[3] lists foreign travellers in Siberia. But this work of his spans only the times from the thirteenth to the seventeenth century, and for this last century he finds twenty-six[4] known and two anonymous voyagers who left descriptions of Siberia. It is neither as useful nor as complete as, e.g., Friedrich von Adelung's account of early travellers in European Russia. Likewise, L. S. Berg's *Ocherki po istorii russkikh geografcheskikh otkrytii*[5] can lay no claim to being a comprehensive survey of the available material. Another list of similar character has been compiled by Georg Henning, who reported in the *Mitteilungen des Vereins für Erdkunde zu Leipzig*[6] on Siberian travel accounts from Sigismund Herberstein's famous first visit to Russia in 1516 to 1518, to the time of the embassy which in the years 1692 to 1695 took Isbrand Ides all through Siberia to the confines of China. Ides's embassy which like most other journeys was undertaken by foreigners in Russian service, is an important and convenient milestone for the historian.[7] It marks the conclusion of the first stage in Siberia's development. There follows a brief transition period during the time of Peter the Great, which includes that part of Peter's reign which was absorbed by western tasks and particularly by the struggle for access to the Baltic Sea. The two volumes of the *Pamiatniki sibirskoi istorii XVIII veka*[8] give a survey of the advances in the knowledge of Siberia made during this transition period; they end with the year 1724. Only toward the last years of Peter's rule did Siberia move again into the foreground; the great embassy of Lev Vasilevich Izmailov in 1719 bears witness of the country's growing significance and Russia's renewed interest in Asia.

It is at this point that the present study begins. It will treat mainly of central Siberia and cover essentially the century that followed Peter's death in 1725 and ended with the death of Alexander I in 1825. The most important older guide for this eventful period is Vladimir I. Mezhov's *Sibirskaia bibliografiia*,[9] which contains in volume II special sections devoted to exploration and travel accounts. Included in these are not only books, but also a number of shorter accounts taken from periodicals, among which the *Sibirskii Vestnik* and the *Severnii Arkhiv* are the most prominent.

Since Mezhov, a number of competent new works have appeared. M. P. Andreev has continued his earlier studies and dealt in detail with the first half of the eighteenth century.[10] Unfortunately, he could not complete his work, which was published posthumously. More than half of it is devoted to the voyages of Gerhard Friedrich Müller, Krasheninnikov, and Steller; yet it provides a valuable guide also to additional travel accounts which either exist in print or were found by Andreev in the archives of the Akademia Nauk and in various Siberian depositaries. However, he very justly emphasizes that many of these accounts, composed as they sometimes were in the later lives of their authors, reflect, rather than personal experiences, a knowledge gained indirectly, and often even simply from the reading of books. Caution in accepting their evidence and further search in the archives seemed to him, therefore, to be indicated.[11]

Another useful work is that of V. G. Mirsoev. His *Istoriografiia Sibiri (XVIII v)* covers the eighteenth century,[12] and a second volume deals with the first half of the nineteenth.[13] The two volumes are not as original and encompassing as Andreev's historiographies and, moreover, bear an ideological stamp which sometimes detracts from their scholarly value. Mirsoev surveys not so much sources as second-hand accounts of Siberia; and even when these were written by men with some personal acquaintance with Siberia, they still retain the character of secondary material. Among the publications which Mirsoev discusses is that of V. N. Tatishchev (d. 1750), one of the "fathers" of Russian history, who derived his knowledge from documentary sources which he studied critically, as well as from some of the travellers. The presentation is useful since Tatishchev made historical as well as geographical contributions to our knowledge of Siberia.[14] Mirsoev further deals with Shcherbatov, whose dependence on Müller he emphasizes.[15] Eventually he discusses the works of the great explorers Müller, Gmelin, Falk, Fischer, and Pallas. Minor accounts, such as that by Fries and others, have been unduly neglected. Mirsoev pays considerable attention to the Far Eastern area and its visitors; he mentions members and activities of the Russian-American Company and he deals with the various expeditions around the world. This extreme eastern area is naturally only marginally considered here because it lies beyond the horizon of the subject of our volume, Jakob Fries.

Of greater use than Mirsoev's two volumes is E. P. Zinner's recent monograph on Western travellers in Siberia.[16] Not only does Zinner identify numerous (though by no means all) Western travellers who left accounts but also analyzes and soberly criticizes their work. He makes many references to the major contemporary publications which came out abroad.

An *Istoriia Sibiri,* which appeared in the same year as Zinner's volume, though placing the accent mainly on population questions, colonization, social conditions, trade and agriculture, constitutes a further valuable guide because it includes a detailed map on which the routes of major travellers are entered—of Messerschmidt, Bering, Gmelin and Müller, Steller, Lindenau, Falk, Lepekhin, Rychkov, Pallas, Georgi, Zuev, and Sarychev.[17] In addition to the *Istoriia Sibiri,* the work by M. M. Gromyko is useful[18] because it brings population data which can serve as a check on the report, observations, and figures which Jakob Fries supplies. A number of differences appear but perhaps do no more than reflect, among other things, the rapid changes which occurred in Siberia. Thus, the development of the metallurgical industries in the Kolyvan-Voskresensky and Barnaul regions (which Fries did not see) accounted for changes in the direction of growth, while natural disasters, and particularly fires which regularly ravaged Siberian towns, caused set-backs.

In the English language, a good guide is Robert J. Kerner's *Northeastern Asia*.[19] Like Mezhov's work, it is a general bibliography and cannot lay claim to completeness with regard to travel accounts, but of the Siberian guides published in non-Russian languages it undoubtedly proves most valuable for research in the field. Another English compilation may be found in Edward G. Cox's *A Reference Guide to the Literature of Travel*.[20] Volume I contains a separate chapter on Siberia, but despite its concentration on travel, it is of considerably less help than either Mezhov or Kerner. To these two must be added Harry W. Nerhood's *To Russia and Return*,[21] a bibliographical list of Russian travel accounts in the English language. Furthermore, the bibliographies of three monographs by Clifford M. Foust,[22] James R. Gibson,[23] and Gaston Cahen[24] are helpful.

By dealing with the geography of Russia's Asiatic realms, a number of other works prove useful, although they do not deal directly with travels and descriptions of central Siberia, but are rather indirectly related to Siberian journeys and the fruit these bore. They are monographs which discuss maps drawn of Siberia—maps which in turn were the results of the work of travellers and their surveys of the land. One such work is the already mentioned article by Georg Henning, published in 1905.[25] The other is by Gaston Cahen, whose book, *Les Cartes de la Sibérie au XVIIIe siècle*,[26] came out in 1911 and ranks as a classic also among Soviet scholars. It gives a significant, yet far more comprehensive picture than Henning's of the growing acquaintance with Siberia's wide areas and the interrelationships of river and mountain systems and chains, as they became known in the era of the Enlightenment. Accompanying texts bear witness to the improvements in map making as well as the more practical issues of Russian road building, travelling methods, and settlements, and furnish us with an indirect approach to a study of Siberian travellers and the accounts of their journeys. Map making was, of course, encouraged, if not altogether organized, by the Russian government, and sometimes the explorer and traveller himself sketched the map, sometimes it was left to special draftsmen, like Berkhan or Lürsenius, who were, as companions of the explorers, assigned to the task.[27]

In any case, the student of travel in Siberia will do well not to rely exclusively on written evidence. Historians have made far too little use of artefacts, illustrations, and other non-literary evidence. Many of the foreign travellers, especially of the two great expeditions into the interior of Siberia and of the Second Kamchatka expedition of Bering, were accompanied not only by map makers, but—in an age before the invention of photography—also by painters, and some of the scientists could themselves paint tolerably well. Their publications were therefore often accompanied by illustrations which inform us, at a glance, of the countryside, people, dress and implements. Well known among the painters was Plenisner, who participated in Bering's voyage and accompanied Steller in Kamchatka, and who later became commandant of Okhotsk.

If, thus, there are various sources but no complete collections of foreign travel accounts and surveys of Western sources dealing with eighteenth-century Siberia, there are still some additional studies, limited as to area or time, which are useful in further inquiries. In 1876, Modest Bogdanov published in the *Russische Revue* a survey of voyages of the Aral and Caspian Sea region[28] which included many travellers who have described parts of Siberia as well. Here we find names such as Messerschmidt, Gmelin, Rychkov, Pallas, Lepekhin and others, who became famous as students of Russian Asia and whose work will presently be discussed. More useful still as a partial guide is the work of Gerhard Friedrich Müller, who published his famous *Sammlung Russischer Geschichte* a century before Bogdanov.[29] This collection of accounts is the result of a very careful investigation of all the then available material and is also based on practical personal experience; Müller gained the latter in his capacity of companion and member of the great scientific Siberian expedition which comprised the Second Kamchatka Expedition of Bering and, besides Bering, the group under the leadership of Gmelin. Müller had access to valuable Siberian archives, parts of which are now lost, and he reprinted and discussed the accounts of expeditions into Siberia beginning with what he termed the first trip, in 1608,[30] and pursuing his topic down to his time. Although he was accused by a contemporary of inaccuracies and omissions,[31] his collection has remained an indispensable source up to the present. Another German professor, Johann Eberhard Fischer, completed in abbreviated form what Müller had started but had never brought into a continuous narrative.[32] Then there is Johann Christoph Adelung, who published at approximately the same time as Müller and Fischer a collection of accounts of sea voyages and other expeditions which the Russians undertook along the northern coasts of Siberia in their attempts to find the North-East passage.[33] With regard to systematic information and special attention to inner Siberia, their accounts are all three surpassed by that of a fourth German scientist in Russian service, their younger colleague Johann Gottlieb Georgi. Like Müller, Georgi based his story largely on personal knowledge and contact, for he had the good fortune to accompany the second great scientific expedition through Siberia, that of Pallas, who revised and continued the task started by Müller's colleague Gmelin. Georgi's work is the only one to include a bibliography which comes close to being a comprehensive survey of travellers at least up to the time of his writing in 1775.[34] Lastly, a younger contemporary published a work which, though not dealing with travel literature, adds a few bits of information here and there because it is an inexhaustable mine of information about so many Russian affairs, namely the *History of Medicine in Russia* by Wilhelm Michael Richter.[35]

Besides the great reports by the Western explorers in Siberia and their friends and students at the Academy and elsewhere in Russia (and among their number, too, is Lomonosov, who worked with Krasheninnikov on an abridgment of the latter's account of Kamchatka), there exists some contemporary secondary material, which came out in Western countries and which, either because of the personal acquaintance of its editors with one or the other of the Siberian travellers or because of the study of the travel accounts and other written materials, constitutes a valuable addition to our knowledge. It comprises collections of travel reports, often provided with critical remarks. These collections bear witness to the real excitement which the explorations and discoveries of the great European scientists journeying in Siberia provoked all over the continent, and the pride which the world of the Enlightenment took in their achievements. Among them is volume X of the *Recueil de Voyages au Nord*[36] which devotes thirty pages to a "description of Siberia". Another is called *Voyages en Sibérie*[37] and contains excerpts from the journals of Gmelin, Pallas, Georgi, Falk, and Lepekhin. Shorter accounts of one point or another are embodied in writings by the astronomer Nicholas Delisle and the scholar Peter Müller. The diplomatic resident of the states of Braunschweig and Lüneburg, Friedrich Christian Weber, published two volumes on Russia, including Siberia.[38] Reference has already been made to Samuel Engel's work,[39] which brought accounts from Delisle, Buache, Gmelin, Müller, and also personal speculations of Engel himself and which came out in several editions. A notable contribution is also the work of Johann Benedikt Scherer, who was born in 1741 and was later a professor in Tübingen and who had for a time lived in Russia, although without visiting Siberia. He was personally acquainted with men like Müller and Fischer and he edited Steller's description of Kamchatka, but unfortunately his account lacks accuracy.[40] Somewhat later appeared the work of William Tooke,[41] a good observer of the Russian scene, but he is to a lesser extent concerned with Siberia.

Little can be learned from more recent general descriptions. N. A. Kubalski, for instance, who published a book called *Travels in Siberia* in 1853 in French, confined himself to giving a very sketchy account of the trips of Gmelin, Benyowski, and a Lithuanian prisoner, General Joseph Kopec. The latter was sent in 1794 to eastern Siberia and Kamchatka, from where he returned once more by way of Siberia, but without leaving more than an oral report. Nor do two twentieth-century publications by Herbert Scurla and A. V. Yefimov add much to our knowledge. The former includes excerpts from German travel accounts,[42] the latter deals chiefly with North Eastern Asia.[43] Likewise, the book by Youri Semionov[44] cannot pretend to be a comprehensive study of Siberia and still less a guide to travel literature, even though it contributes to our awareness of possible sources and acts as a stimulus to further research in the field.

2 Travel Accounts Before 1775

The century under consideration here, from 1725 to 1825, may be appropriately opened with a figure of great fame. His reputation rests, however, on discoveries in remote regions rather than on his travels through inner Siberia; for these travels have contributed little to knowledge of the country inasmuch as he gives no immediate account of them. This is Vitus Bering, who crossed Siberia first in 1725. His trip came at a time when, towards the end of his life, Peter the Great, always known for his western ideas and policies, had begun to reveal his interest also in his vast eastern realms and, aware of the manifold aspects of Russia's role, had turned his eyes and activities towards Asia. Obviously, his concern was not only, and perhaps not even primarily, with potential scientific and cultural achievements, but—in the sense of enlightened philosophy—equally with political and economic aims and with glory; and even Bering's expedition, so widely known for its geographical purpose, was largely determined by economic goals: trade and gold.

Bering's enterprise was not an isolated event; it must rather be considered as the climax of a number of undertakings which characterized Peter's preoccupations after the struggle against Sweden drew to a close. They were marked in the Near East by the campaigns of 1722 and 1723 against Persia, in the farther East by plans for explorations and acquisitions along Siberia's northern and eastern coasts, and by political arrangements with the ultimate eastern neighbours, China and Japan. Negotiations with China had to be committed to special envoys who, notwithstanding the acquisition of Baltic ports and the possibility of sailing from there to the Far East, were generally forced to travel via Siberia to their destination. It is in connection with such embassies that we find the first reports about land and people in Siberia during the eighteenth century. One of these embassies was that of

Lev Vasilevich Izmailov in 1719. It included a young scientist who may fittingly be described as the first of the typical eighteenth-century travellers through Siberia. His name was John Bell, an Englishman, who had his eyes open for observation and his mind disciplined for evaluation. Interest in a far-away land like Asia had stimulated him and good connections had made it possible for him to join Izmailov's mission as a doctor and surgeon. He diligently took notes, kept a diary, and eventually embodied his personal experiences—together with many stories related to him by others—in a work composed by him some forty years later, in 1758 to 1762.[45]

Bell left Moscow in the fall of 1719 and travelled to Kazan; from there he pursued his way by sledge to Viatka and then on via Verkhoture and Tiumen to Tobolsk, where he arrived on December 16. After a month's stay he continued to Tara, Tomsk (February 4, 1720), Eniseisk, Troitsa, Iakutsk, Balagansk, and on to Irkutsk, from where he crossed into China and arrived on November 20 in Peking. In April 1721 he was back in Selenginsk, crossed Lake Baikal on the ice, stayed in Irkutsk until July and then, on October 2, returned to Tobolsk, travelling by boat via Ilimsk, Eniseisk, Narym, the Ob and the Irtysh rivers. At the end of the year, he was back in European Russia. In reporting on his journey he comments on all he sees or hears, whether salt, iron, or asbestos works in the Urals, or animals, peoples, mores, or historical events in Siberia.

Another report of a participant in Izmailov's embassy to China has come down to us from the hands of Georg Johann Unverzagt, a German.[46] Unlike Bell's description, it was published rather promptly after Unverzagt's return. He went in 1719 to Solikamsk, crossed the *grosse abscheuliche Gebirge* which separates Europe from Asia, that is the "big, horrible mountain chain" of the Urals, which has been again and again described by travellers, including Jakob Fries, with more awe than many another part of the whole Siberian trip. By way of Tiumen he reached Tobolsk on Christmas Eve. He talked to Swedish prisoners who lived there and had founded a Lutheran church, and he visited the governor general. Except for some rather superficial remarks on the landscape, the manner of travelling and some of the habits of the natives, he has not much to tell about his further progress via Tomsk and Ilimsk (which he calls "just a hamlet") to Irkutsk and on to Selenginsk and China. On November 20, he was back in Selenginsk and by sleigh crossed Lake Baikal and returned home.

A third China traveller, who likewise left a report about Siberia, was Lorenz Lange. Like Bell and Unverzagt, he was a member of Izmailov's embassy. A Swede by birth, or possibly a Dane or German, he had entered the Russian service at an unknown stage of his life,[47] and as early as 1715 had been sent to China. Leaving St. Petersburg on August 18, 1715, and Moscow on December 22, he crossed the Siberian border and reached Tobolsk on January 27, 1716, Tara on February 16. He describes briefly the natives of the region and their habits, but like so many others bases much of his knowledge on what he heard at second hand. In March he met Swedish war prisoners in Tomsk, then spent two months in Eniseisk, and was on July 11 in Irkutsk, about which, to our disappointment, he has nothing to say. About one year after his leaving St. Petersburg he crossed Lake Baikal and then proceeded to China, spending almost two years in Peking. The report of his trip, submitted to Peter, made such an impression on the emperor that he was sent back with Izmailov in 1719 to serve as Russian consul and resident in Peking. In 1728 he paid a visit to St. Petersburg, but in the thirties travelled again to China, on which his reports, unlike Bell's, have much more to say than on the Russian parts he saw.[48] Later, Lange served with distinction as vice-governor in Irkutsk and continued to attend to the regulation of border questions with China. His duties brought him into contact with members of the great expeditions of Bering and Gmelin. Upon the occasion of an incident caused by Georg Steller, he acted with circumspection and kindness.

At the same time when Bell, Unverzagt and Lange crossed Siberia on their way to China, the first great Western naturalist to explore Siberia started on his six-year-long trip. He himself has not left a description which was published, but his letters and reports to friends have provided an ample basis for a comprehensive picture of his work and his observations. His name was Daniel Amadeus Messerschmidt. He was born in Danzig in 1685 and had studied medicine in Halle. His Siberian trip took from 1720 to 1726, and his achievements were so fundamental that his work remained a model for all scientists who participated in subsequent travels and explorations in Siberia. Although his journey began a few years before the death of Peter the Great (which marks the point at which this narrative starts), it lasted into the period after Peter's demise. In 1719, he left Europe and around Christmas reached Tobolsk. During the next year, he sailed down the Irtysh river to Tara, crossed the Baraba steppe and went to Tomsk and Kuznetsk. He spent the year 1722 in the Enisei region and Krasnoiarsk, 1723 on the Lena and in Irkutsk. In 1724, he crossed Lake Bailkal and travelled to Nerchinsk and into Mongolia, returned to Irkutsk the following year and from there sailed down the Angara river. He then went to Eniseisk and to the mouth of the Irtysh, used the year 1726 to explore the Irtysh mountains and then slowly returned to the Urals. Finally, in 1727, he was back in St. Petersburg.[49] Finding all his work and travails but insufficiently recognized and rewarded, and being by nature a hypochondriac, he left Russia and returned to Danzig. There, too, he found no recognition, rest or satisfaction, and within a few years he once more was back in St. Petersburg. Destitute and dependent upon the charity of others, he died there in 1735.[50] Messerschmidt belongs to the large group of outstanding naturalists who are characteristic of the eighteenth-century Enlightenment; he was a true precursor of the great Siberian and Pacific explorers and, though a jealous government had imposed on him, as on others, secrecy about his discoveries, we owe him—indirectly, on the basis of his notes—our first reliable knowledge of the natural surroundings in Siberia.

For some time Messerschmidt was accompanied on his travels by a Swedish prisoner of war, Captain Philipp Johann Tabbert, who was later raised to the rank of nobility under the name of von Strahlenberg. He wrote an account of his journey[51] which covers the years up to 1722 when, following the peace of Nystad, he was exchanged and returned to his country. He spent part of the year 1720 together with Messerschmidt in Tobolsk; in 1721 he explored with him the Irtysh region and crossed the Baraba steppe, and by the time of his release he and Messerschmidt had reached Krasnoiarsk. In the form of a dictionary[52] he furnishes us with an account of many curiosities which the two had seen, and he gives historical and linguistic data, names, trade measures, descriptions of geography and political and military conditions, and remarks on minerals and other natural objects of Siberia. Much of his information he owed not to personal experience but to information from Messerschmidt, from other travellers, or from natives. Like other travel accounts, his book may thereby have gained in breadth what it may have lost in strict accuracy.

As a Swedish war prisoner who served Russia from the time of the battle of Poltava to the end of the Great Northern War, Tabbert-Strahlenberg is no exception. Actually, some 800 to 900 Swedish prisoners (not all of Swedish birth but also of Dutch or—like Tabbert—of German origin) were sent to the Tobolsk district alone, many of them officers; and altogether over 1100 seem to have lived in the various parts of Siberia—in Tomsk, Ilimsk, Irkutsk, etc. [53] Even after the peace of Nystad, some of them stayed on in Siberia, at least for a few years. They enjoyed considerable freedom, and thus many of them contributed greatly, as Tsar Peter had foreseen, to the cultural development of his eastern empire. Conversely, they contributed also to the knowledge which the outside world sought so eagerly of the far-away country. For a few wrote down their experiences, like Strahlenberg; others recounted their adventures to friends, and various German, French, Swiss and other publications about Siberia, also interested in their personal fate, were based on their accounts. Thus, the *Recueil de Voyages au Nord*[54] brought a contribution under the title "Relation de la Grande Tartarei; Dressée sur les mémoires originaux des Suedois Prisonniers en Sibérie. . . .". Interestingly, it points out that the Siberian prisoners went in groups (*"en troupes"*) into the countryside looking for pre-historic tombs, for mounds of earth with skeletons, and in this way benefited the sciences. A Nürnberg publication of 1720, *Der allerneueste Staat von Siberien* . . .,[55] was based on reports and letters by Swedish prisoners, and Müller collected accounts of theirs in his *Sammlung russischer Geschichte*.

One of the most prominent Swedish prisoners, a friend of Strahlenberg, was a Swedish captain of dragoons, Curt

Friedrich von Wreech. He was sent in 1711 first to
Solikamsk, then to Tobolsk. His report covering the years
1709 to 1722 gives only a few bits of information about the
land and people of Siberia (the Ostiaks), but is of special
interest because it provides an insight into the life of the
prisoners and their relationship to Siberia.[56] They occupied
themselves with various trade activities or worked as
artisans and teachers.[57] Von Wreech founded a school for
Siberian children. Like many of the prisoners, he was
under the influence of Pietism and corresponded with A. H.
Francke in Halle. His memoirs are full of pious meditations.
But not only did he, like others, carry Pietistic views of
Francke and Spener beyond the Urals into the most distant
regions but also much of the worldly spirit of the Enlightenment, of its thirst for knowledge, for the study of nature,
for acquaintance with the East and Eastern philosophical
ideas—interests which Francke's famous school and the
University of Halle likewise represented.[58] Thus, the officers
fulfilled a remarkable double task and constituted a unique
link between Europe and Siberia. Von Wreech's school,
where in 1714 eleven boys and one girl were being taught,
consisted in 1719, together with the attached hospital, of no
less than 134 persons. Notwithstanding constant struggles
for funds, several buildings were erected owing to the
devotion of the teachers and the support of co-religionists
in Moscow, and much of the best Europe had to offer was
taught to the Siberian children. They were also instructed
in German, and taught some Swedish. The end of the school
came when news of the Peace of Nystad reached Tobolsk
in October 1721 and the officers were returned to their
homeland.

Another Swedish captain and prisoner who left an
account was Johann Bernhard Müller. He published a report
on the Ostiaks whom he studied in the region of Beresova.[59]
He described their habits, customs, religion and added notes
on history, geography and minerals. Then there was
Heinrick Fick, born in 1679 in Hamburg, who accepted first
Swedish service in Livonia and, by 1715, having come to
St. Petersburg, entered the Russian service. He was not a
member of the group of Poltava prisoners, but he served
as an important adviser of Peter the Great. He was a freethinker and a remarkable diplomat. Like many others, he

was arrested by Empress Anna in March 1731 and sent first to Tobolsk, where he lived quite well and peacefully, and later to Irkutsk and Iakutsk. Recalled by Empress Elizabeth in 1741, he returned in 1743 and died in 1750. He composed a report on the Iakuts which was recently published. In it he denounces the ill-treatment of these people whose life he studied, their exploitation and the terrible conditions created among them by illness (smallpox) and brutality (especially in the collection of *iasak* by the Russian administration). He is particularly bitter about the Great Kamchatka Expedition under Bering, which, dependent upon native support, inflicted untold hardships upon the poor natives.[60]

Still other reports of Swedish prisoners reached the ears of the scientific world through Gerhard Friedrich Müller, who printed in his *Sammlung* what a Dutchman, Henrik Busch from Hoorn, who had served the Swedish king and whom Müller met as late as 1736 in Iakutsk, had to tell about a trip he had made in 1715 to 1717 from Okhotsk to Kamchatka.[61] Müller also published an account by Johann Christian Schnitscher, a Swedish officer who joined in 1715 the Russian embassy to China. He wrote about the Kalmyks on the basis of his own observations and what he learned from his interpreter. This account was originally published in Swedish in 1744 and then translated.[62] A comment on it was furnished and printed by a Swedish *Stückjunker*, an artillery sergeant by the name of Johannes Gustav Renat. He had been taken prisoner first by the Russians, then by the Kalmyks, and he spent seventeen years with them, until 1733. He is supposed to have taught them how to smelt iron ore and how to found cannons. Becoming their "supreme commander", he led them against the Chinese, and eventually acquired "immense wealth". Through a map of Djungaria[63] he contributed to the knowledge of Siberia. A description of the Kalmyks was also written by a doctor and surgeon, Gottlob Schober, who left his notes with the Russian State Councillor Lerche, who in turn, with the help of the historian August Ludwig Schlözer, published them in abbreviated form.[64]

Yet it is significant for the West's interest in Siberia, suddenly aroused, that the scholarly world of Europe did not even have to wait for the publications of the great scientific expeditions, such as the *Sammlung russischer Geschichte*, or even for the memoirs of the Swedes, but that the news and letters from Swedish prisoners as early as 1720 induced an editor like the one of *Der allerneueste Staat von Siberien* to publish a broad survey of Siberian history and geography, climate, flora and fauna, minerals, towns, etc., and while denouncing, in accordance with enlightened views, all superstitions, to tell—notwithstanding misinformation and superficiality—about the habits of Tartars and Samoieds, Kalmyks and Ostiaks, Tungus and Buriats, Mongols and Kirgizs. Indeed, though the same book does not name the prisoners who furnished the information, it describes at length their school at Tobolsk and the missionary spirit which animated them.[65]

The last of the accounts before Bering's trip, which merits mention here, comes from a Commissary of War, Johann Unkowski, whose very short report covers the period of October 1722 to June 1723. It may likewise be found in Müller's *Sammlung*[66] but it gives us no more than a few descriptions of native ceremonies. Unkowski does not seem to have penetrated into Siberia beyond a point approximately a hundred versts west of the Irtysh river.

Bering himself and his party of thirty-three left St. Petersburg two years later, on February 5, 1725, just a week after the death of Peter the Great. In company of the later Captain Spanberg and with Alexei Chirikov he travelled via Vologda to Tobolsk. He stayed there until the middle of May and spent the summer attending to the shipping of supplies by boat down the Irtysh river and up the Ob to Narym; then he went up the Ket and on to Eniseisk, and from there to Ilimsk, where he spent the winter and from where he visited Irkutsk. The next year he proceeded further and finaly reached Iakutsk.[67] Then he travelled to Okhotsk and, on August 4, 1727, to Bolsharesk on Kamchatka. Neither he nor his companions seem to have felt a desire to describe the so little known country which they crossed; apparently their minds were focused on the greater task ahead of them in the Pacific regions, and it is only about Kamchatka and its inhabitants and the animal life there that we possess accounts from their pens. Thus, the excellent opportunity of learning from capable explorers about regions so little investigated in their time was wasted.

Bering sailed in July 1728 from Kamchatka and a year later was back in Okhotsk, from where he now crossed inner Siberia for a second time without leaving a comprehensive book or report, although an account and maps were submitted to the Academy. On January 10, 1730, he reached Tobolsk via Ilimsk, Eniseisk, Tomsk and Tara, and on March 1 arrived in St. Petersburg. A new expedition, necessitated by his failure to solve the problems set for his first voyage, was eventually decided upon, and in April 1733 he took leave for a second time. Once more he travelled through Siberia, this time spending no less than four years on the trip, for not until 1737 did he reach Okhotsk. It took him an additional three years until his ships could be launched and he could sail on the *St. Peter* on his last successful but fatal voyage.[68] No account of his own of these seven years of work, experience and observation has been left.

After Bering's death, the command fell to Sven Waxell, a Swede who, supported by Steller, brought the remnants of the expedition of the *St. Peter* back to Kamchatka. He had left St. Petersburg in 1733, together with the approximately five hundred men who were assigned to the support of the explorers and scientists making up the expedition. To this number were added some five hundred soldiers, many of whom were deportees. Waxell travelled via Tobolsk, Eniseisk, Ust-Kut and Iakutsk and reached Okhotsk in 1739. His description deals chiefly with the dispositions that during these long years had to be made for the trip itself and furnishes only indirectly a picture of conditions in the country.[69] His further account of Spanberg's voyages to Japan and his own to America do not deal with Siberia, but he did give a description of Kamchatka. He was one of the few who, after sixteen years, could finally return to St. Petersburg, and he died as a captain commander when in his sixties.

At the time Bering left St. Petersburg for the second voyage, the Russian authorities had decided not to confine their investigations to Pacific and American problems and to Japan, where Spanberg sailed three times—in 1739, 1741, and 1742—(like Bering, he left no description of the

Siberian part of his journey),[70] but to supplement the planned sea voyages by great land expeditions into Siberia. They therefore undertook to equip scientific expeditions for the systematic description of the huge territory which lay between the Urals, China, and the Pacific Ocean. As a result, not quite four months after Bering had departed from St. Petersburg, a group of scientists under the leadership of Johann Georg Gmelin got under way. Born in Tübingen, southern Germany, in 1709, Gmelin had gained early fame in the field of natural history. He left Tübingen in 1730 in order to join the Academy of Sciences in St. Petersburg and was encharged with the first great mission to Siberia for its scientific exploration and description. The expedition included the German historian and professor Gerhard Friedrich Müller, a French astronomer, Louis de l'Isle de la Croyère, a Russian student, Stephan Krasheninnikov, who came from Moscow and later became a professor at the Academy of Sciences, and a number of others, the total party amounting—apart from servants—to sixteen. Among them was also, for a time, the young German botanist Georg Steller, Bering's famous companion. The party did not travel in one body, but different tasks were assigned to the individual members according to their special interests or the orders of Gmelin. If ultimately the expedition turned out to be of tremendous importance, it certainly owed much of its success to the work of (largely unknown) predecessors, both Russian and foreign. But these predecessors provided hardly more than oral news or internal reports which reached Russian and Siberian administrative agencies, and failed to give to the world printed and comprehensive scientific information such as Gmelin's expedition supplied.

Gmelin started on his Siberian trip on August 8, 1733. He proceeded first to Tobolsk, where he arrived the following January. During the year 1734 he explored the region of the Irtysh river to Kolyvan, then went to Kuznetsk, Tomsk, and Eniseisk. In 1735 he travelled from there to Krasnoiarsk, Irkutsk, Nerchinsk, and back to Irkutsk. In 1736, he visited the region of the Angara river, of Ilimsk and Iakutsk, in 1737 that of the Lena river. The year 1738 found him again in Irkutsk and in Eniseisk, where he met Steller. The year 1739 was employed with studies along the Enisei river and with the return trip to Krasnoiarsk. 1740 Gmelin spent in Tomsk and neighbourhood, 1741 in the Baraba steppe and Tobolsk, 1742 in the Urals, and finally, after ten years of exhaustive work and of privation, he reached St. Petersburg again. The great amount of scientific data and the outstanding results of the expeditions were embodied in a four-volume description of his trip through Siberia[71] and in additional works which he wrote after a total stay of almost twenty years in Russia. Nothing illustrates better the importance of his work than a poem which Albrecht von Haller, himself an interested student of nature and a true child of the eighteenth-century Enlightenment, wrote and which prefaces Gmelin's *Reise durch Sibirien:*

Wo Russlands breites Reich sich mit der Erde schliesset
Und in den letzten West des Morgens March zerfliesset,
Wohin kein Vorwitz drang; wo Thiere fremder Art
Noch ungenannten Völkern dienten;
Wo unbekanntes Ertz sich künftgen Künstlern spart,
Und nie besehne Kräuter grünten;
Lag eine neue Welt, von der Natur versteckt,
Biss Gmelin sie entdeckt.

Gmelin's work is a mine of information, the first comprehensive and accurate account of Siberian natural surroundings, geography, botany and zoology. A peculiar leaning toward the investigation and description of all kinds of folk customs, witchcraft, and shamans is evidenced which sometimes strikes the reader as rather unscientific but had its place in eighteenth-century anthropology and does not overshadow the great merits of his other investigations. In 1747 Gmelin returned to Tübingen, became a professor of botany and chemistry, and died in 1755 at the early age of forty-five.

A less prominent member of the expedition was a Frenchman, Louis de l'Isle de la Croyère, half-brother of two famous astronomers and geographers, Guillaume and Joseph Nicholas de l'Isle. The latter was a member of the Russian Academy of Sciences and it was he who secured for his step-brother Louis the position of astronomer and physical observer on Bering's staff. Louis started on the trip as a member of Gmelin's expedition, yet retained his chief interest in Siberia's eastern regions and the Pacific and therefore eventually proceeded farther east; he met Bering's other companion, Georg Steller, and the two undertook part of their travels together. Finally, the great moment came: in the spring of 1741, de l'Isle de la Croyère sailed with Captain Chirikov on the *St. Paul*, reached with him the shores of America and returned with him on the tenth of October, 1741. But the dramatic end was near; at the ninth hour, the *St. Paul* anchored in Avacha Bay, and at ten o'clock de l'Isle died of scurvy.[72] He has left us no account of his travels. What we know of them has come to us through the reports of others, for his observations have become part of the accounts of Gmelin's, Steller's, Bering's, and Chirikov's voyages. But they were not highly regarded by the other naturalists, who—notwithstanding the praise bestowed upon him, at the expense of others, by his step-brother Nicholas—found them superficial and unreliable. Nor did the others care for the foppish Frenchman with his Parisian clothing and peruke, who also drank too much. Müller mentions the low opinion which Buache, too, had of his compatriot de la Croyère.[73]

A third famous member of Gmelin's expedition was Gerhard Friedrich Müller, the historian to whom we owe a most exhaustive study of Siberia, which he embodied in his nine-volume *Sammlung russischer Geschichte*.[74] Müller was born in 1705 in Westphalia and at the age of twenty had become a lecturer at the Academy in St. Petersburg. In 1731 he became a professor of history, but differences and strife with colleagues made him offer his services to Gmelin as a civilian historian. Despite illness which forced him in the winter of 1737 to 1738 to ask for his recall, Müller actually stayed abroad for nine and a half years. However, while at first he had generally followed the course taken by Gmelin, he was more independent after his illness began. In 1738 he visited the Angara region; much of 1739 he spent together with Steller; still later he travelled along the Enisei river, and returned towards the end of the year to Krasnoiarsk; during the year 1740 he worked mainly in the archives at Tomsk and slowly made his way westward to Tiumen; in 1741 he spent his time in the Isets province, where he again met Gmelin; he used the year 1742 chiefly for recuperation in the Urals, and finally returned to St. Petersburg. Largely because of his own difficult character he met there with new problems; eventually, in 1765, he moved to Moscow and died in 1783. His work on Siberia contains a wealth of information. It includes material on numerous aspects that are conspicuously lacking in the accounts of the natural scientists and it serves to give us insight into the political scene of Siberia, into the country's administrative divisions, towns and municipalities,[75] as well as into economic questions, trade routes, and trade possibilities.[76] Much has been written on Müller and the importance of his work, on his own observations, his reports of the undertakings of others he knew, and his historical research in Siberian archives. Judged harshly by some for certain prejudices and also disliked for his complicated nature, he is yet recognized by all as the leading authority of his time.[77]

The political part of Müller's work was later both enlarged upon and abridged and edited by Johann Eberhard Fischer, who, like Müller, did not base his account on theoretical studies only but also holds a place as a traveller in Siberia; for in 1740 he himself joined Gmelin's expedition, spent 1741 in the Krasnoiarsk and Irkutsk regions, the next years in the areas of Iakutsk, again Irkutsk and Tobolsk, and did not return to St. Petersburg until 1747. He thus speaks from personal experience.[78] His reports on ethnographic questions as well as his critical investigations of Siberian archives are valuable, even though his colleagues estimated neither his scholarship nor his industry highly. Like others, he too met with personal difficulties and for a time was, for political reasons, under arrest.

Among the "younger" members of the expedition—even the senior members were still in their twenties when they started out from St. Petersburg—were Stepan Krasheninnikov and Georg Wilhelm Steller. Krasheninnikov was born in Moscow in 1712 and undertook the journey as a "student". Not much is known about his origins; essentially, he was a self-made man and later proved to be no less difficult a person than others. Only upon his return did he become adjunct and subsequently professor of botany and natural history, in which position he was little liked because of his lack of consideration of others and his brutality. Like so many of the members of the Bering-Gmelin expeditions, he died at an early age, in 1755. Gmelin relied considerably upon him and in 1737 allowed him to proceed on his own to Kamchatka. It is there that, during the year 1738, he made his separate and special contribution to the success of the expedition through his study of the natural history of the far-away peninsula. He eventually published an extensive account of his travels,[79] dealing with the botany and zoology of the country, the conditions of the soil, and the customs of the inhabitants. What gave his work special importance was his collaboration with Steller, which afforded him access to the vast amount of material which Steller collected, with inadequate opportunity for publishing. It is this association also which justifies his inclusion here in an account of the travels of foreigners.

Steller, a "rare genius", as all his contemporaries considered him, is no doubt the most interesting and dramatic figure among Gmelin's—and Bering's—companions.[80] Born in Windheim in southern Germany in 1709, he had early shown extraordinary abilities. He had studied in Halle, first theology then natural sciences, had moved to Berlin in 1734 and then to St. Petersburg, where in 1737 he became "adjunct" (associate) at the Academy of Sciences. He married the young and gay widow of Daniel Messerschmidt—a marriage that turned out a sad disappointment, for his wife had little interest in the work to which both her first and her second husband devoted themselves, and despite earlier promises refused to accompany Steller on the great scientific expedition, which he was allowed to join at the end of the year 1738. Thus he travelled alone; in autumn 1738 he reached Tomsk by way of Narym rather than Tara, and in January 1739 he came to Eniseisk. In March he proceeded to Krasnoiarsk—the gate to a "new" country that was no longer like Western Siberia—and then he spent a year in the Irkutsk region, exploring in particular the surroundings of Lake Baikal and visiting Kiakhta on the Chinese border, partly in order to secure from the Chinese urgently needed paper for his correspondence, notes and collections. In 1740 he went on the 2700 km-long track to Iakutsk and then on to Kamchatka, and in the following year succeeded in joining Bering's expedition on the *St. Peter*. His share in the accomplishments of Bering's second voyage, before and after the commander's death, are well known. After reaching Kamchatka again, he spent additional years there and in Siberia, incessantly working, discovering, describing, until his tragic end in 1746. He never returned. Arrested on his way after passing the Urals, sent back to Siberia, freed again and once more on the journey back, he succumbed to illness at the age of 36 before he could reach St. Petersburg and report. Plants, fishes, land animals, mountains—and the famous sea cow—are named after him and testify to his achievements. He was strong-willed, difficult to work with, and Gmelin himself had considerable trouble because of his insubordination.[81] But his enthusiasm, devotion to his studies, and willingness to endure every hardship for their sake were unique, and the loss of the diary of his trip through Siberia [82] would have been a still greater calamity, had it not been for Krasheninnikov's writings. Krasheninnikov who knew but little German, apparently had someone translate Steller's notes, some of which were then incorporated in his report.

Also fascinating is a man by the name of Jakob Lindenau, born in 1706, who travelled in the company of Müller, Fischer and, after Fischer's arrest, with Steller. Later, having accepted the task of studying the ethnography of Siberian peoples, he continued his journey alone. Much of his time he spent in the region of Iakutsk and in 1743 he came to the Okhotsk region. As one of the last members of the Second Kamchatka Expedition, he returned to St. Petersburg in 1746. Later he went back to Siberia and despite his excellent work and Laxmann's vigorous intercession in his favour with the Academy, he died, poor and forgotten, at the age of ninety, during a fire that razed his lonely cabin on the banks of the Angara river. He left no publication of his own.

Notwithstanding the participation of other good scientists, such as Alex Philipp Martini, who like so many outstanding members of the Academy had come from Tübingen University and who accompanied Gmelin's expedition for a while, there exists no other comprehensive report on Siberia. A number of smaller contributions of the period deal with the Ural and Orenburg regions, in which much interest was shown because of the need for their political, military, and economic integration into the Russian empire. Thus, Wilhelm de Hennin wrote on the industries of Western Siberia, which he visited.[83] But knowledge of Siberia was not furthered beyond that gained from Gmelin and his companions. Following his expedition, scientific and historical investigation in Siberia was almost at a standstill for approximately thirty years, and Ludwig Holberg justly complains in his preface to a good travel account of European, if not Siberian, Russia by his compatriot Peter von Haven (1715–1757):[84] "It would be desirable that more of our countrymen would record with equal industry what they see and learn on their travels abroad: However, we must regret that among so many hundreds of travellers no one can be found who upon his return has informed his countrymen in a similar manner [as the author]". Indeed, we have to wait for the period of the second great expedition, undertaken by Pallas and his group of naturalists, to find anything that compares in significance with the investigations of Gmelin and his companions.

No more than three or four travellers can be mentioned who, during the period between the two expeditions, left accounts of Siberia, and they have not contributed much to our knowledge. One of them was the Abbé Chappe d'Auteroche, a French astronomer born in 1722. In 1760 he had become a member of the French Academy of Sciences and in the same year was sent by this institution to Tobolsk in order to observe the transit of Venus over the Sun. He travelled via Ekaterinburg, Beloiarsk and Tiumen and arrived in time for his observations in Tobolsk. Upon his return he published a book on his voyage[85] which shows a singular lack of insight and is disappointing for a man of Chappe's standing. He included some measurements of elevations, such as Gmelin had taken before him, some paragraphs on mineralogy, a few statements about visits which he made to the famous mines of the Demidov family in the Urals, and he added a volume of maps as well as a translation of Krasheninnikov's report. But the exactitude of his observations and statements, even in his own field of astronomy, was challenged even by his contemporaries, and many of the descriptions he gave of what he saw were sharply censored for their bias. He was accused of arrogance, unfairness towards the Russians, and incorrectness in much of his historical data.[86] A few years after his journey to Siberia he went for the sake of new astronomical observations on a second distant expedition, this time travelling to California. There he fell ill and died in 1769.

Another account referring to the same period is that of Johann Ludwig Wagner, which was, however, published only thirty years later.[87] Wagner was a postmaster in Pillau when, during the Seven Years War, Russians invaded Prussia and, in February 1759, took him prisoner as a spy. He was sent to Tobolsk and to the small place of Mangasea in the northern Enisei region where he arrived after more than a year's travel and where he spent three years. Released in 1763 he returned to his home country. His memoirs make pleasant and worth-while reading and illustrate conditions which scarcely came under the scrutiny of the natural scientists, and which can give us a few occasional glimpses of daily life among the people of Siberia, both indigenous and Russian.[88]

Two other travellers merit mention: Peter Ivanovich Rychkov and Erik Laxmann. The former, a Russian, born in 1712, became commander of large iron works in the Urals and with his seat in Ekaterinburg had an opportunity of seeing some of the eastern slopes of the mountains. He has left a careful description of the topography of the Orenburg district,[89] which includes a small part of Siberia's most western regions and which adds to the information that could be gained at the time from Messerschmidt and Gmelin. The other, Erik Laxmann, was a native of Finland who became a pastor of the German community in Barnaul at the mines of Kolyvan. He later accepted a professorship in chemistry at the Academy of Scienes in St. Petersburg and eventually became Councillor of the mining industry (*Bergrat*) in Nerchinsk. He died in 1796. Georgi accuses him of having been "a lazy writer"[90] but this judgment seems too harsh. Laxmann led a busy life. He had a keen interest in many things, travelled widely, and occupied himself with many new scientific problems and inventions.[91] His travels took him not only all the way east through Siberia to the Amur river (his wife died in Kiakhta and was buried in Selenginsk), but likewise south to the Altai mountains and up to the northern parts of European Russia. While he did not publish his travel accounts in book form, he gave much of the information he gathered in his letters. Some of these were printed by August Ludwig Schloezer in 1769,[92] others almost twenty years later in the *Neue Nordische Beyträge*.[93] The former refer to the years 1763 to 1767 and were addressed to men like the great Linnaeus, Schloezer, or the mathematician, philosopher and economist, Professor Beckmann; they contain observations on native languages, on insect collections, meteorological studies, and the like. The later letters, covering the years 1786 to 1790, were likewise addressed to scientists and deal with similar observations. In addition, Laxmann contributed short articles to periodicals.

Before coming to Pallas's expedition, a Count Mauritius Augustus de Benyowski should be mentioned. He was a Pole of doubtful character and little trustworthiness, who wrote an uninspiring account of his travels in Siberia,[94] which contains a few general observations and which, because of his adventurous life, aroused the interest of his contemporaries; Augustus von Kotzebue later even wrote a play about him. Benyowski was born in 1741; during the wars led by the Confederation of Bar he was taken prisoner by the Russians. He was sent to Tobolsk, which he reached on January 20, 1770. From there he travelled over less frequented roads via Berenovsk, the rivers Om and Jurga to Tomsk, where he arrived by April 17, and then proceeded via Krasnoiarsk and along the Angara river to Ilimsk and down the Lena to Iakutsk. On October 16 he finally reached Okhotsk. Later he went to Kamchatka, where he was well received in the household of the governor, Nilov. But desirous to escape, he not only seduced the daughter but also saw the governor killed in the scuffle, and then the knave, together with others, sailed for Macao and China. After his return to Europe he set out in 1784 for Baltimore, Maryland, and engaged in trading activities with Africa. For this purpose he sailed via Brazil and the Cape of Good Hope to Madagascar, but became involved in illegal activities and was killed in 1786.

Benyowski's adventures in Siberia are the last to be recorded before we come to Pallas's important mission. A professor of surgery, Peter Simon Pallas was born in Berlin in 1741, where he also died one year after his return, in 1811. At the age of twenty he paid a visit to England and quickly gained so great a reputation that within two years he was made a member of the Royal Society in London and of other eminent scientific bodies. From 1763 on he stayed for three years in Holland and in 1767 accepted a call to St. Petersburg to become a professor of natural history and lead an expedition into south-eastern Russia and Siberia. About thirty years had passed since the last great exploratory work had taken place; many of the fruits of Gmelin's and Steller's work had been lost in the course of the years, and advanced methods and new understanding alike demanded new investigations. On June 21, 1767, Pallas left St. Petersburg, some of the members of his expedition having started on their way earlier. Again, the government had commissioned very young and very outstanding scientists—only one, Falck, being over thirty years of age.

The task set to the expedition consisted of the investigation and description of the natural surroundings in Siberia, of its geology and geography, plants, animals and minerals, and of the life and customs of the native populations.[95] For the duration of the trip the participants were assured double salaries, and orders of the government entitled them to every possible support by the Siberian authorities. They were to have free transportation, free quarters, and priorities on both. Obviously, though easily forgotten, the scientific endeavours had their price: again, they meant a great burden for the native population.

In 1768 Pallas reached Simbirsk; in 1769 he continued his work in the Volga and Ural regions, which he revisited in the following year. In 1771 he left Europe and travelled along the Tobol and Irtysh rivers to the province of Kolyvan with its important mining district, then down the Tom and Enisei to Krasnoiarsk. 1772 he spent around Irkutsk and Krasnoiarsk; in 1773 he was back in Tobolsk and the Ural mountains and the next year he returned to St. Petersburg. His students undertook a number of side trips and combined their reports with his. The sum of his investigations, Pallas published in a most thorough and studious work[96] which became the standard reference book on Siberia's natural history. It deals primarily with manifold investigations of plant and animal life, lists and describes minerals and factories in which these were processed, and fulfilled in a most satisfactory way the tasks set by the government and the Academy. Like all the great naturalists of the eighteenth century in their accounts of Siberia, Pallas studiously avoids in his writings a discussion of those conditions which might serve the historian as a guide for a social history of the country.

Following the precedent of Gmelin, Pallas's work was supplemented by a number of publications which his chief companions brought out. Among these companions we find Johann Peter Falck (Falk), Johann Gottlieb Georgi, Ivan Lepekhin, Nicholas Rychkov, D. Samuel Gmelin, and Anton Güldenstädt—all of them prominent men who hold distinguished places in the history of the natural sciences.

Falck, born around 1727, was Swedish by nationality. As a tutor in the house of Linnaeus he came into close contact with the great botanist and was himself engaged in the study of natural history. After a number of travels in northern Europe he went to St. Petersburg to become a professor at the Imperial Medical College. Despite ill health he decided to join the scientific expedition which was to study south-eastern and Asiatic Russia and left on September 5, 1768. Perhaps he hoped to recover mental and physical vigour in the more healthful parts he intended to visit. He journeyed to Moscow and, in 1769, down the Volga to Samara, Saratov, and Tsaritsyn and there met Pallas, Lepekhin and Güldenstädt. In the following year he was joined by Georgi and visited Astrakhan, Samara, and Orenburg, studying carefully, despite his illness, every detail, according to his instructions. In 1771 he went partly over the same ground that Pallas and Rychkov had investigated, travelled in the Kalmyk steppe, the Isets province, to Omsk (where he arrived in July), the Kolyvan mine district, and finally reached Tomsk. Here he separated from Georgi and in 1772 slowly returned via Tara, Tobolsk, Tiumen, and Viatka to Kazan. Again, increasing ill health notwithstanding, he persisted in continuing his investigations. He also sacrificed the following year to his work and once more visited the Volga region; but early in 1774 his despondency reached such a point that he put an end to his sufferings with a pistol shot. His friend Georgi prepared from his copious, though unorganized notes an excellent three-volume description[97] which is constructed along the same lines as Pallas's report and supplements the main study with observations in regions Pallas had not seen. Volume I contains two interesting maps tracing the routes followed by several of the great eighteenth-century travellers in Siberia.

Falck's companion Johann Georgi, likewise a student of Linnaeus, was born in 1738 in Pomerania, where he became a pharmaceutist. He came to St. Petersburg in 1769 and was sent to join Falck, whom he accompanied on his travels and with whom he was connected by the bonds of a sincere friendship. He left Falck in Tomsk and on February 27, 1772, proceeded to join the main expedition of Pallas at Krasnoiarsk, spending the rest of the year on and around Lake Baikal. In 1773 made his way slowly back to the Volga via Krasnoiarsk, Tomsk, and Ekaterinburg and travelled the major part of the next year in the neighbourhood of Astrakhan and up the Volga to Moscow before he returned to St. Petersburg. He incorporated his very careful general physical and geographical descriptions and his special observations along Lake Baikal in two large volumes which were published in the course of the following thirty years.[98] His accounts are systematic, rather dry, and full of information on the natural wealth of Siberia, her plants, animals, inhabitants, and geography, and also on the habits and ways of one people after another that inhabited Siberia. It also serves as one of the best guides for scientific activities in Siberia and summarizes to a certain extent the achievements of half a century of work. In 1783, Georgi became a professor of chemistry in St. Petersburg, where he died in 1802.

Ivan Lepekhin was the most prominent member of Russian descent among Pallas's party. Born in 1740, he became a student at the Academy of Scienes and took his doctor's degree in medicine in Strassburg. In 1768 he was named associate at the Academy and three years later became a regular member. His death occurred in the same year as that of Georgi, ending a life of somewhat less accomplishment than his friend and colleagues had hoped for in his youth. It was in 1768 that he started on his Siberian trip, proceeding first via Moscow and Simbirsk to Orenburg and making a number of side trips. He saw little of Siberia, though, for he spent the year 1769 in the region of Saratov and Tsaritsyn and the steppe parts of the Urals, and in 1770 he visited the iron and copper works in and beyond the Ural mountains, combining his studies of industries with those of peoples, birds and insects. After a visit to Tiumen and Verkhoture in 1771 he travelled independently in European parts of the empire. The results of his trips were embodied in a diary which appeared in Russian and was soon made available to the learned world through a German translation.[99]

Like Lepekhin, Nicholas Petrovich Rychkov (1746–1784), a son of Gmelin's companion, and D. Samuel Gmelin (1744-74), a nephew of the famous naturalist, participated in Pallas's expedition only to the extent of its European phase. Both went to the Volga and Urals regions, Gmelin continuing then to the Caspian Sea, where he was overtaken by disaster: rebellious tribes seized him as a prisoner, and before Empress Catherine succeeded in having him ransomed he died of disentry in 1774, at the age of thirty. Rychkov accomplished his task after visiting the Belaia and Kama districts, Ekaterinburg, the Kirgiz steppe, and Orenburg, and soon after his return, in 1771, published a diary that was less of a learned account than a description, in a simple, pleasing style, of what he had seen. It offered little that was new.[100]

The last of Pallas's important companions, Johann Anton Güldenstädt from Riga, went—like Gmelin the younger—to Astrakhan, but then turned westward toward the Dnieper. He died early, before having had time to publish his discoveries which, however, would have had but little bearing on the increase of our knowledge of inner Siberia.

3 Travel Accounts After 1775

The second scientific expedition into Siberia concludes a great enterprise which had extended over fifty years—from the time of Bering and Peter the Great to that of Pallas and Catherine the Great—and which had had as its objective the exploration and description of the enormous empire that Russia had politically gained in the preceding century. Soviet authors tend rather mechanically to divide the century in the middle, and when periodizing the Siberian explorations they also speak of the first half and the second half of the century. Yet they themselves are aware of the fact that only a generation later, at the beginning of the last quarter of the century, after the conclusion of the great Pallas expedition, one age had closed and a new era had begun.[101] At the beginning of the period of exploration discussed here, i.e. around 1725, almost nothing had been known of the territory's actual value, nor indeed of its very extent, shape, and content; at the end, around 1775, Siberia's confines were ascertained, its peoples and natural wealth made known. However, this was not enough. The great minds of the Enlightenment were not only anxious to gain an understanding of the world through sober, yet imaginative investigation of its natural forces and to provide merely a broader knowledge of facts, such as the travel accounts of the eighteenth century convey. Nor were they satisfied with basing their descriptions on the investigation of reality rather than on acceptance of legend.[102] They also had a moral purpose. By extending their investigations and applying their knowledge to the human race, and by occupying themselves with descriptions of human society, they envisaged its improvement. This purpose, pursued through their labours in France as in America, in Germany and Sweden as in England, had, however, during their endeavours in Russia, to be subordinated to material aims. The political and social structure of the tsarist empire, with its institutions of autocracy, service nobility and serfdom, made the advancement of a new moral order impossible, and the scientific minds of the age have correspondingly left unsatisfied our desire for more knowledge about Russian life and institutions proper. We learn little of conditions prevailing within the Russian society in Siberia; mainly native populations were observed, and they were treated like plants and animals.

The new era, at the threshold of which stands Jakob Fries, the man whose travel account is reproduced in the present study, brought little change in this respect. After nature had been "discovered" according to the tenets of the Enlightenment, natural surroundings described, and the original thirst for knowledge of the working of nature satisfied, no important new stimulus can be traced; the time had not yet come when "man" was to be discovered, or his place in nature and evolution; neither had the overwhelming interest in him, and in society and sociological aspects, been kindled to the extent to which it came to be later. A period thus intervened during which a compelling and driving spirit for the fufilment of an important task and the discovery of an essential new field were lacking. This holds true also for Siberia, where we fail to trace between 1775 and 1825 any important objectives which outstanding figures set themselves as aims for their travels and observations.

Numerically, the travel accounts of these fifty years do not compare unfavourably with those of the preceding period. As to content, they furnish us with comparatively little. If we learn anything, it refers mainly to the Pacific Coast and Alaska, where great foreign as well as Russian sea expeditions were undertaken, or where members of the Russian-American Company, which included no foreigners, travelled; or it refers to the southern confines of Siberia along the Altai mountain range and the Chinese border. All these reports deal at best only incidentally with the great central Siberian highway from the Urals to Lake Baikal, on which the centres of civilization in Siberia were located and on which Fries travelled.

Perhaps it is the type of foreign observers who published accounts of what they saw in Siberia which accounts for the fact that the content of their reports is less satisfactory.

If we look back upon the men who contributed so much to the exploration of Siberia in the half century from 1725 to 1775 and the work they accomplished, we are struck by their extraordinary personal qualities and professional ability, as well as by the individualistic traits which characterized them. They were, almost without exception, men of difficult character. Some were brutal and officious, some irascible and arrogant, foppish and lazy, morose and peevish, ambitious and greedy. The conditions under which they worked were incredibly hard, even when a train of servants was assigned to them and when they had relatively adequate food, good wines, and comparatively comfortable sleeping equipment. They were separated by thousands of miles from their homes and families; and young, as most were, they had to forego the close company of women—unless they exposed themselves, with venereal disease rampant, to the gravest risks. They were dependent upon, and restricted to, the company of each other, and, no matter how far away, were under the surveillance of a central government which, merely on the basis of misinformation often malevolently given, could ruin their later lives. They were exposed to the ill will and lack of cooperation of lower officials in Siberia, to the harsh climate, to lack of medical care, to the most varied plagues and illnesses, and to incessant psychological pressures. They had to spend five, ten, or even more years abroad and were forced to rely, at their rather youthful age, upon those inner resources which upbringing and strength of character had to provide. Few entertainments were available to them other than those shallow ones which parties with endless drinking bouts offered on those occasions when they could stay in the crude Siberian main towns.

Yet it seems almost petty to mention their personal shortcomings or to refer to the stupendous hardships they endured. In their reports and publications, they hardly mention their sacrifices. They showed, with only a very few exceptions, a devotion to their work, a knowledge of their professions, a willingness to accomplish their tasks, a wisdom, courage, and perseverance which is almost beyond comprehension. The voyage of Bering, with all it demanded of the participants, is well known, but seldom described are the similar difficulties that many had to face in inner Siberia, along the Ob, the Enisei or Lena, on the way from Iakutsk to Okhotsk, or crossing the Baraba steppe, Lake Baikal or dangerous rivers such as the Selenga. Could the satisfaction of tasks successfully achieved—tasks which, because of the disheartening imposition of secrecy, they could generally not even freely discuss and which, therefore, often deprived them of their share of glory—make up for the "lost" years of their youth, if they ever returned alive?

If, in contrast, we look at the travel reports which we possess for the second period, 1775 to 1825, they come chiefly either from the accidental visitor, whether prisoner or exile, or from a new type of individual, the globetrotter, who travelled for the sake of amusement and whose interest lay chiefly in the performance of some spectacular enterprise. He seldom had the inclination or the ability to furnish us with sober accounts or to increase our knowledge; he rarely had scholarly interests or saw a great task before him; it was not often that he showed a willingness to endure hardships in the service of the Russian government. Indeed, there were perhaps no more than two or three travellers who help us in forming a picture of Siberia as it existed around the turn of the eighteenth century. To them may be added an administrator who should at least be mentioned because of his outstanding personality. He was a Russian, Count M. M. Speransky, who spent the years 1819 to 1822 as governor general of Siberia,[103] but whose special position precluded the possibility of his giving accounts in the sense in which they have been collected and listed in this essay.

The first travel report proper of the second half of the century under consideration here concerns the tribe of the Buriats, their lives and customs, and a brief dictionary of their language. It was composed by a Swiss teacher, Regnier (Ren'e). Peculiarly enough, he is not mentioned by Fries, although he was a countryman of his, who as a tutor of the children of the then governor, von Brill, had been in Irkutsk shortly before Fries himself came there. This report was written in 1774 and handed to a Professor Schaden in Moscow, who in turn sent it to a German publisher who brought it out in a historical collection in 1780.[104]

Next we find the Russian A. M. Patrin, a corresponding member of the Academy of Sciences, who visited the province of Kolyvan and the Altai mountains in the summer of 1781 and who wrote an account of his trip shortly before his return from Barnaul to Tomsk in 1782, which was published in German.[105]

At the same time as Patrin was inspecting the Kolyvan and Altai regions, an Englishman, Samuel Bentham, also visited those parts. His manuscripts are preserved but have not been printed. A description of his trip to Siberia on the basis of these papers was, however, published in 1958.[106] He went to Siberia "to mend his fortunes" and for this purpose envisaged entering the Russian service. At the same time, he wanted to satisfy his curiosity, his *Wissbegierde*, as Pallas, who met him, calls it, and gain in technical experience. He spent almost half a year (in 1781) on an estate of the Demidov family and interested himself in the Demidov mines and iron works. In January 1782 he crossed central Siberia by way of Tobolsk, Tara, Tomsk, Krasnoiarsk and Irkutsk and spent almost two months close to the Chinese border in Kiakhta, Selenginsk and Nerchinsk. On his way back he made a detour to visit Barnaul with the intention of acquainting himself with the industries established there. Essentially, he achieved his various purposes. For he stayed on in Russia for another eight years and rose to the rank of brigadier general. After his return to England he was, however, not able during his career in the British navy to put his experiences to good use, and disappointed (and disliked for his criticisms of the British establishment) he spent more than a dozen years as a voluntary exile in France. He died in 1831.

Four years after Patrin and Bentham, Peter Ivanovich Shangin likewise travelled to Barnaul and the Altai regions. He, too, merits mention because an account of his was published in German.[107] Yet neither his nor Patrin's, nor occasional letters by various individals of Russian origin, who refer to specific observations in Siberia, though published in foreign languages, can claim our special attention.[108]

Of greater significance is Captain Joseph Billings, an Englishman born about 1758. He accompanied Captain Cook on the latter's last voyage, during which Cook visited Petropavlovsk in Kamchatka.[109] He then joined the Russian navy, and despite his youth and comparative inexperience was to his own surprise placed in 1785 in command of an expedition to the north-eastern parts of the Empire—an expedition which pursued, as Bering's before him, not only geographical but also political aims. He proceeded from St. Petersburg to Ekaterinburg and Tobolsk, where he arrived on January 22, 1786, and then, without spending much time or paying attention to his surroundings, continued on his way via Tomsk (February 4) and Irkutsk (February 14) down the Lena river to Iakutsk. Here he began to engage on his proper mission which concerned the exploration of the northern Pacific shores. His companion and secretary, Martin Sauer, published an account of Billing's voyages which is interesting in many respects but does not differ from the descriptions of others engaged in tasks not directly connected with Siberia, offering but little with regard to the regions through which they passed.[110]

Another companion of Captain Cook likewise crossed Siberia. This was John Ledyard, who was born in 1751 in Connecticut, had studied theology, but then preferred exploration and adventure and had joined Cook's expedition. After eight years of travel he returned to his home country and engaged in trade; but soon his spirit of enterprise drove him to new excitements. As a typical sensation-hungry globetrotter he seems not to have cared very much about the type and direction of his next undertaking. He first decided to cross the American continent, but when he met with difficulties that were put in his path by the American authorities, he changed his mind and, while in Paris, determined to cross the Asiatic continent instead. With the help of Jefferson and some other friends he raised money for a journey via Siberia to Kamchatka and from there across the Bering Straits.[111] He started out late in 1786. In March of the following year he met Pallas, with whom, as he proudly relates, he dined in

St. Petersburg, and then went on to Moscow. He joined there a Scotch physician who was about to leave on a mission to the province of Kolyvan, and he travelled with the doctor via Kazan, the Urals and Tobolsk to Barnaul. He then left for Tomsk, Krasnoiarsk and Irkutsk, visited Lake Baikal and then sailed down the Lena river. In Iakutsk he reached Captain Billings, whom he had, of course, known before through their common participation in Cook's voyages. Ledyard joined Billings' party, but found his chief very incapable and apparently made himself rather obnoxious. He was eventually arrested and sent back via Siberia to Kazan. Later he travelled to Egypt and up the Nile, where he died soon after in 1789. His journal of the Siberian trip was poorly kept,[112] which is all much the more regrettable as Ledyard was not a Russian nor in Russian service, and therefore might have reported freely where others, because of censorship— either from above or self-imposed—could not help but show a considerable amount of caution.

Besides Ledyard there were two others whose path crossed that of Billings and who left a few notes on Siberia. One of them was Billings's lieutenant, Gavrila Sarychev. He left St. Petersburg in September 1785, went via Tobolsk to Irkutsk, from where he started in December for Iakutsk. His trip through Siberia is briefly mentioned by him in connection with a more thorough account of north-eastern Siberia, Kamchatka, the Kodiak islands, and North America, which begins with his leaving Iakutsk in 1786.[113] The other was Jean Baptiste Barthélémy de Lesseps, a Frenchman born in 1766, who participated in the expedition around the world of La Pérouse and in 1787, while in the Far East, was commissioned to bring news of the exploration to France.[114] Though asked to hurry he was forced to spend the winter in Kamchatka. Not until June 1788 did he reach Okhotsk. He then proceeded to Iakutsk, where he met Billings and dined with him, spent a short time in August in Irkutsk, and returned via Tomsk, Tobolsk, Ekaterinburg, and St. Petersburg. Early in the autumn he was back in Versailles. He later served several terms as consul in St. Petersburg, and he died in 1834. His *Journal historique*,[115] despite its two volumes, deals, like other accounts, essentially with regions other than central Siberia. He himself regretted his lack of study and confesses that his journey to St. Petersburg was "so rushed . . . i.e., from the tenth of August to the twenty-second of September that it has been impossible for me to write [my notes] with my original exactness".[116]

The next traveller was a man of whom we know little, but whose contribution to our knowledge of Siberia is far above that of his predecessors. His name was Johann Sievers, who became a member of the Academy of Sciences and died in 1795. He had studied to become a pharmacist and he may be considered an heir of the Enlightenment rather than a representative of the new age. As a member of an expedition charged with looking for places suitable for planting the valuable rhubarb, he travelled without haste, without desire for spectacular effects, and with the intention of observing and reporting. He left Moscow on February 13, 1790, and went along the main route through inner Siberia to Irkutsk which he reached in April and which, as he judged from Georgi's and other naturalists' accounts, he found considerably changed since their time. He enjoyed the beauty of Lake Baikal and proceeded on to Kiakhta. In 1792 he was ordered to investigate whether or not rhubarb plantations could be started farther west also on the Enisei or Irtysh, and he therefore returned to Irkutsk, left in February for Krasnoiarsk and then turned south. Later he went back to Krasnoiarsk, visited Tomsk, Barnaul, the Altai mountains and the Kirgiz steppe. He embodied careful descriptions of what he saw in letters to his friends and former teachers. These letters have been published and are the first source since the Pallas expedition and Jakob Fries's journey to give us more than superficial impressions of late eighteenth-century Siberia.[117]

After Sievers's publications, the yield of Siberian travel accounts resumes its disappointing character, although a constant flow of travellers to Siberia—most of them on official missions—continues. There is not much of interest about Siberia, except for some remarks on social life and the theatre in Tobolsk, in a report of the Englishman John Parkinson, a fellow of Magdalen College, Oxford, who accompanied the later first Lord Skelmersdale on a Russian tour, which at first was scheduled to reach China but which in fact did not get beyond Tobolsk; nor do we learn much from a brief account edited by Kisak Tamai about a sojourn of four shipwrecked Japanese prisoners who were sent to Irkutsk in the year 1796 and who were detained there for eight years.[118] They proceeded later to St. Petersburg and finally, in connection with Admiral Krusenstern's expedition around the world, they were allowed to return home.[119]

Little information can be gained from another French abbé who visited Siberia and who left a "Journey in Siberia". His name was de Fabruy. Born in 1750, he left France in 1791 during the revolution since he refused to take the oath on the new constitution, and he spent a number of years in Belgium, Germany and Russia. In the summer of 1798 he accompanied a M. de Vioménil, whom Paul I had named head of a regiment of dragoons in Siberia, and on August 16 he arrived in St. Peter, in Kirgiz territory. Almost all he has to say of his experiences concerns his and his master's personal affairs. A few notes which contain remarks about the Kirgiz add nothing to our knowledge. His stay in Siberia was not long; by 1802, he was able to return to France.[120]

Some information may be gathered from the poet Augustus von Kotzebue, who wrote in pleasing style a book, *The most remarkable year in the life of Augustus von Kotzebue,* which enjoyed much favour at the time of its appearance.[121] *Kotzebue* was born in 1761 in Weimar; in 1781 he came to St. Petersburg and secured a place in government service. His interest in the stage led him in 1798 to Vienna, where he was offered a position at the theatre. From that time on he devoted himself entirely to the theatre and to writing. On a visit to Russia in 1800 he was suddenly arrested and taken to Siberia, and it is in this connection that he wrote an account of his travels in this country. He was first sent to Tobolsk, where he arrived on May 10, then to Kurgan, but with no more information than he had formerly been given for his arrest, he was released on July 7, 1800, and returned to Weimar. He remained active in the political and literary life of Germany during the great times of liberation from the French yoke, but he seemed little interested in the new spirit and, suspected of reactionary activities and of spying for Russia, he was murdered in 1819 by an enthusiastic young liberal.

The other available travel accounts of Siberia during the Napoleonic era belong mainly to a group of voyagers who in one way or another were connected with the Russian-American Company, founded by Emperor Paul I for the development of Alaska.[122] Among them were two imperial fleet officers, Khvostov and Davydov, who crossed Siberia in the years 1802 and 1803. Gavrilo Ivanovich Davydov was only eighteen years old at the time of his journey; he left a description which was published in German a number of years later, after the author himself had died at the early age of 25.[123] It constituted a promising first effort, makes enjoyable reading, and contains information about conditions in central Siberia which, though not abundant, is worth while. However, Davydov's real interest centred around the eastern parts of Asia, which he saw on his trip from Irkutsk to the Kodiak Islands. He and his companion travelled via Ekaterinburg, Ishim, Shadrinsk, and the Baraba steppe to Kainsk and Tomsk, which they reached in June 1802, then to Krasnoiarsk and Irkutsk, and down the Lena river. The return journey in 1803 followed the same route, except for the last part which led via Tobolsk.

The next traveller is Dr. Georg Langsdorff, likewise connected with the Russian-American Company, who as a botanist accompanied Admiral Krusenstern on the famous Russian sea expedition around the world.[124] He was born in 1774 in Heidelberg, had received his doctor's degree in medicine in Göttingen in 1797 and had practised medicine in Portugal, where he also served as surgeon-major to to English auxiliary troops. He was named corresponding member of the Academy of Sciences in St. Petersburg and succeeded in joining Krusenstern's fleet when passing through Copenhagen. He left the expedition and stayed for a while in Alaska and the Far East. In 1807 he returned via Siberia, travelling to Irkutsk, Kiakhta and back to Irkutsk (November 22), then to Krasnoiarsk (November 27), Tomsk (December 1), through the Baraba steppe, and to Tobolsk, where he stayed from December 11 to the end of January 1808. He reached Kazan on the first of March. The dates suffice to indicate how little time there was for observation. Langsdorff himself says in his memoirs later:[125] "A hasty winter progress, such as mine was, furnishes ... few observations and occurrences worthy of being recorded"[126]—a sad comment on the change of times from the age of the Enlightenment when travellers, even when on business, would not forego the pleasure to stop, to observe, to describe. The fact that Langsdorff did not may be all the more regretted as his brief four-page description of life in Irkutsk, with the poignant remark: "Here are many Oriental customs, and very little happiness",[127] indicates his ability to furnish us with sidelights which bear on social conditions about which we learn so little from other available sources. Langsdorff died in 1852 in Freiburg, Germany.

Several times Langsdorff refers to his friend D'Wolf. John D'Wolf was an American from Bristol, Rhode Island, where he was born in 1779 and died in 1872. As a sea captain he sailed in 1806 to Alaska, but sold his ship there to Dr. Langsdorff in order to be free the next year to continue his voyage via Asia and return by land, crossing Siberia and Europe. He accomplished his plans, went to Okhotsk and arrived by the end of July 1807 in Iakutsk. He then sailed up the Lena river to Irkutsk, where he arrived in August. On September 6 he was in Krasnoiarsk, on the tenth in Tomsk, on the nineteenth in Tobolsk, on the twenty-fourth in Ekaterinburg, from where he went to Kazan, Moscow, and St. Petersburg. D'Wolf did not speak Russian and learned little; as he says, he was "for eight days and nights in succession"[128] lying on his back in a carriage, thus, like Dr. Langsdorff, allowing us little to expect from his observations. His writings give us no sensible clue for the hurry, unless it was his desire for a sporting feat rather than a worth-while experience that drove him on. He published his adventures in 1861—more than half a century after his return.[129]

During the period covered by these voyages there occurred a number of embassies to China and Japan which, as of old, had to cross Siberia. Among them was that of Count Golovin to Peking and that of Nicholas P. Rezanov to Japan.[130] The reports they sent home referred to official business rather than to observations of social conditions and natural phenomena of the country they passed on their journey. However, the Golovkin embassy had—after the example of Izmailov's and Raguzinsky's—a scientist attached whose account of the trip through Siberia constitutes, together with Sievers's letters, a foremost source of information. This was Julius Heinrich Klaproth, born in Berlin in 1783, a man with sharp powers of observation, scientific training, and a great ability to write. He had the inclinations and abilities of a polyhistor, was interested in philosophy, history, mathematics, linguistics, and several other fields, and specialized in Oriental studies. He became an associate of the Academy of Sciences in St. Petersburg in 1804 and early in 1805 travelled via Moscow, Ekaterinburg, Tomsk and Krasnoiarsk to Irkutsk in order to join the embassy of Count Golovkin. On this trip he studied the native populations, their languages and customs, and observed carefully whatever he encountered. Together with Golovkin he crossed Lake Baikal and proceeded via Kiakhta into China. The embassy was soon turned back and on the return trip Klaproth again travelled part of the way alone; he went to Ust Kamenogorsk and into the Altai mountains, the Irtysh region, the Kalmyk steppe, and to Omsk, and did not return to St. Petersburg until 1807. He died in Paris in 1835.[131]

The last account of a traveller crossing Siberia during the Napoleonic period is that of Peter Dobell. In 1830 he published a two-volume account of his travels in Kamchatka and Siberia during 1812,[132] but he has nothing to offer regarding the central and western parts of the country. In its own way, a very different type of record may be worth mentioning here, a little volume which appeared in 1819. This contains a series of drawings of places in Siberia, which the painter Andrei Martinov published after a trip that he undertook via Tomsk and Irkutsk to the Chinese border.[133]

The last decade of the period under consideration offers several travel accounts which contain more descriptive material than most of those of the four preceding ones. The first one is that of Johann Friedrich Erdmann, who was a doctor—later in Saxon service—and who made a trip into the Tobolsk government in 1816. His book, which was published in 1825 and 1826,[134] contains careful descriptions particularly of the Ural regions and its iron works, and some general remarks which apparently were considered unfriendly to Russia, but which give us welcome glimpses of aspects that escaped earlier visitors or which it was thought either not worth while or not prudent to publish.

The next two accounts are written by two globe-trotting Englishmen hungry for sensation, trying to outdo each other, and ending up with a ridiculous quarrel over their respective merits. The one was John D. Cochrane, a descendant of one of England's well-known families, an adventurer and braggart, who by later standards may be classified as "a sportsman". The special venture which he thought of consisted of crossing Siberia on foot—an enterprise which might have afforded him, and us, with a wealth of interesting observations had his mind been receptive, his eyes open for essentials, and had he executed his plan instead of indulging in what is nowadays termed "hitchhiking". He left an inaccurate and supercilious account, which is distinguished mainly for the very unfavourable picture Cochrane gives about most of the places he visited, and the unfriendly description of the Russians. He took the customary route via Omsk, Krasnoiarsk, Udinsk and Tomsk to Irkutsk, from where he travelled northeastward, retracing his steps some two and a half years later, and marvelling then at the rapidity with which changes were taking place in Siberia. In 1824 his book was published.[135] The author himself died one year later on a similar venture which took him to South America.

The other was James Holman, a former naval officer, a fellow of the Royal Society, born in 1786, the title of whose account suffices to indicate the limitations of his work: *Travels through Russia, Siberia, Poland, Austria, Saxony, Prussia, Hanover . . . 1822, 1823 and 1824 while suffering from total blindness.*[136] Cochrane said about Holman that "any information . . . is not implicity to be relied on, particularly situated as he is, possessing hardly a sufficient knowledge of the Russian language", to which Holman replied that "physically blind as the Author is, he cannot but be sensible to the mental obscurity of Captain C."[137] We may admire the courage of the man whose loss of eyesight, suffered at the age of twenty-four, did not prevent him from undertakings such as the Siberian trip, but we must agree that his ignorance of the Russian language added to his physical handicap constituted too much of a curb on his powers of observation to allow his travel relations, interesting and well written though they may be, to touch more than the surface of things. Holman left Moscow in June 1823, just when Cochrane was returning, and travelled from Ekaterinburg to Tobolsk, then to Kainsk, Tomsk, Krasnoiarsk and Irkutsk. From there he intended to proceed via Kamchatka, but without being given a definite reason he was ordered to return by the shortest route and to quit the country. On January 18, 1824, he left for Omsk and crossed the Siberian border in February. In his account he reports chiefly on his visits in the houses of various prominent Russian officials and their social life, and he gives some descriptions which he must have learned through others. He later undertook additional journeys and died in 1857.

Holman's Siberian excursion ended in 1824. After this date, the interest of travellers as expressed through substantial accounts shifted to new regions. The government had an influence on this shift, for it desired further information on the navigational possibilities along the coasts of Siberia on the Arctic and the Pacific Seas. F. P. Vrangel's trip bears witness to this change of interest.[138] Moreover, Central Asia attracted new attention. E. Eversmann in 1825, and in 1829 Alexander von Humboldt, who visited Siberia in company of two other German scholars, Chr. Gottfried Ehrenberg and Gustav Rose, made some contributions to the knowledge of their times by giving accounts of these parts. And a new report on the Irkutsk government and the region of Lake Baikal, as well as on trade in that area, written by M. Hedenström,[134] likewise dates back to these years. Perhaps it is only fair to add two more travel descriptions of Siberia, although they, too, are a few years beyond the period under consideration here. They come from the Prussian physicist Georg Adolph Erman (1806–1870), who had studied in Berlin and Königsberg and later became a professor at the University of Berlin, and from his companion, a Dane by the name of Christoph Hansteen. Erman left a careful and learned description in which he dealt particularly with northern Siberia,[140] discussing, as once Gmelin and Pallas had done, though now on the basis of modern science, the geology, zoology, and anthropology of the regions he visited, and contributing to improved surveys and measurements in Siberia. He travelled in 1828 to Tobolsk and from there on to Tara and Tomsk (unfortunately, he too hurried along this eight-hundred-versts-long stretch of road, covering it in six days) and then undertook a side trip to the province of Kolyvan. After his return to Tomsk he proceeded to Krasnoiarsk, which had greatly increased in importance since the introduction of Speransky's reforms. From Krasnoiarsk Erman followed the road to Kansk and Irkutsk, crossed Lake Baikal and arrived, via Selenginsk, in Kiakhta and Maimachen on the Chinese border. His further route led him to the north eastern regions of Siberia, from where he returned in 1829. His extensive travel report is supplemented by that of Hansteen, which concludes the list of accounts of Siberia here presented.[141]

4 Hans Jakob Fries

Almost exactly at the half way mark of the hundred years of our discussion, a trip through Siberia from the Urals to the Chinese border took place, undertaken by a young Swiss doctor and described by him in an interesting account. He was Hans Jakob Fries (or Vries), born in Zürich in 1749, the oldest son of a carpenter who lived in relatively meagre circumstances and who died in 1799 as a pensioner (*Pfründner*) in St. Jakob. There were thirteen children in the family, of whom only three survived to a mature age. Among them was Jakob's brother Johannes, who also became a carpenter and, a prosperous man, died in 1815 without leaving any children.

Like many of his compatriots, Hans Jakob could not envisage a promising future in his beautiful and beloved, but narrowly confined homeland,[142] and therefore decided to seek his fortune elsewhere. Perhaps he also hoped to make himself in this way useful to his family; at least, he indicated such a desire in a letter from Russia, in which he expressed his intention to support his parents.[143] It is possible, though, that, as Erica von Schulthess has discovered through recent valuable research, a concrete reason existed for his emigration.[144] When seventeen years old, in 1766, he was arrested by the police and accused of having stolen books in various book shops, and of having resold them. Fries confessed and was expelled from school. Forced to earn a living, he worked on a job which offered him neither satisfaction nor an attractive goal in life. Seeing a desirable career impossible at home, he left Switzerland on April 1, 1770. He was barely twenty years old. He had with him introductions to friends in Germany, who in turn gave him recommendations to others in Russia, including the family of Fries's famous compatriot, Leonhard Euler.[145] Fries travelled via Leipzig and Potsdam to Berlin where, as he later thankfully acknowledged, he was shown much courtesy and friendliness, and then proceeded to Stettin, Königsberg and St. Petersburg. On September 1 he arrived in the Russian capital. He was well received, particularly in the German and Swiss colony there, and he found a friendly welcome also with the Eulers.

After a three months' stay, Fries left for Moscow shortly before Christmas 1770, and thus happened to be there at the time when a terrible epidemic of the plague had struck the city. According to Fries's description,[146] which is quite detailed, there were no less than 58,091 dead in the city and some additional 91,000 in the surrounding province. Whether it was under the impression of this event or whether planned earlier,[147] Fries began to take up the study of medicine, preparing at the General Military Hospital to become a surgeon. He combined his medical studies with work in the field of botany. In 1773, he passed his first examinations and became an assistant surgeon. In this capacity he accompanied during the following year a regiment of Orenburg dragoons on its campaign against the Turks, and in 1775 he participated in an expedition sent out to suppress a revolt of the Zaporogian Cossacks. After the conclusion of this undertaking he received orders to accompany a recruiting officer, Major Riedel, a fellow Swiss,[148] on a mission to Siberia; Riedel was to select and draft soldiers from the forces stationed in Siberia in order to refill the ranks of the European regiments. Fries was elated at the opportunity of seeing the strange and faraway land, and it was this trip which he has described in the account published here.

After his return from Siberia he resumed his studies, working at the Admiralty Hospital in St. Petersburg, where he passed his final examinations, and in 1780 he became a state surgeon. He married a Fräulein Mechelmann and had two daughters, both of whom later married Russian officers. He himself was eventually promoted to inspector of the medical police in the Vologda district, and in 1797 became a Councillor of State. His interests extended beyond his own field of medicine; he published a description of the Vologda district for the *Severnyi Arkhiv* and he wrote some thirty-seven historical, geographic, ethnographic and statistical studies, among them one on the city of Ust Veliki, another about the river system in northern Russia, and still others about meteorological questions. Most of his studies bore on problems of the Russian national economy, and several of his articles were printed by the Archaeological Institute of St. Petersburg in the *Vestnik Arkheologii i Istorii*. The Academy of Sciences named him a corresponding member. On November 8, 1801, he died in Vologda.[149]

In addition to his publications in Russian, Fries wrote, as mentioned, for the *Archiv gemeinnütziger physischer und medizinischer Kenntnisse* about the pest in Moscow. This is part of a series for the years 1788 to 1791 which contains what he called a diary covering the first eleven years of his stay abroad.[150] He describes therein his departure from Switzerland, his voyage through Germany, his experiences in Russia, his trip in Siberia, and his studies after his return. It is, however, not a day-by-day account based on notes made at the time; it rather represents not always reliable reminiscences interspersed with a good deal of second-hand information gathered at the time of writing from books and statistics.

An immediate and more exhaustive account of Fries's travels may be found in a long, precise letter which he wrote to his parents upon the completion of his journey through Siberia and which contains only personal observations. This letter covers the five years from 1774 to 1779, during which Fries apparently had failed to send any news to his parents. A version of it is preserved in the *Zentralbibliothek* in Zürich, Switzerland. It is doubtful that even this version is the original—which may no longer exist at all.[151] A. Hug, whose Feuilleton about Fries in the *Neue Zürcher Zeitung* is mentioned in note 143, in any case used another copy, or a similar report which comprised 261 pages. Obviously he was not aware of the document here published. J. J. Egli, who published several articles in the *Zeitschrift für wissenschaftliche Geographie*,[152] likewise used another copy. His articles are confined, though, to mainly historical and geographic observations which Jakob Fries reported and which Egli compares with what was known a century later. The version here reproduced did not come to the attention of the authorities of the

Zentralbibliothek until after the Second World War, when a reorganization of the materials took place.[153]

The letter may be divided in three parts. The first five pages refer to family news and inquiries about friends and relatives in Zürich; they are of no particular interest and have no bearing on historical events in Russia or Siberia. The second part comprises approximately twenty-three pages and deals with Fries's participation in the Russian campaign of 1774 against the Turks. A map has been added to the present volume to illustrate the route taken by the regiment to which he was assigned. The third and most important part is that which describes Fries's journey through south eastern Russia and Siberia. This journey led the young Swiss to regions which had been opened up to systematic investigation and exploration only a few decades earlier, through the work of the first great scientific expedition of Gmelin. Fries's own journey almost coincided with the second scientific expedition, undertaken by Pallas during the years 1769 to 1774.

The route which Fries followed through Siberia differed to a considerable extent from the customary one. The earliest trade routes from Russia into Siberia had generally led along trails and rivers far to the north; for it was there in the forests of the north that furs, the chief objective of the traders from Pskov, Novgorod, Suzdal and Tver, were most abundantly to be found.[154] These northern routes had the additional advantage of being least dependent upon the Tartar hordes who dominated Russia and Siberia and who, for strategic reasons, were interested in controlling the direct lines connecting with Mongolia and China. When Tartar domination had come to an end and the systematic penetration of Siberia by Russians got underway, the passes across the central Ural mountains and the rivers farther south began to supplement the previous northern routes.[155] Yet, even then the north remained the chief link to Siberia and the East because of the good interconnections between the various river systems. Thus, the envoy Isbrand Ides travelled in the late seventeenth century considerably farther to the north than Fries and his contemporaries were to do later on. So did most of the other voyagers—

including Vitus Bering—until well into the eighteenth century.

Only gradually did a change take place. Overland routes were laid out and provided with postal relay stations and inns.[156] They replaced water routes, and afforded the increasing number of visitors and administrators permanent, direct and shorter communication lines. Toward the end of the reign of Peter the Great, the route through the Urals via Solikamsk and Verkhoture, which had first been establish in 1598 and which led into central Siberia, became the most important one. New routes were introduced still farther south when Russian domination along the Yaik (Ural) river became firmly established and towns and frontier fortifications were built there. The development of the southern roads was, however, artificially checked, for in an attempt to control and supervise all exports and imports to and from the East, laws were made according to which all trade had to be centred on the Verkhoture road. Not until 1761, toward the end of Empress Elizabeth's reign, was the southern route via Ekaterinburg reopened.[157]

As it turned out, neither Solikamsk nor Ekaterinburg served as the point of departure for Jakob Fries. His route lay still farther south, for it was from Orenburg that Major Riedel and he were to set out for their Siberian expedition. They travelled along the Sakmara river to Upper Uralsk and from there almost exactly due east, crossing the steppe regions and heading directly for Omsk. They did not gain the main road until they reached Vozdvyshensk. Then they followed the main road, passed through Tomsk, Krasnoiarsk, Irkutsk, crossed Lake Baikal, and proceeded via Selenginsk to Kiakhta and Maimachen. They returned along the same route, but after reaching Upper Uralsk they turned westward and visited some of the iron works in the mountains and finally reached Orenburg from the north rather than the east. The total distance they travelled amounted to 12,588 versts.[158] Obviously Fries could orient himself, like Pallas, by "verst columns" (mile stones) found along the roads. He kept a careful daily record of all distances, and these coincide well with those given by other sources and particularly by Pallas.[159]

As to Fries's mode of travelling, it did not differ from

that used for many centuries. Most of the way was covered in wagons for which horses were provided at the numerous postal stations. Long after Fries, Adolph Erman pointed out how little the ways of travelling had changed in the course of the centuries; the sledges used by him were essentially still of the same type which Sigismund von Herberstein had once described for early sixteenth-century European Russia. [160]

Fortunately Fries was not as rushed on his journey as De Lesseps, Langsdorff, D'Wolf and others.[161] Yet even he complains, justifiably, of the speed with which he had to proceed, blaming it mostly on the lack of curiosity which his superior officer, Major Riedel, evinced in regard to his surroundings. It must, however, be considered that Riedel was on an official mission for whose prompt execution he was held responsible. The formidable supervision of the Russian government and its heavy hand were felt everywhere in the vast empire. In reading the various travel accounts one finds again and again the control which the central authorities at St. Petersburg, thousands of miles and months of travel away, could exercise even in the most distant parts and over the most petty decisions. Fear of later being accused of neglect of duty, of being subjected to degradation and possible banishment to Siberia necessarily affected the measures taken by those in charge of expeditions. In view of the costs involved in all Siberian expeditions, haste characterized their actions, and the peculiar pressure for speed and for bringing a task once undertaken to a prompt conclusion was just as great in the days of horseback and wagon travelling as it was later with ever faster railroads or airplanes.

For Fries himself the situation was, however, different. Bearing no responsibility for the accomplishment of the mission he could and, having the mind and ability, did use the opportunity for looking not only toward the successful conclusion of the enterprise and the end of the road, but also at the road itself and those things that the enterprise had to offer while it lasted. It is for this reason that his account commands the interest of posterity.

Notes to Part I

1. University of California publications in history, XXX (1943).
2. *Ibid.* XXXI (1043).
3. Irkutsk, 1941.
4. Alekseev, p. xxii. Alekseev includes in his list writers who never saw Siberia, such as John Milton.
5. Published by the Akademia Nauk, Moscow, 1946.
6. "Die Reiseberichte über Sibirien von Herberstein bis Ides", Leipzig, 1905.
7. E. Ysbrants Ides, *Driejaarige Reize naar China*, Amsterdam, 1710 (In English: Evert Ysbrandszoon Ides, *Three Years Travels from Moscow . . . to China*, London, 1706).
8. Published by Arkheograph. Kommissia, St. Petersburg, 1881–85.
9. 2 vols., St. Petersburg, 1891.
10. *Ocherki po istochnikovedeniiu Sibiri . . . XVIII vek (pervaia polovina)*, "Nauka", Moscow-Leningrad, 1965.
11. *Ibid.*, pp. 11, 45.
12. Kemerovskoe knizhnoe izd., 1963.
13. *Istoriografiia Sibiri, Pervaia polovina XIX veka*, 1965.
14. I, 56–80.
15. I, 80–84.
16. *Sibir v izvestiiakh zapadno evropeiskikh puteshestvennikov i uchenikh XVIII v.*, Vostochno Sibirskoe knizhnoe izd., 1968.
17. Ed. by A. P. Okladnikov, V. I. Sunkov *et al.*, vol. II, "Nauk", Leningrad, 1968.
18. *Zapadnaia Sibir v XVIII veke*, Novosibirsk, 1965.
19. 2 vols., Berkeley, 1939.
20. 3 vols., University of Washington, 1935.
21. Ohio State University, 1968. Important for Siberian studies are also Sergei V. Bakrushin's works, but his accent is also on the seventeenth century. For a complete list of his works, see S. V. Bakhrushin, *Nauchnie trudi*, Moscow, 1952, pp. 9–20.
22. *Muscovite and Mandarin: Russia's Trade with China . . . 1727–1805* Chapel Hill, 1969.
23. *Feeding the Russian Fur Trade . . . 1639–1856*, Madison, 1969.
24. *Histoire des relations de la Russie avec la Chine, 1689–1730*, Paris, 1941.
25. pp. 373–394.
26. *Nouvelles Archives des Missions Scientifiques . . .* Nouvelle sér., I (Paris, 1911).
27. A map of Tobolsk province and of Irkutsk between 1726 and 1737 were, for instance, published by Lee Bagrow, "Ivan Kirilov, Compiler of the First Russian Atlas, 1689-1737", *Imago Mundi*,

NOTES TO PART I

II, 78 ff. Likewise in *Imago Mundi* (XII, 157–159) is an article by Nicholas Poppe, "Renat's Kalmuck Maps". Johan Gustav Renat, a Swedish artillery sergeant made prisoner in 1709 and sent to Siberia, spent 17 years there, mainly among the Kalmyks, and brought home two maps.

28. "Uebersicht der Reisen und naturhistorischen Untersuchungen im Aralo-Kaspi-Gebiet, seit dem Jahre 1720 bis zum Jahre 1874", vol. VIII (St. Petersburg, 1876), pp. 145–159; 440–459; 558–576.
29. 9 vols., St. Petersburg, 1732–64.
30. Müller, IV, pt. vi, 473 ff.
31. [Samuel Engel], *Mémoires et observations géographiques et critiques sur . . . pays septentrionaux*, Lausanne, 1765. Cf. James R. Masterson and Helen Brower, *Bering's Successors, 1745–1780*, University of Washington, 1948, pp. 14 f.
32. *Sibirische Geschichte*, 2 vols., St. Petersburg, 1768. The work ends with 1761. A careful Russian edition appeared recently, with S. V. Bakhrushin as co-editor.
33. *Geschichte der Schiffahrten und Versuche . . . zur Entdeckung des nordöstlichen Weges . . .*, Halle, 1768. Especially part VI, "Versuche und Reisen der Russen in Norden und Nordosten von Asien", pp. 505–704.
34. *Geographisch-physikalische und naturhistorische Beschreibung des russischen Reiches*, 3 vols. in 6, Königsberg, 1796–1802. Bibliography in vol. I, pp. 32–48.
35. *Geschichte der Medizin in Russland*, 3 vols., Moscow, 1813–1819.
36. Amsterdam, 1738, X, 69–99.
37. Two volumes, Bern, Switzerland, 1791.
38. *Nouveaux Mémoires sur l'état présent de la Grande Russie ou Moscovie*, Paris, 1725.
39. Cf. note 30.
40. *Georg Wilh. Stellers Beschreibung von dem Lande Kamtschatka . . .*, Frankfurt-Leipzig, 1774. Probably Scherer wrote his account on the basis of Steller's own papers, which he had received from Jakob Stählin in St. Petersburg. See "An Early Account of the Russian Discoveries in the North Pacific", transl. and ed. by James W. van Stone in *Anthropological Papers of the University of Alaska*, VII, 2 (1959), p. 94: Historical Researches . . . by J. B. Scherer, Paris, 1777.
41. *View of the Russian Empire*, 3 vols., London, 1800.
42. *Jenseits des steinernen Tores, Entdeckungsreisen deutscher Forscher durch Sibirien . . .*, Berlin, 1963.
43. *Iz istorii russkikh ekspeditsii na Tikhom Okeane, pervaia polovina XVIII v.*, Moscow, 1948.
44. *La conquête de la Sibérie*, Paris, 1938. Semionov refers on p. 370 to a book by "le colonel de Belcourt", which I have not been able to trace. He also mentions p. 329, Xavier de Maistre's popular *La jeune Sibérienne*, which somewhat illustrates contemporary knowledge, understanding and illusions about Siberia.
45. *Travels from St. Petersburg in Russia to diverse parts of Asia*, 2 vols., Glasgow, 1763.

46. *Die Gesandschafft . . . von Gross-Russland an den Sinesischen Käyser . . .* 1719, Lübeck, 1725.
47. Foust, p. 26 n. For Lange's trip to China in connection with the embassy of Count Sava Vladislavich Raguzinsky, who lived in Dalmatia (in Ragusa), cf. *ibid.*, p. 24 n.1-2. Also William Coxe, *Account of the Russian Discoveries between Asia and America,* London, 1780, p. 205. Lange (whose name is also spelled "Lang") is clearly identified by his companion Unverzagt as of Swedish birth.
48. "Journal du Voyage . . . Laurent Lange" in Weber, II (1725). An English translation made by John Bell in his *A Journal from St. Petersburg . . . to Pekin . . . , 1719,* Glasgow, 1763. For the German edition, cf. *Neue Nordische Beyträge,* 7 vols., St. Petersburg-Leipzig, 1781-1796, II, 83-159.
49. "Nachricht von D. G. Messerschmidts siebenjähriger Reise in Sibirien", *Neue Nordische Beyträge,* III, 97-158. An extensive edition of Messerschmidt's writings has recently been prepared: *D. G. Messerschmidt: Forschungsreise durch Sibirien,* 1720-1727 *(Quellen und Studien zur Geschichte Osteuropas,* VIII), ed. by Eduard Winter, N. A. Figurovsky, G. Jarosch *et al.,* 4 vols., Berlin, 1962-1968.
50. Cf. Georgi, I, 51.
51. *Das Nord- und Ostliche Theil von Europa und Asia,* Stockholm, 1730. An English version: *An Historico-Geographical Description of the North and Eastern Parts of Europe and Asia* was published in London in 1736.
52. *Ibid.,* 308 ff.
53. Zinner, p. 68 Albert Hämäläinen indicates that of the several thousand captured officers perhaps not more than a quarter returned. "Nachrichten der nach Sibirien verschickten Offiziere Karls XII . . . ", Suomalais-ugrilainen seuran, *Aikakanskirja (Journal de la Société finno-ugrienne),* XLIX (1938).
54. Vol. X (Amsterdam, 1738), pp. 10, 69-99, *passim.*
55. *Der allerneueste Staat . . . nebst einer Historischen Nachricht von . . . gefangenen Schweden,* 1720.
56. *Wahrhavte . . . Historie von denen Schwedischen Gefangenen in Russland und Sibirien . . . nach . . . Pultawa,* Sorau, 1728. Cf. Hämäläinen, pp. 2-10.
57. Co-prisoners mentioned by Wreech were Captains M. W. Albedyl, Andres Stolhammer, C. v. Creutz and H. A. Morton, Lieutenants J. Schöning and C. Palm, Baron Griepenhielm, G. O. von Berch, C. G. Ochs, Melchior Paul, etc.
58. Cf. Eduard Winter, *Halle als Ausgangspunkt der deutschen Russlandkunde,* Berlin, 1953.
59. "Les moeurs et usages des Ostiacks" in Weber's *Nouveaux Mémoires.* Originally published in Berlin, 1720: *Johann Bernhard Müllers . . . Leben . . . der Ostiaken.*
60. "Unterthänigste Vorstellung . . . betreffende der . . . in Nord-Syberien . . . unterworffenen . . . völcker, besondern grossen Gravationen", *Tartu Uelikooli Toimetused* [Dorpat University]

ed., *Acta et Commentationes,* B Humaniora, XVII (1930).
61. G. F. Müller, *Sammlung,* III, 102–110.
62. *Ibid.,* IV, 275–364. (In Swedish: *Berättelse om Ajuchinska Calmuckiet,* ed. Lars Salvius).
63. *Ibid.* IV, 228.
64. "Auszug aus Dr. med. Gottlob Schobers . . . Memorabilia Russico-Asiatica", *Ibid,* VII, 47–71. August Ludwig Schlözer (1735–1809) had come to St. Petersburg in 1761 and remained there for about six years. At first, he worked as an assistant to Gerh. Fr. Müller, later, in 1765, he became a member of the Academy and professor of Russian history. He left St. Petersburg in 1767 in order to become a professor at the University of Göttingen. His colleague Johann B. Beckmann (1739–1811), a philosopher with many inclinations similar to Schlözer's, had also been in St. Petersburg, having arrived there in 1763. For two years he held there the position of professor of natural history. His most famous work is a *Münz-, Geld- und Bergwerks-Geschichte des russischen Kaiserthums,* 1700–1789 (Göttingen, 1791). He also brought out a *Literatur der älteren Reisebeschreibungen,* 8 pts. (Göttingen, 1807–10), which goes up to 1705 but has nothing to offer about Siberia. It constitutes more of a curiosity than a serious scientific enterprise.
65. According to this account, the missionary movement began with the getting together of about thirty Swedish officers in Tobolsk in order to read religious books. This happened in 1711. Then, one of them took on a pupil, and gradually a school was built, then enlarged. By 1715, it had two teachers of religion and the three Rs and two Latin teachers, offering also instruction in drawing and sewing. In 1716, the number of the teachers had climbed to eleven.
66. "Auszug aus dem Reise Journal des Herrn Ober-Kriegs-Commissarii Johann Unkowski von der Calmueckey", *Sammlung russischer Geschichte,* I, 141 ff.
67. There are many accounts of Bering's travels. Cf., e.g., John Harris, *A complete collection of Voyages and Travels,* 2 vols., London, 1744–48; *Sammlung russischer Geschichte,* I, 1 ff., III, 112 ff., P. du Halde, *The General History of China,* 3rd ed., 4 vols., London, IV (1741), pp. 429 ff. About earlier trips of discovery along the Pacific coast of Siberia by Dezhnev and by Gvozdev, see Frank A. Golder, *Russian Expansion on the Pacific,* Cleveland, 1914, pp. 67–95 and 159–162.
68. F. A. Golder ed., *Bering's Voyages,* 2 vols., New York, 1922–25. L. S. Berg devotes to Bering's voyage a considerable part of his *Ocherki po istorii russkikh geograficheskikh otkryty,* Moscow, 1946.
69. *The American Expedition,* London, 1952. (A German edition: *Brücke nach Amerika,* Olten-Freiburg, 1968.).
70. George A. Lensen, *The Russian Push toward Japan: Russo-Japanese Relations, 1697–1875,* Princeton, 1959.
71. Johann Georg Gmelin, *Reise durch Sibirien, 1733–43,* 4 vols., Göttingen, 1751–52.

72. Golder, *Bering's Voyages,* I, 310 f. Chirikov died likewise young, in 1748.
73. *Sammlung,* III, 273. F. Buache, royal cartographer in Paris, wrote "Mémoires sur les pays de l'Asie" and "Considérations". Cf. Monsieur [Nich.] de l'Isle, *Explication de la carte des ... découvertes au Nord de la Mer du Sud,* Paris, 1752, and the remark made, p. 11, about Buache, who in 1750 had added outlines of new discoveries to the map made by Delisle in 1731.
74. Vol. I (St. Petersburg, 1732) includes an account of Spanberg's voyages to Japan. The explorations between Asia and America, transl. into English by S. Müller, are found in *Voyages from Asia to America,* London, 1761.
75. Cf. *Sammlung,* II, iv, pp. 231 ff.
76. *Ibid.,* III, v-vi, pp. 413 ff.
77. Cf. Andreev, pp. 73–164; Mirsoev, pp. 126–163.
78. "Akademiki Mueller i Fischer i opisanie Sibiri", *Chtenia v imperatorskom Obshchestvo istorii ... pri Moskovskom Universitet,* III (1866), 15–30. See note 32.
79. *History of Kamtschatka ...,* transl. by James Grieve, Glocester (sic), 1764. (An original Russian edition published in St. Petersburg, 1755.)
80. Cf. Leonhard Stejneger, *Georg Wilhelm Steller,* Cambridge, 1936; also Golder, *Bering's Voyages, passim.*
81. Gmelin, III, 361 ff. and *passim.*
82. Stejneger, p. 135.
83. *Opisanie Uralskikh i Sibirskikh Zavodov, 1735,* ed. by M. A. Pavlov, Moscow, 1937.
84. *Reise in Russland,* Copenhagen, 1744.
85. *Voyage en Sibérie .. 1761,* 4 vols., Paris, 1768. (English translation: *A Journey into Siberia ... in 1761,* London, 1770.)
86. A lover of Truth, *The Antidote or an Enquiry into ... A Journey into Siberia ... by the Abbé Chappe d'Auteroche,* London, 1772. Zinner is among the few authors who takes a rather kindly view of Chappe d'Auteroche. P. 209.
87. *Mémoires* (transl. from the German), Bern, 1790.
88. The second part of the memoirs consists in general descriptions gathered by the author during his time of exile. He mentions a "M. Sujef, de qui nous avons une relation d'un voyage en Sibérie" from the year 1772. See Georgi's map. Vassilii Fedorovich Zuev (1754–1794) had studied abroad, in Leiden and Strassburg, and later became adjunct and professor at the Academy of Sciences in St. Petersburg. He took part in Pallas's expedition and in February 1771 travelled on his own from Cheliabinsk north via Berezov to Kara Bay. Only in January 1772 did he join Pallas again in Krasnoiarsk. His report is incorporated in that of Pallas (III, 14–38).
89. *Topografiia Orenburgskoi Gubernii,* 1762, Orenburg, 1887.
90. Georgi, I, 59.
91. In one of his letters, Laxmann complains that after constructing instruments for meteorological observations he sent them

NOTES TO PART I

to various places in Siberia, but apparently they were not put to the right use and served decorative rather than scientific purposes. Later in his life he became interested in glass making, invented or adopted new methods and founded glass works in the Baikal region.

92. M. Erich Laxmann, *Sibirische Briefe,* ed. by Aug. Ludw. Schloezer, Göttingen-Gotha, 1769.
93. III, 159–177; V, 302 ff.; VI, 252–256.
94. *Memoirs and Travels,* 2 vols., transl. from the original, Dublin, 1790. A new edition: London, 1904. A later traveller, de Lesseps, criticized Benyowski's lack of veracity and his behaviour and wrote that "cet Esclavon s'y étoit dit François, & s'y étoit comporté en véritable Vandale". *Journal,* I, 154.
95. Chappe d'Auteroche's observations being more than a little unsatisfactory, and a new transit of Venus being expected, investigations in this connection were also made an objective of the expedition. Cf. Hartwich Ludwig Christian Bacmeister, ed., *Russische Bibliothek,* I (St. Petersburg, 1772), 40–59, 89–104, 376–378.
96. *Reise durch verschiedene Provinzen des Russischen Reiches,* 3 vols., St. Petersburg, 1773–76.
97. Johann Peter Falck, *Beyträge zur Topographischen Kenntniss des Russischen Reichs,* 3 vols., St. Petersburg, 1785–86.
98. See note 34. Also: *Beschreibung aller Nationen des russischen Reiches,* St. Petersburg, 1776–1780 (English edition: *Russia, a . . . Historical Account of all the Nations which comprise that Empire,* 4 vols., transl. by Wm. Tooke, London, 1780–1783).
99. *Tagebuch der Reise durch verschiedene Provinzen des Russischen Reiches, 1768–1771,* transl. by Chr. H. Hase, 3 vols., Altenburg, 1774–83.
100. Nikolaus Rytschkow, *Tagebuch über seine Reise durch verschiedene Provinzen des russischen Reichs, 1769–1771,* transl. by Christian Heinrich Hase, Riga, 1774.
101. Cf. Zinner, p. 206; also *Istoriia Sibiri,* p. 350.
102. Zinner, p. 6.
103. Cf. V. Vagin, *Istoricheskia svedenia o diatelnosti Grafa M. M. Speranskogo v Sibiri, 1819–1822,* 2 vols., St. Petersburg, 1872. Also Marc Raeff, *Siberia and the Reforms of 1822,* Seattle, 1956.
104. "Beschreibung der Buräten", in: Johann Georg Meusel, ed., *Beyträge zur Erweiterung der Geschichtskunde,* 2 vols., Augsburg, 1780–1781, I, 119–180.
105. *Neue Nordische Beyträge,* IV, 163–198.
106. Walther Kirchner, "Samuel Bentham and Siberia", *Slavonic and East European Review,* XXXVI (1958), 471–480. I should like to thank Mr D. R. Bentham of Loughborough, England, for additional information about Samuel Bentham which is not contained in my article. He has identified the lady mentioned in the article as Sophia Golitsyn, and he gives among Bentham's achievements the construction of a new type of "planing

machine which was of real importance in the history of technology".
107. *Neue Nordische Beyträge,* VI, 28–112.
108. *Neue Nordische Beyträge, passim.*
109. *The Voyages of Captain James Cook round the World,* London, 1813; see *ibid.,* VII, 192, regarding maps drawn by Plenisner and Krasheninnikov.
110. Martin Sauer, ed., *Joseph Billings Account of a geographical . . . Expedition to the Northern Parts of Russia. In the Years 1785, etc. to 1794,* London, 1802.
111. Jefferson spent the years 1784 to 1789 as minister plenipotentiary in France. Ledyard visited him there in the summer of 1786 in order to submit to him his plans. Jefferson found Ledyard personally attractive and, through the good services of Baron de Grimm, intervened in his favour with Catherine II. But she refused permission for Ledyard's trip. Nevertheless, he started on his journey. Marie Kimball, *Jefferson, the Scene of Europe, 1784–1789,* New York, 1950, pp. 260 ff.
112. Jared Sparks, *Life of John Ledyard,* Cambridge, 1829. About Ledyard's journal, cf. *ibid.,* p. 264.
113. *Putechestvie flota kapitana Sarycheva . . . pod nachalstvom . . . Billingsa, 1785–1793* g., 2 vols., St. Petersburg, 1802. Cf. same, *Putechestvie po severovostochnoi Sibiri . . .,* Moscow, 1952 (English translation: *Account of a Voyage of Discovery to the North East of Siberia,* 2 vols., London, 1806). *Gawrila Sarytschew's achtjährige Reise im nordöstlichen Sibirien,* transl. and ed. by Johann Heinrich Busse, Leipzig, 1805.
114. Jean François, Comte de la Pérouse (1741–1788?), was in 1785 charged by the French king to attempt the North West Passage and to explore the Pacific Ocean. As commandant of two ships, he sailed via Alaska, Sakhalin, Hawai, the Philippines and New South Wales and reached the Hebrides, where apparently his ship was wrecked, and he was lost. In 1797, Lesseps published an extensive account of the voyage.
115. *Journal historique du voyage de M. de Lesseps,* 2 vols., Paris, 1790.
116. *Ibid.,* II, 329.
117. Johann Sievers, *Briefe aus Sibirien an seine Lehrer,* St. Petersburg, 1796. Cf. *Nordische Beyträge,* VII, 145–370.
118. John Parkinson, *A Tour of Russia, Siberia and the Crimea, 1792–1794,* ed. by William Collier, Frank Cass, London, 1971; cf. A. G. Cross, "An Oxford Don in Catherine the Great's Russia", *Journal of European Studies,* X (1971). *Karawanen Reise in Sibirien,* Berlin, 1898; cf. Stewart Culin, ed., "Across Siberia in the Dragon Year of 1796", *Asia,* XX (June, 1920).
119. Another trip across Siberia by Japanese sailors was made in the years 1731–1732.
120. L'Abbé de Fabry, *Mémoires de mon Emigration (Société de l'histoire de France,* No. 66), Paris, 1933.
121. London, 1802.
122. See Semen B. Okun, *Rossiisko-amerikanskaia kompaniia,*

NOTES TO PART I 61

Moscow, 1939 (English translation: *The Russian-American Company*, Cambridge, 1951).
123. *Reise der russ.-kaiserl. Flott Offiziere Chwostov und Dawydow von St. Petersburg durch Sibirien nach Amerika und zurück in den Jahren 1802, 1803 und 1804*, Berlin, 1816.
124. Adam Joh. v. Krusenstern (1770–1846) was a native of Estonia. Having gained experience while serving with the English fleet and participating in various voyages, he returned to Russia in 1800. He was put in charge of the Russian Expedition around the World (1803–1806), which was to serve political and economic purposes and the advancement of geographical knowledge. Chief objects of his explorations were Kamchatka as well as the regions of the sea around Japan, Sakhalin, and China. Krusenstern himself published an account of the voyage and its results and brought out a scientific atlas.
125. *Voyages and Travels . . . 1803–1807*, Carlisle, 1817.
126. Langsdorff, p. 616.
127. *Ibid.*, p. 615.
128. Wilfred H. Munro, *Tales of an old sea port*, Princeton, 1917, p. 185.
129. John D'Wolf, *A Voyage to the North Pacific and a Journey through Siberia*, Cambridge, 1861.
130. Rezanov died at Krasnoiarsk on his return journey, having fallen with his horse. Langsdorff, p. 547.
131. *Allgemeine Deutsche Biographie*, XVI (1882), 51 ff. Klaproth's *Reise durch Russland und Sibirien* (Tübingen, 1815) has not been available to me, although other writings of his were, which however do not refer to Siberia in any useful degree.
132. *Travels in Kamtchatka and Siberia*, 2 vols., London, 1830.
133. *Zhivopisnoe puteshestvie ot Moskvi do Kitaiskoi granitsi*, St. Petersburg, 1819.
134. *Reisen im Innern Russlands*, 2 parts, Leipzig, 1825–1826.
135. *Narrative of a Pedestrian Journey through Russia and Siberian Tartary*, London 1824.
136. 2 vols., London, 1825.
137. *Ibid.*, I, x.
138. F. P. Vrangel, *Putechestvie po Severnim beregam Sibiri, 1820–1824 g*, 1948.
139. *Otryvki o Sibiri*, St. Petersburg, 1850.
140. *Travels in Siberia*, 2 vols., Philadephia, 1850 (London edition: 1848).
141. *Reise Erinnerungen aus Sibirien*, Leipzig, 1854 (original Danish: *Reise-erindringer . . .*, Christiania, 1859).
142. Walther Kirchner, "Emigration to Russia", *American Historical Review*, LV (1950).
143. A. Hug in *Neue Zürcher Zeitung*, Feuilleton, No. 66–73, March 7–14, 1882.
144. "Ein Zürcher Chirurgus im Reiche Katharinas II", Part I, *Neujahrsblatt der Hülfsgesellschaft in Zürich*, 1955.
145. The mathematician Euler (1707–83) from Basel had, in 1727, received a call to the Academy of Sciences in St. Petersburg

at the instigation of Daniel Bernoulli. In 1730 he became a professor and in 1733 a member of the Academy. He left St. Petersburg for Berlin in 1741 and stayed there for a quarter of a century, but returned to St. Petersburg in 1766 to spend there the remaining twenty years of his life. For the last fifteen years, he was almost blind. His fame rests on his achievements in the fields of calculus and trigonometry. At the time Fries visited him, his family, once numbering fifteen, had, owing to the death of ten children, dwindled to five. See also: Eduard Winter et al., eds., *Die deutsch-russische Begegnung und Leonhard Euler*, Berlin, 1958, and A. P. Jushkevich, Eduard Winter et al., eds., *Die Berliner und die Petersburger Akademie der Wissenschaften im Briefwechsel Leonhard Eulers*, 2 vols., Berlin, 1959-61, I, 1-34, passim.

146. *Archiv gemeinnütziger physischer und medizinischer Kenntnisse*, ed. by Johann Heinrich Rahn, II, pt. I (1789), 668-677.
147. The ravages of the pest left a deep impression. Cf. *Russische Bibliothek*, V (1778), 287-325. Also Walther Kirchner, "Zur Geschichte der Pest in Europa: Ihr letztes Auftreten im russischen Heer", *Saeculum*, XX (1969), 82 ff. Same, "The Black Death . . . 18th Century . . .", *Clinical Pediatrics*, VII (1968), 432-36.
148. Not much is known or published about Major Riedel. Without giving her source, E. v. Schulthess remarks that he was from Silesia. His name was Johann (Ivan Ivanovich), and he became, under Emperor Paul, chief of a Cuirassier regiment (see p. 153, note 98).
149. For Fries's life, cf. *Dictionnaire historique et biographique de la Suisse*, vol. III (Neuchatel, 1926); *Entsiklopedisheskii slovar*, vol. LXXII (XXXVI A, 1902), 797; *Spisok Chlenov Imp. Akad. Nauk, 1725-1907*, ed. by B. L. Modsalevsky (St. Petersburg, 1908), p. 158. Jakob Fries should not be mixed up with Jacob Friese (1699-1755), mentioned by Richter, *Geschichte der Medizin in Russland*, III, 188 and 499, who was likewise a surgeon in Russian service.
150. Vols. II, pt. 1, 658-726; III, pt. 1, 2-97; III, pt. 2, 269-340.
151. Erica von Schulthess has examined the question of the original and possibly still extant copies and variants, and has published a list of all the material she found. She believes that the original letter is no longer in existence.
152. Vol. III, pts. 3 and 4 (1882).
153. At that time, Director Forrer called also my attention to the letter.
154. Robert J. Kerner, *Urge to the Sea*, Berkeley, 1946, p. 29. Cf. Fisher, 158 ff.
155. *Ibid.*, p. 69.
156. In 1719 John Bell still complained that they found neither houses nor inhabitants along their road for up to six days. Cf. I, 216.
157. Strahlenberg has suggested in his account, p. 254, that Prince Gagarin, governor of Siberia in the time of Peter the Great,

NOTES TO PART I

was instrumental in closing all roads except via Verkhoture because, in preparation for making himself an independent king of Siberia, he wanted to control not only the trade, but also all news reaching St. Petersburg. There is little proof for this story. Apparently, Chappe d'Auteroche has followed a similar account of Gagarin's activities. Cf. I, 111.

158. 1 verst is about 1.066 km or about 0.664 English mile.
159. A list (in German) of the postal stations and their distances in Siberia has been published in St. Petersburg in 1761: *Anzeiger der Post Stationen durch Russland und Sibirien*, p. 37 ff.
160. Erman, p. 86.
161. In addition to the passages mentioned above, cf. D'Wolf, p. 183; "Desirous of reaching St. Petersburg before the close of navigation in the autumn, I was prepared to travel day and night, and of course passed many towns and villages without noticing them".

PART II
Hans Jakob Fries's Journey Through Siberia, 1774—1776

PART II

Hans Jakob Fries's Journey Through Siberia, 1774—1776

Tenderly beloved parents, sister, brother, and relatives:

More than five years have passed since I received a letter from you, my dearest, my most beloved father, in which you once more assured me of your paternal love—a matter which evoked an indescribable joy in my soul, spurred me to a thousand good resolutions, and reminded me in the most moving way of the obligations and duties which I owe most particularly to you, my dearest father, and which I shall owe you throughout all my life.

No doubt you will remember that I wrote to you from Romanov, where I was stationed as an assistant surgeon[1] in a field hospital under the command of Baron Obreskov, how much I desired you to share with me in my funds and fortune which at the time seemed to be increasing. You also sent me your thanks for this intention of mine. However, fate has not permitted me to fulfill this wish of yours and mine. Just at the beginning of March, 1774, I was moved away from Romanov and transferred to the Astrakhan Carabineer Regiment. Without further delay I had to travel to Bucharest, the capital of Wallachia, and after having presented myself to General Count Ivan Petrovich Soltikov, commander in chief of the third division of the great Russian army,[2] I had to go on to the regiment to which I was assigned and which occupied winter quarters not far from Bucharest, on the south eastern slopes of the Carpathian mountains. I was indeed most lucky in finding here great patrons and friends in the colonel of the regiment as well as in all the staff and ranking officers. However, I was also compelled to use up my savings for things which became indispensable now that I had to march with the regiment and that I had to participate in the campaigns. Subsequently it pleased all-directing Providence to decree that I experience the most varied kinds of fortune and to support and aid me all-powerfully on trips to the remotest parts of the world. You will learn from what follows in this letter all that has happened to me since you last received news from me; into what parts of the world I have subsequently travelled, and all that I have had to experience within the last five years during which you could not receive any news from me.

As mentioned, I was sent to the Astrakhan Carabineer Regiment as a new junior assistant surgeon at just the time when the regiment had received orders to move from its winter quarters. Hardly did I have sufficient time to put into decent order all the equipment needed for the coming march. Already on May 6, 1774, we left winter quarters. On the twelfth of the same month we camped near Bucharest; on the eighteenth we joined the rest of the Soltikov division, and then we encamped at various places along the Argis river. On the sixth of June we crossed the Danube near Tutukey,[3] and though we had to stand a heavy cannonade from the side of the enemy we still succeeded in reaching safely the other bank of the Danube, in Bulgaria. After we had dispersed thereupon the enemy's forces without encountering much resistance, we made ourselves master of a redoubt on the hills of Tutukey from where the Turks had fired upon our ships while they were crossing the river. On the seventh of June the Russian and Turkish outposts got into a scuffle. This led to a skirmish, the first one in my life in which I participated or rather where I was to be an onlooker. Hardly had the action ended to the advantage of our division that a courier arrived whom Field-Marshall Count Rumiantsev[4] had sent to our commanding general and through whom I received to my greatest surprise a letter from you, my very dearest father. It is impossible for me to describe to you the joy which I experienced upon its receipt. I read it. . . .[5] This, I hope, suffices in answer to your letter. Permit me now, my dearest parents, to continue with my account, with the story of my life and of my travels. I hope that the reading of my letter will not tire you,, and I leave it to you to decide whom else you will allow to see this letter; however, concerning this, I shall express myself further at the end.

The Soltikov Corps broke camp on the ninth of June 1774, and day after day marched on the Bulgarian side from Tutukey up along the Danube. I am unable to describe in all detail through what paradise-like regions we had to

1 Russian sledges used for travelling and for conveying baggage, provisions, etc. in winter

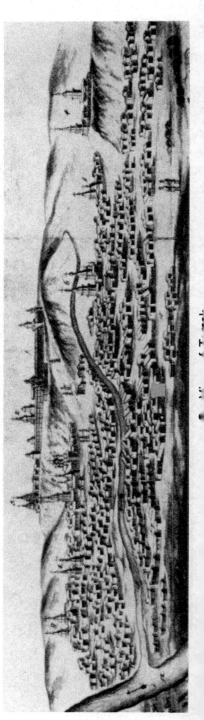

2 View of Tobolsk

march: through gardens without end, full of the most beautiful fruits and wild grapes; through forests densely wooded with splendid and majestic cedars, pines, and walnut trees; and through fertile plains, shaded by mulberry trees, and filled with the loveliest Turkish and Bulgarian Christian villages.[6] These, however, were being devastated before my very eyes through the violence and the laws of war. Heaven—of what inhumanities was I an eye witness here; deeds which make all nature tremble. Halt, therefore, my pen, and rather pull a curtain over these horrors! The Russian soldier is once and for all the world's greatest barbarian, if one lets him loose to act and roam as he pleases in enemy territory. His officer is not infrequently his teacher, and, in regard to gentlemen of higher rank, I have had sufficient opportunity to observe that instead of maintaining discipline, the generals find a good deal of joy, amusement, and advantage in the perpetration of all kinds of injustices.

Meanwhile half of our regiment together with several hundred Cossacks was sent out and was ordered to attack an enemy corps hidden in the forest. Soon thereafter our victorious partisans returned with five hundred captured Turks, their families, and several thousand head of cattle—sheep and goats. I was assigned sixty-five riflemen to dress their wounds, and with the aid of my three barber-surgeons I was soon finished with them. Since, however, I was also ordered to visit the wounded captives, it was not until a late hour that I was finally done for the day. I was taken to these poor people, who moaned and wailed so horribly in their misery that one's heart wanted to break in two. I found most of these unhappy ones completely naked. Once having defeated the enemy, our Cossacks treat him so inhumanly that they do not even leave the shirt on his back. Only the women, among whom there were several very distinguished ones, still had something left with which to cover themselves. For this, however, the Cossacks were undoubtedly well paid with ducats. Accordingly I searched for my wounded Turks among this naked group. There were ninety-three of them, all miserably wounded by the musket fire of the Cossacks. I did not have enough linen with which to dress their wounds adequately. Thereupon the good women came to my assistance; they gave me their handkerchiefs and the shawls from their heads, some of them even tore off pieces of material from their long shifts, with which to dress the wounds of their sick menfolk. My solicitude for these unhappy wounded made such an impression upon the captured company that wringing their hands they called upon their prophet Mohammed—called upon him to repay me for my cares. "God bless you for it," said an old Turk while I dressed a wound next to his throat; and he kissed my hand while a tear from his eye fell on it. That much gratitude and that much virtue were displayed by a people whom we call barbarian! What a horrible connotation the name Turk carries with us; and how noble, how Christian—what shame on the title of Christian!—how virtuous is many a one who carries the name Turk.

Meanwhile the captured party screamed for water with which to quench their thirst in the horrible heat. One handed them after much begging and moaning the . . . from the Danube. The count, however, sent them a good deal of . . . for their refreshment. I cannot tell you enough how happy the prisoners were with this countly gift. They immediately fell upon it and burned and cooked it as well as they could in the midst of the disorder in which these good people found themselves. They permitted me—their doctor, as they called me—to eat the best of all.

On the tenth of June the captured Turks were sent to Russia. On the eleventh we captured an entrenchment located on the Danube near Marntiny [Martin] or Taben; on the very same day we moved on to the Bulgarian capital of Rostik, or Roschttschuk [Rushchuk] also located on the Danube, which was at once formally invested.[7] The main camp was about a half hour's distance east of the city; from its right wing to the left it was fully an hour in length, extending from the banks of the Danube to the highest parts of the vineyards of Rohttschuk. Our regiment occupied approximately the middle of this line, being at a place at which it could easily have lost its last man—if only the Turks had begun to fire from one of their fear-inspiring batteries. Since, however, the Seraskian commander of the city was in negotiation with our count, each side refrained from attacking for the moment. Meanwhile I, together with several other officers of our regiment, nearly lost my life in punishment for a thoughtless temerity. The young major of our regiment, a Prince Meshchersky,[8] was standing with many officers on a haystack in front of our lines and looked through his perspective glass at the city to whose protection the above-mentioned battery contributed very much and which had stood, so to speak, before our very noses—fully provided with readied 24-pound cannons. I joined this group of officers the very moment that a cannon ball fired from one of the cannons of the battery whistled over my head, and, although it did not hit anyone in our group, it killed immediately behind our front line three horses belonging to our senior major. Thereupon we immediately moved our camp and initiated other measures against the enemy city, to which the brave Major Perret from Solothurn, in his capacity as chief quartermaster of our division, contributed the most and the best. Repeated bombardments took place and by and by we cut off the Turks from their lines of communication and supply, so that they saw themselves forced to risk occasional sorties, in which they consistently came off the loser and were driven back with great losses. As a rule, the count attempted to avoid the spilling of blood, since new peace neogtiations were held, and these were actually concluded on the thirteenth of July, to the great joy of both parties.[9] After an extraordinary and luxurious feast, which was celebrated by our own corps and the now reconciled enemy, we left the formerly besieged city of Rohtschuk as early as the fourteenth of July and recrossed the Danube.

Thereafter we no longer spent much time in the Turkish provinces and, on the sixth of October, completed the last summer campaign, which had found us in different camps along the Wallachian rivers Argis and Dembovich. We were assigned cantonment quarters along the upper parts of the Pruth river, which we reached on November 1st by way of the cities of Bucharest, Fokshany, Berlat, and Jassy, entering then the city of Albeste. While we were on the march I had ample opportunity to attend the Wallachian and Moldavian country fairs. Hereabouts, this formerly so joyous season was this time hardly given to much festivity. The people were quite naturally fearful of the Russian soldiers, coarse guests as they are, and were therefore very much on their guard against them. I saw half of a squadron of a certain regiment break into a wine press where they swept down upon the large stands laden with quarts of wine. They drank as much as they could hold and then, as token of their gratitude, overturned the remaining half-empty stands. Imagine, dear father, how much these poor peasants must have suffered here—what damage the entire army must have done if one half of a squadron alone could cause so much misery and harm.

In Wallachia, they have a different way of making wine and cider from that customary in our country. Instead of using cross bars they use here large bags into which they throw the grapes and then stamp on them with their feet, until all of the juice has been extracted. In fact, the indigenous peasants cause themselves little trouble in the cultivation of the vine. Just as nature lets the grapes grow, so the grapes grow for them, without ever being attended by human hand. Moldavia and Wallachia could perhaps be the most exquisite country of Europe, if nature, which here produces everything in abundance, were assiduously and skillfully given a helping hand. To be sure, things looked rather sad here at the present time, for, as I said before, wherever Russian soldiers busy themselves for seven years, little good remains.

As a whole, the Wallachian peasants are very stupid, negligent, and superstitious, and have much in common with the customs of the Turks, to whom they have become enslaved. Most of the inhabitants are followers of the Greek religion, but they are not permitted to make use of church bells for public services; instead they beat on wooden boards which are hung in the church steeples, and these boards produce a sound just like that produced with us by the coopers when they beat firmly upon their barrels. Yet, ever since the Russian army has come into the land, they have begun to make regular use of bells. However, the kindly Wallachian Christians were most unlucky in this, for the habitual greed of the Russian soldiers was so great they they spared not even the bells in the church towers. Thus once our carabineers, sent out on a search for provisions, brought to our sutler a bell cast in Nuremberg and still quite new; for which he gave them a hundred pounds of meat; the bell, however, he sold to some Polish Jews for 150 ducats. Thus I could go on mentioning many other impressions of mine, were it the main purpose of my letter to touch only upon Wallachia. Since, however, I have to tell you of completely different and more important incidents, I shall let the matter rest with what I have told you thus far of our doings with the army.[10]

As you see, I was still with the Astrakhan Carabineer Regiment, in which Colonel Prince Meshchersky, Lieutenant Colonel Sakretsky, First Major Baron von Schenk from Darmstadt and Second Major Riedel were serving. These were the most noble and eminent persons in the regiment. They made up the staff and were all so well disposed toward me that I could always count upon their fairness, generosity and friendship. I was their daily guest, and no matter who happened to be invited to their table, I was always welcome, even though the site of the hospital was as much as three miles away from staff headquarters. Since the colonel and the lieutenant colonel were seldom with the regiment, I came more often into contact with Majors Schenk and Riedel. It was with the latter that I was called upon, as you will learn later, to travel through the greater part of the Asiatic world. In addition I had various friends and good acquaintances among the captains of the cavalry and the subaltern officers. On the other hand, the regimental surgeon Schmidt was, alas, a most wretched creature, one who understood nothing but wanted to give the impression of understanding everything; one who knew how to make the impression of being the most honest type of man but who in reality was the world's basest creature. Therefore he was little liked by the regiment. He was kept at the hospital, and I, at staff headquarters.

It would be an injustice were I to overlook here the regimental farrier Lemke, the saddler Meissner from Brunswick, and the belt-maker Heimann from Breslau—all of whom showed me countless favours, even though I could have but little contact with them. Thus I was as well-off with the regiment as I could possibly have wished. On the other hand I had to be very thrifty with my resources. For with a yearly salary of 120 rubles, or about 240 Zurich Gulden, a Russian imperial assistant field surgeon cannot go very far. The greatest part of the pay is spent for carriage and horse, clothing, linen and laundry. It costs 10 Zurich shillings to have a single cuffed shirt laundered and one always has to look neat, trim and smart. One pays

6 fl. for an ell of mediocre cloth; 15 Gulden for a piece of linen sufficient to make about a half dozen shirts; 1½ Gulden for a pair of twined cotton stockings; all of this notwithstanding other expenses for darning and mending, for shoes and boots, for surgical instruments, servants' wages, tips, etc. Dear God—how often it would have been helpful had I learned in my youth various things that are practically indispensable to an unmarried man in foreign countries, such as knitting stockings, or darning them adequately, or sewing a little, shaving oneself, dressing one's hair—all these are things of great importance; and I assure you that had I been able to do for myself the many things that often I have not been able to have had done at any price, I would be at least 50 Gulden each year to the good. Thus I have sometimes ripped to shreds within one week a pair of brand-new stockings, only because I could neither sole nor mend them, and could not find anyone either to whom I could have given them to be mended. Even being able to cook is important for a young man. Parents, therefore, are committing a great wrong when they tie the ladle around their children's necks or when they call them kitchen spongers; they should rather teach them to prepare some simple, useful dishes. Dear God, how glad I was, and still am, that, whenever I was not invited for dinner, I was able to prepare for myself all kinds of soups, dumplings, rolls, etc.

As I have said, on the first of November we had moved into the last Moldavian cantonment quarters. As early as the first of December we received orders to vacate the Turkish countries completely and to pass the winter in Poland. We marched therefore in the direction of the little town of Sarona in order to cross there the river Dniester. Since, however, the formation of ice was already too strong, we had to wait until the river was completely frozen. On the eighth of December we arrived in Sarona; on the ninth, firm ice began to form on the Dniester; on the tenth the river froze entirely, and on the eleventh our regiment together with three other regiments crossed this river into Poland. Here we were assigned winter quarters in the province of Brachow [Bratzlav, Bratislav], between the cities of Winizo [Winnitza, Vinitsa] and Nimerow [Nemirov]. We moved into these at the end of the year

1774, and now recuperated from the continuous hardships which, during the preceding eight months, had greatly taxed our strength, partly while we were on our marches, and partly while in camp.

Our quarters belonged to the estates of a Polish nobleman, a Baron von Grocholsky, who lived only about twenty minutes from staff headquarters. I soon became acquainted with the local provincial physician, Doctor Golz, to whom I owed the good fortune of gaining the favour of the whole household of Baron Grocholsky by means of a minor but successfully executed operation. Doctor Golz entrusted me with the cure of a noble lady by the name of Coslobsky, who lived there. For three years she had been bothered by an ingrown toenail on the left foot. With the consent of the doctor I resolutely removed the afflicted toe of this delicate woman, caused the wound to heal within a short time, and thus gained the special favour of the master's house. I was rewarded in cash with fifteen Dutch ducats and, among other things, with various pieces of her own handicraft; with cuffs, night caps, stockings, etc. In addition to Doctor Golz and an ex-Jesuit, Pitgesky, whom I came to like very much and who became a very good friend of mine, I had the honour of coming into contact with several members of the Polish nobility. Among the many other magnates who frequented the home of Grocholsky, there were the real brother and sister of the king of Poland,[11] Mr. Boniatowsky [Poniatowski] and his sister. I can pride myself upon the special privilege of having met with the greatest kindness and affability from the side of this just-mentioned brother of the king as well as of all the other great men of this kingdom with whom I became acquainted. He very often entered into conversation with me, praised Switzerland, my native land, and called me, whenever he saw me, "petit bon Suisse". The ladies stoutly desired that I remain with them and that I marry; in fact they presented me with many really excellent offers of marriage, which I would not have refused, had I been able to keep my religion in the process. But they would have left me no peace, had I not changed it in due time. A Lady Branyzky [Branitski] once asked me: "Est ce que c'est grande chose, pour devenir heureux, d'etre bon Catholique?" To that I heartily answered:

"C'est, ce que je ne sçais pas, Madame. Mais je sçais tres bien, que pour être heureux il ne faut pas justement devenier [sic] Catholique, et que c'est grande chose, d'etre moins heureux et tant bon reformé."

Although at first the fact surprised me that in this region everyone is received so readily and in such a friendly manner, I came to realize the more the longer I was there, how beautiful and how becoming to humanity these Polish ways and manners are—manners for which one searches in vain in other places and which one finds just the same in a corner of the world, which we back home consider to be the home of the worst barbarians. Polish women excel the women of all the rest of the world in good behaviour and urbanity. The best part of all is their inborn inclination for work. I cannot possibly describe how well they understand it to choose for themselves all types of handiwork, how excellent their taste is, and how, with all this, they are always mindful of cleanliness; so much so that here the lowliest chamber or kitchen maid is never seen in a soiled chemise or in a torn, dirty dress. It would be most necessary to introduce this virtue of diligence and cleanliness into Russia. Because there the most noble lady as well as the lowliest craftsman's wife is ashamed to sew shirts or to knit stockings. They are only interested in having many servants and in living in great state, without caring the least bit about either their own dresses or the dresses and linen of their servants. For this reason one sees in the Russian empire so many idle male and female servants, clad in soiled linen and torn dresses; for this reason too there are so many lice in Russia. The Polish peasantry—at least in those sections through which I travelled—live happily and are very well off. And who is to doubt that Poland is everywhere and has been at all times a blessed land?

We vacated our winter quarters on the first of May, 1775, when we had to leave Poland and march on a secret expedition against the Zaporozhian Cossacks. These people, who are known in Germany by the hated name of "Heydemacken", used to live solely from robbery and from the booty which they had obtained through armed raids on the borders of Poland and Russia; they lived according to their own laws, in a desert between Russia, Poland, and

Crimean Tartary. The Russian crown deemed it necessary to put an end to the useless state of this evil rabble, and therefore ordered Lieutenant General Teggeli to take the command of a strong corps, into which our regiment was incorporated.[12]

Consequently we marched from our winter quarters through various towns, inhabited by poverty-stricken Jews, in the direction of the small Polish border town of Targowize [Torgovitsa]; from here we crossed the river Siencha [Sinjucha, Sinucha] and reached the fortress of Elizabeth [Elizabetgrad] on the Ingul river in New Servia. Here our entire division encamped on the fourteenth of May. The division consisted of eight infantry regiments, three Carabineer regiments, three regiments of hussars, one regiment of pikemen, or hussars with long spears, one regiment of artillery, and four regiments of Don Cossacks; hence all together twenty regiments, which on the nineteenth of this month were spread all over the entire country of the Heydemacken. A bulwark formed by the waggons and carriages as well as the field hospitals of the entire division was established close to the fortress of Elizabeth. The field surgeon Tobler, a native of Appenzell, who at that time saw service with the heavy artillery, asked me, since he was ill, to remain with him in the waggon fortification and to aid him because of his wasting fever.[13] Major Schenk granted permission and ordered me to stay with our field hospital at the waggon city. Here I came under the command of our divisional surgeon Schmidt, who had been administering to my dear fellow countryman Tobler for the past two years. Tobler died on the first of July, after I had spent practically day and night with him for six weeks. I had him buried and myself preached the funeral sermon; for if we do not wish to be buried after the Russian manner, we have to perform the services of a field chaplain ourselves. My friend, may he rest in peace, left a fortune of 2,000 Gulden which, however, was lost because he had entrusted it to unknown and dishonest hands. Of this, however, I gave a careful account to his friends and fellow countryman, Pastor Mesmer in Dresden. To me Tobler gave a silver watch, six new shirts, and his bed linen. His remaining equipment together with the military pay still due to him remained with artillery headquarters, which will unquestionably have given a proper account to the proper authorities. At least I have all the confidence in artillery Lieutenant Colonel von Brikmann that he will have taken it upon himself to see to it that the money was properly transferred to Tobler's parents.

The joy which my little inheritance originally gave me, soon changed into a very great sorrow. For a hussar, who had spent some time with acquaintances in my quarters, made me the target of one of the most frightful tricks, in that he stole everything I owned down to my last shirt. Because of the terribly great summer heat and in order not to be bothered during the night by bed-bugs, I had put up my tent behind the house where I stayed, underneath a pretty wine arbour. Once when I lay down to sleep I forgot to lock the door to my chamber. "Durch Schaden wird man klug," it is said, and so it was with me. The thief found what he wanted—an open door, and in the room everything lying on the table and hanging on the wall. He packed up everything, even my writings and my briefcase containing instruments, and escaped with them across the border. I had to suffer with great patience this misfortune by which I was struck, the more so as it was difficult for me to put myself into my previous condition. My thanks go, however, to a few of my friends in the regiment, who aided me in the most generous manner and eased my worries.

Apart from this I passed this rather unfortunate summer in a comparatively quiet manner. I did not have many patients, and none was sent to me from the regiment. Quite often I took walks into several villages in the surroundings of Elisabeth; these villages had been founded by Greek Christians who had escaped from Turkey. In fact, I found some very pretty sections in this wilderness, although I noticed in many places a great lack of timber. With the exception of the Black Sea and the rivers Dnieper and Bog, which form the boundaries of this country, I have seen neither large lakes nor rivers. Nevertheless, there grows everywhere here incomparable grass, and vermin are found here in horrible quantities. Occasionally I have seen two or three snakes on the little hill in front of my sleeping quarters. The most dreadful of all spiders, the tarantula, is equally common here; and although tarantulas are not as harmful as is commonly believed, their appareance in itself is horrible enough. Not so long ago I saw one of these monsters of nature climb up my tent pole. Furthermore, there is no lack here of grasshoppers of the first magnitude. The newly-founded Greek colonies here are so well-to-do and numerous that within a very short time the entire wilderness may be crowded with people. Likewise, the newly-founded hussar regiments have been moved here and have been distributed among Greeks and so have the newly conquered Zaporozhian Cossacks. They have been ordered to settle here, to marry according to the law, and to till the soil. All this after the leader of the Zaporozhian army, together with his secretary, had been brought in as captives and his subordinates had been reduced to complete obedience, and after the expedition, which had succeeded without the spilling of blood, had been brought to a conclusion.[14]

While we were hopefully counting on decent winter quarters either here or in the nearby provinces of Little Russia, our dear Astrakhan Carabineer Regiment was ordered instead to march to Nischynowograd [Nizhni Novgorod] on the Volga. Since this was a march of more than two hundred hours, we had to supply ourselves with good furs, in order not to freeze to death on so long a winter journey. The regiment withdrew the cordon which it had formed along the Bog river down to just below Olchkon [Olviopol?] and toward the end of September arrived again in Elisabeth, where our colonel, Prince Meshchersky, began the necessary preparations for the march before us. It is from this point, my dearest parents, that I began the long journey, which I made at first with the regiment into the innermost provinces of Russia, and then with Major Riedel into the most distant parts of the Russian empire, way into northern Asia; a journey which, so far as I know, no one from Switzerland has yet made. I shall take the greatest pains to give you herewith a good description of it; thus you will not object to my adding all of the places through which I travelled, their distances from one another, and the proper dates. After many walks and with the aid of English watches, I have found that five Russian versts, seven of which are equivalent to a German mile, constitute exactly one hour's walk; that,

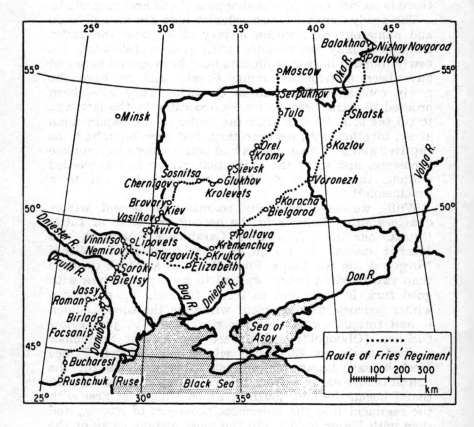

1 Fries's journey from Moscow to Wallachia and back to the Volga, 1773-1775.

furthermore, one hour's walk is equivalent to 7,500 of
my ordinary steps, and that, accordingly, one Russian
verst contains 1,500 of my steps. Thus I prefer to speak of
distances in hours, as customary with you. In the final
analysis the figuring adds up to the same thing, whether
I figure five versts to an hour or seven to a German mile.
In order to give you a clear picture of all my travels
through Russia, I shall first mention those which I made
in the years 1770, 1773, and 1774.

TRAVELS THROUGH THE RUSSIAN EMPIRE
First journey from Petersburg to Moscow, in the year
    1770, which I made in the company of Herrn Fluri,
    from Glaris.

				hours	minutes
Decembris	From	Petersburg			
Jan. 8	To the city	of	Nowogorod [Novgorod]	37	12
10	,,	,,	Waldey [Valdai]	24	–
12	,,	,,	Wischny Wolotschok [Vishny Volotchok]	25	12
14	,,	,,	Torschok [Torshok]	14	–
16	,,	,,	Twer [Tver]	13	12
18	,,	,,	Klin	16	–
20	,,	,,	Moscow	16	24

From Petersburg to Moscow, 146 hours or 730 verts or
104 2/7 German miles

That I dedicated myself to the study of surgery in Moscow
and that I learned the French language at Pastor
Brunner's[15]—all this together with other news I have
already reported to you in a letter which I sent from
Romanov, Ao. 1774.

Second journey from Moscow to Wallachia, which I under-
    took as an assistant surgeon by order of the Imperial
    College of Medicine and at the expense of the imperial
    treasury.

1773				hours	minutes
Decembris		From Moscow			
the 4th	To the village	Tulskoy Pachra		6	48
5th	,, ,,	Lopasne [Lopasnia]		6	36

5th	To the city Serpuchow [Serpukov] on the Occa		5	36
	During the years 1771, 1772, and 1773 ten days quarantine were held here because of the contagious disease among the soldiers.			
6th	To the village Sawode		6	48
6th	„ „ Woschen		4	–
6th	To the city Tula		7	–
	Here are powerful iron works and magnificent lock factories, in which there are manufactured all types of products by locksmiths and iron masters. It is from here that the major part of the army obtain their needed muskets and firelocks.16			
7th	To the village Solowa		8	–
7th	„ „ Sergiewsky [Sergijevo]		4	24
7th	„ „ Minschoy Skuratow [Skuratovo]		5	24

1773
Decembris From Minschoy Skuratow
the 7th To the village Bolschoy Skuratow

	[Bolshoi Skuratovo]		3	12
7th	To the city Amtschemsky [Mezensk, Mzensk?]		5	24
8th	„ „ Orel, on the Occa		11	24
9th	To the village Kromach [Kromy]		6	36
10th	To the city Siewsky [Sievsk]		15	36
	Here was six weeks of quarantine.			
11th	To the city Gluchow [Glutchov], the capital of the Russian Ukraine and the residence of Count Rumiantsov		22	48
12th	To the village Tuligow		4	–
12th	„ „ Krolewza [Korolevetz, Krolewez]		3	48
13th	„ „ Obolonaja [Obolonje]		5	48
13th	To the city Sosniza [Sosnitsa]		6	–
14th	To the village Meny [Mjena]		3	48
15th	„ „ Beresnago [Beresna]		5	12
15th	To the city Tschernigow [Chernigov] on the the Dessna [Desna]		6	36
20th	To the village Oluschewsky		6	–
20th	„ „ Tschemera		4	–
20th	To the city Kaselza [Koselets]		4	48
20th	To the village Semipolok [Semipolki]		5	–
20th	„ „ Prowarow [Brovari]		5	48
20th	To the city Kiev. On the right shore of the Dnieper river which one must cross here		3	36
	I received my further army orders from General Burmann17 and inspected here the			

JAKOB FRIES'S JOURNEY, 1774—1776

	holy relics in a church whereto, year in and year out, pilgrimages are made from all corners and all ends of the Russian empire.		
25th	To the border town Wasilkowa [Vasilkov]. The great eight-week quarantine took place here.	6	–
	From the border town Vasilkov:		
26th	To the first village in Poland, Motowylowsky [Motowilowka]	6	24
26th	To the village Chwestowa	3	12
26th	,, ,, Romanowsky	4	–
26th	,, ,, Skwyry [Skvira]	5	–
27th	,, ,, Morosowsky	5	–
27th	,, ,, Spylschynez [Spitschinzy]	4	–
27th	,, ,, Lipowka [Lipovets]	3	–
27th	,, ,, Boytowyz	3	–
28th	To the city Niemerow [Nemirov]	4	–
28th	To the market town Petschora, on the Bog [Bug] river	6	–
28th	,, ,, Lepowky	6	–
28th	,, ,, Thomaspol	6	–
29th	To the last Polish village Jeleza	6	–
29th	On the Dniester river, across from the Moldavian town Sarocco	7	24

1774
Jannuarii

	The strong formation of ice necessitated my spending two days on the left shore of the river. In the night of the first of January 1774, the river froze completely, and I was the first one who dared, at daybreak, to cross to Sarocca [Soroki].		
the 1st	To the village Kagnarow	4	–
	,, ,, Belsa [Bieltsi]	5	–
	,, ,, Obrescha	4	–
	,, ,, Tabor on the Pruth river	5	–
	To the capital Jassy in Moldavia	9	–
	As newly appointed assistant surgeon I was introduced here to Field-Marshal Count von Rumantsov and was transferred to the hospital in Romanov by the field surgeon Baron von Asch.[18]		
7th	To the market town Turca Formasa	8	–
	To the little town Romanov [Roman] on the Moldau river	6	–
	Here I took over the position of assistant surgeon Mueller from Schafhausen, formerly assigned to the hospital and deceased only a short while ago. In addition to the hospital I had to take care of the house-		

		hrs.	mins.
	hold of Baron Obreskow, who was then assigned to here, until, in the month of March, I was transferred to the Astrakhan Carabineer Regiment.		
Martius			
the 25th	To the city Fokshany	24	–
26th	To the capital Bucharest, in Wallachia	42	–

From Moscow to Bucharest, 365 hours or 249 miles or 1,828 versts.

	Upon the request of the divisional surgeon Zubert, I received orders in Bucharest from the commander-in-chief, General Soltikov, to join the Astrakhan Carabineer Regiment, and accordingly I set out to the headquarters of the same.		
the 28th	To Cosleste [Costesci?] on the Dembowitsch river [Dimbovnik, Dambovnik]	16	–
Magus	Marches of the Astrakhan Carabineer Regiment		
from the 6th to the 12th	To Bucharest	16	–
from the 20th to June the 6th	Marches of Soltikov's division, along the river Argis [Ardzes, Arges] to the Danube	12	–
	Crossing of the Danube by the division, and march of the same to a fortification on the elevation of Tutukey	1	–
	Marches of the Corps to Taban or Marutiny	11	–
	March near Rostik, the capital of Bulgaria	1	–

Julii	Third journey, which, upon completion of the Turkish wars, I undertook with the Astrakhan Carabineer Regiment on various expeditions.		
the 16th	Departure of Soltikov's Corps from Rostik, across the Danube, into a camp on the Argis, between the cloisters of Nygoste and Franchoneste	7	–
Septembris			
the 1st	March to a camp on the Jalomiz, near the cloister of Franconeste	1	–
Octobr.			
from the 6th to the 19th	Marches across Bucharest, through numbers of destroyed villages, to the city Fokshany	40	–
1774 October to the 24th	From the city Fokshany		
	Marches across the Serret river, through Berlat, to Jassy	30	–

4 View of Irkutsk

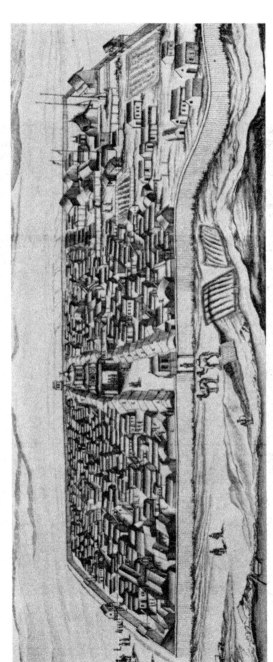

5 View of Chinese frontier town, Maimatschin, with the brook Kiakhta, taken from the West

6 Interior of a Russian dwelling at night

to the 31st		
	Marches of the Astrakhan Carabineer Regiment to its cantonment quarters, near Albeste on the Pruth river, from Jassy	12 —
Decembr. from the 1st to the 8th		
	Marches to Sarocca, on the right bank of the Dniester	23 —
	From Rothschuk on the Danube to Sarocca on the Dniester, 113 hours or 80 miles or 565 versts.	
1774 Decembr. from the 11th to the 20th		
	Departure of the regiment from the Turkish provinces, and marches across the Dniester river into the Polish winter quarters around Woronowize, in the sector of the city of Winize [Winnitsa]	37 —
1775 May from the 1st to the 6th		
	Marches of the regiment from the winter quarters to the small Polish border town of Targowize, on the Sinucha river	20 —
	From Sarocca [Soroki] to Targowize [Torgovitsa] through the Polish province of Braclaw, 57 hours or 40 miles or 285 versts.	
	Marches of the regiment from Targowize to the fortress Elisabeth on the Ingul river, in New Servia	20 —
Octobris		
	Fourth journey with the Astrakhan Carabineer Regiment from Elisabeth to Balachna on the Volga, in the province of Nischynowogrod.	
	From Elisabeth to the country town Krukow [Kriukov] on the Dnieper river	23 —
	From Krukow across the Dnieper to the city Krimentschuk	1 —
	The pontoon bridge which connects here Russia and New Servia is 1,200 of my steps long, or ten minutes.	
	From Targowize to Krimentschuk [Krementchug][19] via Elisabeth, and through all of New Servia, 44 hours or 31 miles or 220 versts.	

A SIBERIAN JOURNEY

from the 28th to Novembr. the 2nd
    From Krimentschuk to the city Pultawa
    [Poltava].   20   –
        In the vicinity of Poltava one can still see many remnants of the battlefield where Emperor Peter I gained a glorious victory over the Swedes.

November
from the 3rd to the 10th
    From Pultawa to the country town Barisowka [Borissowka]   30   –
from the 15th to the 19th
    Via the city Bielgorod to the little town Korotscha [Korotcha]   26   –

Decembris
the 14th To the little town Jablonowa   2   24
    15th To the country town Ekaterinskaja   2   –
    18th To the village Lagschansky   4   –
    19th To the city Starago Okola [Staroi Oskol]   6   –
    21st To the country town Bogorodize   5   –
    22nd To the village Perscherna   4   –
    24th „ „ Endabeste   6   –

        On the 25th the headquarters' staff moved to the town of Worones [Voronets], three hours distance from here. Since I accompanied this group, I had the honour to enjoy a magnificent Christmas noon-meal at the home of the here-residing governor general, Potapov.[20] The town, prosperous and built according to new plans, is among the best I have seen so far in Russia.[21]

    27th To the village Schiwotna   4   –
    28th „ „ Stupina on the Don river   4   –
    30th „ „ Deschina   3   36
    31st „ „ Dresgy [Drjasgy]   5   –

1776
Jannuary
the 2nd To the village Kosowlewe   6   –
    3rd „ „ Peskowatny   4   –
    5th „ „ Isberde, near the city Coslow [Koslov]   3   –

        Up to here, for the past few days, the cold has been so ferocious that we lost many men—men who lost their faces, hands, and feet.

    16th To the village Cheleowa   6   –
    17th „ „ Jepantschina   4   –
    18th „ „ Glasowa   4   –
    19th „ „ Jerseowa   4   –
    22nd „ „ Bogaky   5   24

23rd	,,	,,	Sareow	4	–
25th	,,	,,	Taptilowa	4	–
26th	,,	,,	Stucha	3	–
Januarii the 27th	From Stucha To the village		Skorodea, near the city Schatska [Shatzk]	4	–
29th	,,	,,	Agyschywoy	3	48
30th	,,	,,	Sassawa [Sassovo]	4	–

Many rope-makers live in this large and wealthy village, who send most of their products to Archangel.

Februar the 2nd	To the village		Penkowa	6	24
3rd	,,	,,	Tschotowa	4	–
4th	,,	,,	Tengusowa	4	–
6th	,,	,,	Naryschkina	4	–

They raise here—or rather in the entire province of Arsamasia—the biggest and fattest geese in the entire empire; possibly one cannot find anywhere in Europe geese as excellent as those raised here.22

7th	To the village		Tscherewatowa	6	–
8th	,,	,,	Soksowa	5	–
11th	,,	,,	Lesunowa	9	36
12th	,,	,,	Pawlowa [Pavlovo] on the right bank of the Occa	6	–

This is one of the largest, most beautiful, and most wealthy villages in all of Russia. All of its inhabitants are either merchants or master locksmiths, gunsmiths, and tanners, whose products are exported far and wide. They trade along the navigable Occa and reach many Russian cities, especially Kazan and Astrakhan. They are serfs of Count Sheremetov, who owns not less than 180,000 all over the empire. Therefore, whenever one speaks in Russia of a wealthy man, he thinks of Count Sheremetov, just as one speaks in Zurich of the wealthy Oeri—although there is all the difference in the world between the two.23

14th	To the village		Isbylez	5	–
15th	,,	,,	Tschernewa	4	–
16th	,,	,,	Gabrilowa	3	–
17th	,,	,,	Kosina [Kasino]	4	–
18th	To the city		Balachna on the Volga	2	–

From Krimentschuk to Balachna, 244 hours or 174 miles or 1,220 versts.

From Elisabeth to Balachna, 268 hours or 191 miles or 1,340 versts.

In Balachna the Astrakhan Carabineer Regiment joined with the Nishni-Novgorod Carabineer Regiment; meanwhile there arrived from the Imperial War College an order, according to which both were to be reformed into a dragoon regiment in the Royal Prussian tradition. It was to be called the Nischigorodian [Nizhni Novgorod] Dragoon Regiment and to be under the command of Lieutenant General Kaminsky.[24] Since, however, this new Nizhni-Novgorod Dragoon Regiment was to consist of ten squadrons and each squadron of 136 men, and since the firing power of the combined Carabineer regiments was too weak, the above mentioned Major Riedel was given the order of the very highest empress herself to select the best men from the dragoon squadrons scattered here and in Orenburg and Siberia and to join them to the regiment. Furthermore, the assistant surgeon of the regiment was to accompany the major; the major himself, however, was to be permitted to select according to his own judgment the necessary commissioned and non-commissioned officers for the mission. Upon receiving the order Major Riedel had me called and, since he had always been accustomed to treating me intimately and kindly, he immediately described to me his task and told me of his orders to take me as assistant surgeon along to Siberia; he did this with such signs of satisfaction that I could at once notice how pleased the major was to have me as his travel companion. A journey such as ours could not possibly be undertaken without loss of courage, hope, or strength unless you enjoyed the companionship of a good acquaintance and possessed all the necessary supplies for comfort as well as for the care of the body, which is exposed to all kinds of accidents. On the one hand this new event in my life was most unexpected since, immediately upon our arrival, I had very definitely decided to apply for my surgeon's examination so that I could be promoted; on the other hand, however, I was very well pleased to have such a good opportunity to see distant regions and to undertake a journey from which I could expect nothing but the greatest advantage for broadening my knowledge and experience. And God be thanked who thus far has led me so wonderfully that now, upon the successful completion of my journey with all of its expected advantages, I find myself in a position to achieve my final goal and to look forward to the happy days when I can live as regimental army surgeon of the Russian Crown; may heaven grant that in this position I can also benefit my fatherland.

While we ate our noonday meal and decided to be ready for the journey on the 28th of February, Major Riedel wished me—and I him—luck for the coming journey. Thereupon I attended to a number of things which I happened to think of and which might be useful. Then, however, I took leave from the colonel and from all my patrons and friends in the regiment. For after all, one who is about to undertake a journey of 1500 hours is more, or at least equally, justified in taking real leave than are certain dear people in Zurich when they travel to Bern, to Basel, or at the most to Frankfurt on the Main.

Major Riedel selected an ensign, a sergeant, and a corporal. No one was permitted to carry with him any unnecessary equipment. Each one of us, therefore, limited himself to a portmanteau for the most necessary pieces of clothing. We either sold our remaining belongings or left them with the regiment, for who wants to drag many odds and ends on such a terribly long journey as we now had before us, especially since we were to travel not in our own carriages but on post coaches or rather farmers' carts, which are exchanged at each station. In addition, everyone among us would be a thousand times exposed to the danger of losing his equipment, and for its sake, even his life.

When all of us were ready for the journey I reported to the major on the 27th of February and early on the 28th of February, and in the name of God, we began together our journey to north-eastern Asia. On the route from Balachna to Kazan we had to pass through the following towns and villages:

Fifth journey, to several provinces of the Russian empire, through Asia. In the company of Major Riedel.

1776			hours	minutes
Febr.	From Balachna			

| the 28th | To the village Great Kosina | 2 | — |

28th	To the city Nizhni Novgorod, on the Volga			3	–
28th	To the village Beswodna			5	48
28th	„	„	Stadinez	5	24
29th	„	„	Stachina	6	24
29th	„	„	Fakina	6	24
29th	„	„	Sumka	6	48
Marti the 1st	To the city Kusena-Demianska [Kosmodemianski]			4	–
2nd	To the village Ilyeskoy Pustina			6	–
2nd	To the city Tschubachshary [Tchoboksar, Tschebokssary]			5	12
From Tschubachshary					
1st	To the village Kusnikow			6	24
1st	„	„	Bielowolsk	7	–
2nd	To the city Swyask [Sviask]			6	–
2nd	From Swyask to the city Kazan[25]			4	–

From Balachna to Kazan, 75 hours or 53 miles or 372 versts.

Nizhny Novgorod was the first town along my journey which deserves mention. Here we received from Governor General Stupichin[26] the passport necessary for our further journey. Since the town is situated in an angle where the Occa flows into the Volga and thus forms a natural ampitheatre, one has from the summit of the mountain one of the most exquisite views of the Occa and Volga and of the regions farther down which lie between these mighty rivers.

If we wanted to take full advantage of the already thawing sledge-roads we could not afford to pause at any place without good reason. We hurried therefore in order to reach Kazan on the already breaking ice of the Volga. This road on the frozen river was approximately fifty hours shorter than the customary highway, but, because of the mild weather which was setting in, it was now very dangerous. In fact several travelling merchants who left Nizhni Novgorod only two hours later than we, undertook their last journey. All of the above mentioned towns lie on the right bank of the Volga and among them I have seen several pretty and well built villages. We had to remain in Sviask for an entire day because of lack of horses.

After Nizhni Novgorod, Kazan was the second notable town worthy of my attention during this journey. Since it was totally burned during the famous Pugachev rebellion of 1774, it is now in the process of being newly and splendidly rebuilt.[27] The above rebellion, great misfortune though it was, nevertheless supplied the town with the groundwork for a far happier existence. Kazan is now already splendid, and soon it will hold the third rank among Russia's cities. We reported to the imperial governor, Prince Platon Stepanovich Meshchersky,[28] and received our papers for the further unimpeded journey through Kazan province. Besides, I had the fortune of meeting here a gallant fellow countryman, Herrn Roder from Bern. He holds the position of a public teacher in the local *Gymnasium* and keeps a boarding school for twelve boys of the nobility.[29] Kazan owes him a debt of gratitude for not having been completely destroyed during the days of the internal disorders. Since the entire citizenry was called up in order to hold back the enemy, Mr. Roder was placed in charge of the town militia, having to defend at the same time a strong battery. Through him I obtained several significant items of information which are too important not to be included in my diary.

From Herrn Roder I first learned to what extent Kazan had suffered, and how much innocent and dear German blood had been spilled there. Even the amiable wife of my friend, who indeed deserved everyone's respect because of her virtuous and modest bearing, had, because of the horrible excesses committed by the Pugachev commando, to go through a pregnancy so filled with fear and sorrow that I cannot understand how she survived it, although by now she will have received the reward of virtue in another world. Among other things, Frau Roder told me that in 1774, when Pugachev was already in Kazan, determined to become emperor of Russia and consequently ordering all those who did not recognize him as such[30] to be executed, especially if they were members of the Russian nobility—that then all males were called to the defence of the fortifications and consequently the poor women were left to themselves and to their fate, and had to remain helpless in their homes. However, Pugachev, out of revenge, had all those to whom the administration of the empire was entrusted, miserably deprived of their lives, and that included everyone who had merely the name or appearance of nobility. Consequently, even women of lower social status, and among these many of the merchants and tradesmen, were looked upon by the murderous rebels as members of the nobility, merely because they were of clean and orderly dress; and these, together with the others, constituted horrible sacrifices of war.

All this gave the unfortunate and solitary lady the idea of dressing herself like a peasant woman in order to escape, in this manner, the sword of the deceived bloodhounds. Under this mask of a peasant woman, Frau Roder dared to leave her house and, holding her twelve year old daughter by the hand, to rush to the fortifications into the arms of her husband. She had just taken the first steps from her fine stone house when Pugachev and some Cossacks, who had not yet wiped off the blood of murdered innocence from their swords, happened to ride past. He immediately stopped Frau Roder and asked her whose house this was. Frightened, she answered him while acting like a maid: The house of my master. Pugachev got down from his horse and ordered her to accompany him into the house and to prepare for him a cup of tea. Now he was determined to see the mistress of the house. Frau Roder fully realized that she could no longer remain undiscovered; consequently she threw herself at the feet of her formidable guest, made herself known and said that she herself was the mistress of the house, that this was her daughter, and that she was ready to die with her and with the as yet unripe fruit of her womb. Here the barbarian was overcome with pity. He saved Frau Roder and her daughter from death and then waited for the tea which he had demanded. The good woman served her guest as well as she could, whom, although he could neither read nor write, a disloyal half of the Russian empire had already made its emperor. Pugachev thanked her for the tea and asked Frau Roder how he might be of service to her. Since she had already been served sufficiently in that she could be assured of her life, she merely asked His Tsarist Majesty—for thus one had to address the rogue—for a sign by which his commando might recognize that she had his favour. He advised her thereupon to stay for the time being in his camp, where she would best be taken care of. Thus, the pregnant Frau Roder was taken to Pugachev's camp not far from Kazan, where she was well guarded and exquisitely fed. Meanwhile many other women, whom Pugachev had spared from death because of their beauty, were kept there as pityful prisoners, and were used by the barbarians for the exercise of all sorts of sensual pleasures. In Pugachev's own tent Frau Roder gave birth to a little son, who, however, did not live for longer than two hours. Shortly thereafter the courageous Michelson liberated the unfortunate town of Kazan, and with it also the poor captive women.[31] In gratitude for a similar favour, which the Lutheran minister of Kazan, like Frau Roder, had had an opportunity to do for the rebels, his Reverendship was selected by Pugachev himself as Brigadier and Commandant of Kazan—and, according to a good old Cossack custom, his head was cut off [am Kopfe beschnitten].[32]

In addition, I have cast as good a glance as our short stay in Kazan permitted on other no less remarkable things there. The Kazan Cathedral, in which the Virgin Mother is said to have appeared and once to have wept,[33] attracts almost as great a crowd as the Kiev Cathedral, and in the Greek church there is held a high yearly holiday which is dedicated to this unusual occurrence—although the same Virgin Mother is said to have appeared and wept also in many other churches. A large portion of the Kazan population is made up of Tartars, among whom I became acquainted with many of rank who, contrary to the laws of the Mohammedan religion to which they belong, have already adopted many of our customs and manners. Many Tartars keep tutors for their children, who teach them not only the Russian but also the French and German languages and instruct them as well in the foundations of the various fields of the *belles lettres*. Most of the Tartars are already willing to have their wives seen in public and by now generally marry only one wife. I asked a rich merchant about the reason for this and received the following answer. An only wife gives enough trouble to me, why then should I take for myself more than one? I have seen rather Fr—— and well dressed Tartar women at the local theatre.

All together, the Kazan way of life is far better than that in many places of the empire and the prince-governor goes to much trouble to introduce order and manners among the people. He is the kindest but also the most just man in all the world. Before him, rich and poor are all equal. He helps wherever he can and is himself the first guardian of his territory. One may speak to him at any time. And he also permits every man, without exception and without difficulty to appear before him, and speaks in an equally friendly manner to the general as to the peasant. In like manner he always walks through the city and notices with a hawk's eyes everything that is contrary to the law and orders of the police. Thus one can see him in the market place, among the tradesmen, at the *Gymnasium* and in the schools and the homes just as often as in the chambers of the court. He is, in one word, Kazan's father. All this I was told by Herrn Roder, and he added that Kazan honours him as its father.

I did not have an opportunity to speak with the local minister of the Lutheran church; however, he was described to me as a man in whom the qualities of a shepherd of the Christian flock are to be desired rather than that they can be expected. A tax ought to be imposed on all Christians of the German nations for those German families in Kazan who have met with misfortune during the internal disorders. Their misery is too great to give them hope to be able to recuperate without outside aid, especially since the wealthy Christians in Moscow and Petersburg behave in a most unChristianlike and coldhearted manner towards their German brothers.

We continued our journey from Kazan to Orenburg and came

1776 Martii		From Kazan	hours	minutes
the 3rd		To the village Kabanow	4	12
3rd		,, ,, Jegoriewa	3	36
3rd		,, ,, Imeninowa	4	48
3rd		To the fortress Alexiewsky [Alexjejevsk] on the Kama river	5	48
3rd		To the village Tulkischinowa	5	–
4th		,, ,, Kottuschinowa	4	36
4th		,, ,, Bielogory	6	–
4th		,, ,, Jerikly	5	–
4th		,, ,, Kusankiny	6	36
4th		To the outpost Kutschuewsky [Kitchuisk]	4	36
5th		To the village Achmetowoy [Almetewa]	5	36

5th	,,	,,	Karabasch	5	36
5th	To the city Bugulmu [Bugulma]			5	36
5th	To the village Dymskoy			4	12
5th	,,	,,	Candis	3	48
6th	,,	,,	Scholta	4	36
6th	,,	,,	Usmanowoy	4	12
6th	,,	,,	Jakupowoy [Yakupova]	5	12
6th	,,	,,	Asurowoy	2	–
6th	,,	,,	Kutlimetowoy	2	48
6th	,,	,,	Nayrasowoy	7	–
7th	,,	,,	Dusmetowoy	4	36
7th	,,	,,	Sarmanowoy [Surmanaievo]	4	12
7th	,,	,,	Mustasanoy	4	24
7th	,,	,,	Isawoy	6	24
7th	,,	,,	Bekulowoy	7	36
8th	To the city Sakmara [Sakmarsk], on the Sakmara river			6	12
8th	To the city and frontier fortress Orenburg on the Ural river			5	48

From Kazan to Orenburg, 140 hours or 100 miles or 700 versts.

On the large and new road from Kazan to Orenburg we found everywhere large and well built Tartar villages. And I must admit that I liked it no less with the Mohammedan subjects of the Russian empire than with the Christians. After a time I had several opportunities to mix with the Tartars and to get to know them better.

Bugulma is the only city between Kazan and Orenburg. It has nothing of importance to show except this—that during the Pugachev disorders General Bibikow[34] lost his life here; Herr Fuessli from Schaefli has at present a nice position as tutor with the children whom the general left behind. Near the Tartar village of Usmanawoy we experienced a horrible north-eastern gale, the like of which one finds often in this sector. These gales cause such fearful snow storms that the air is darkened, that entire villages, all streets are covered, and that man and beast are exposed to the greatest dangers of life and limb. No-one is able to continue his journey in such terrible weather. Therefore the mail is sometimes interrupted three or four consecutive times and for this reason, too, so many couriers are lost. Whenever travellers are surprised on the road by these storms, they immediately stop, unbridle the horses from the sledges, put up the shafts so that they stick into the air, and then they themselves lie down in the covered sledge and wait for the storm to pass by. These storms sometimes last for more than twenty-four hours. When the storm has passed they dig themselves out of the snow or, if they have been snowed under too deeply, depend on the aid of people passing by, who can judge by the poles sticking into the air that on that spot someone has been buried in the snow. However, such unfortunates seldom escape with their lives. For since the snow is sometimes piled up to heights of ten feet or more, it may take three or four days, or indeed a whole week, until the roads can again be used. Meanwhile the travellers buried in the snow must perish helplessly. I have lived in these parts of the earth for three years, and have always noticed that these storms are followed by a clear sky, a strong north wind and terrible cold.

Between Sakmara and Orenburg, along the Sakmara river, lies the incomparable Tartar village of Kargala, which is certainly one of the most beautiful villages in the world. The inhabitants of this village are engaged in constant and prosperous commerce with Persia, India, and China. Here too is the seat of the highest church official of all the Mohammedans in the Kazan and Orenburg governments. Even closer to Orenburg we passed to our right the village of Berdea, where the headquarters of Pugachev were located during the siege of Orenburg in 1774.

It was thus on the eighth of March that we arrived in Orenburg, one of the most important cities in the Russian empire. We reported there to the Governor General von Reinsdorf[35] as well as to the Commanding Divisional General Mansurov.[36] Both of these men were very necessary to our mission, because we were to begin here with the levying of the dragoons. Since, however, the local squadrons were at present all together, we postponed the levy until our return from Siberia.

Orenburg lies on the right bank of the river Jaik—now known as Ural—and is one of the most excellent fortifications along the Asiatic frontier's line of the Russian empire, which extends for more than 6,000 hours along the Turkish, Persian, Kirghiz, and Chinese borders, from the Black Sea to the Oriental Sea.[37] It is covered almost uninterruptedly by fortifications, outposts, and

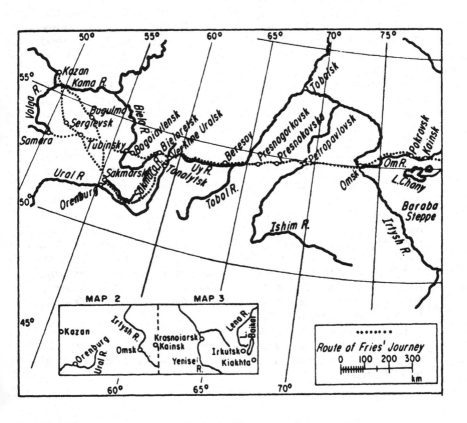

2 Fries's journey through Western Siberia from Kazan to Kainsk (for continuation through Central Siberia, see Map 3), and his way back to Samara, 1776.

border patrol stations.[38] Where this line runs, for example, along large rivers or across high mountains, it is not as imperilled as where it leads through flat country and where an enemy crossing is impeded by rivers, woods or mountains. Likewise, the line along the border of peace-loving Chinamen is much safer than it is in the neighbourhood of predatory Kirkhiz[39] or gangs of roving Tartars from the Cuban.

The Orenburg line begins at the mouth of the Ural on the Caspian Sea and continues along the rivers Ural and Ui along the Kirghiz border until it reaches the Tobol river. It is occupied by regular as well as irregular forces, whose headquarters are always located in Orenburg.[40] The Pugachev rebels have caused great damage to several spots along the line and have totally destroyed others. Efforts are therefore now being made to restore these completely. Since I myself became more and more acquainted with Orenburg after a certain time, because I had to travel there quite frequently, I shall recount later the unique things that I have seen there. The circle of the local Lutheran minister Huebner from Memmingen made my first stay in Orenburg very pleasant and has made me indebted to him for many kindnesses and favours. Herr Huebner will remain one of my dearest and best friends for the rest of my life.[41]

In the midst of newly set-in winter weather we got ready for the continuation of our journey, which was to take us now to the fortress of Omsk in Siberia, across the Ural mountains.

1776 Martii	From Orenburg	hours	minutes
the 10th	To the little town Sakmana [Sakmarskaja]	5	48
10th	To the redoubt Zebanka	2	24
11th	To the fortress Pretschistinskaja	4	12
11th	To the redoubt Nikitinskoy	4	36
11th	To the fortress Wosnesenskaja [Wosdwishenskaja] on the Sakmara river	4	24
11th	To the post station Skaminskoy	5	–
12th	To the redoubt Karagaytugaya	4	48

12th	To the destroyed copper mine Twerdaschowa [Tverdashov]	6	–
12th	To the post station Barakan	5	48
12th	To the fortress Selayrkaja [Zilairsk, Salairskaja]	3	36
13th	To the post station Jurminsky	2	24
13th	„ „ Kurtschawoy	5	–
13th	„ „ Turminsky	6	–
14th	„ „ Ewanewsky	6	–
14th	„ „ Tanalyk [Tanalyzk][42]	6	–
	From Tanalyk		
the 15th	To the fortress Ober Uralsk [Werchne Uralsk, Werchjaizkaja][43]	7	24
16th	To the destroyed fortress Karagayskaga [Karagaiskaja Krepost]	6	24
16th	To the post station Kolokowky	4	–
16th	To the fortress Uyskaja [Uisk]	4	–
16th	To the market town Warlomoy	10	24
16th	To the fortress Koylskaja	2	48
16th	„ „ Jemanschelinskaja	6	–
17th	„ „ Koytskaja-Iatkulskaja	3	36
17th	To the village Retschkylowy	3	36
17th	To the Tartar village Mansurowa	5	–
17th	To the village Suchaborsky	5	–
17th	„ „ Beresowa	4	–
17th	„ „ Ptsyzowa	5	–
17th	„ „ Wusley	4	–
17th	„ „ Dolgowsky	6	–
17th	To the Sloboda Kurtamischewsky	5	–
17th	To the village Jarkaja [Jarkovskaja]	5	48
18th	To the market town Kamynskaja	2	–
18th	To the village Protoschynoy on the Tobol river	2	48
18th	To the redoubt Peschttschanoy on the Siberian line	7	–

From Orenburg to the first Siberian redoubt, 160 hours or 113 miles or 795 versts.

the 19th	To the fortress Presnogorkowskaja	4	48
19th	To the redoubt Presnogorkowskoy	4	48
19th	To the fortress Kabanaya [Kabanja]	4	36
20th	To the redoubt Presno-Ibanowoy	3	24
20th	To the fortress Presnowskaja	4	36

1776   hours minutes
Marty

the 20th	To the redoubt Priballotnoy	4	12
20th	„ „ Sinsarskoy	4	24
20th	To the fortress Stanawaja	6	36
20th	To the redoubt Gagariowa	3	48
20th	„ „ Skopinoy	2	48
20th	To the fortress Petri Pauli [Petropavlovsk] on the Ischym [Ishym] river	5	–

21st	To the redoubt Ploskowoy		5	12
21st	To the fortress Poldnaja		5	48
21st	To the redoubt Medweschoy		6	48
21st	„ „ Tschistoy [Tchistij]		4	—
21st	To the fortress Lebeschuja [Lebjashija]		3	12
21st	To the redoubt Losowoy		4	—
21st	To the fortress Nikolskaja		5	24
21st	To the redoubt Woltschiwoy [Woltschi]		5	12
21st	To the fortress Pokrowskaja		2	48
21st	To the redoubt Kurganskoy		4	—
21st	„ „ Melnischnoy		2	24
22n'd	To the fortress Omsk on the Irrtisch [Irtysh] river		4	12

From Orenburg to the fortress Omsk, 275 hours or 195 miles or 1365 versts.

From Orenburg we crossed a large portion of the Ural mountains, along the rivers Sakmara, Selayr, and Ural.[44] The path across these mountains was almost everywhere extremely difficult and dangerous. Now we sank with our horses and sleighs so deep into the snow that we could hardly dig ourselves out again—and now we slid off fearful heights and fell into abysses, where, without the manifest aid of Heaven, we would have been smashed into a thousand pieces or would have been crippled throughout our bodies. And since, with the exception of sad remnants of the Pugachev rebellion, of destroyed redoubts, fortifications, mines, and wretched huts of Bashkir Tartar border guards, we encountered no inhabited homes where we might have found anything for our comfort or nourishment—all this made the miserable mountain road all the more difficult, inasmuch as we lacked even those things which were indispensable for the preservation of our lives and the strengthening of our bodies. Indeed, we had supplied ourselves in Orenburg with a few hams, several smoked tongues, with bread, and a dozen bottles of wine, but even this small reserve did not last us long. The hams and tongues which had been packed somewhat carelessly into my sleigh were suddenly stolen by the dogs; and the bottles of wine broke and burst through the frequent overturning and bumping of the sleighs. When we came to the fortress of Salayskoy [Salairskaya] we spent the night with the commanding officer of the Orenburg field batallion, Lieutenant Colonel Beutling [Peutling], who had been known to us since the Turkish wars and who now proved an excellent host to his half-starved and miserably weakened guests.

Closer to the fortress of Upper-Uralsk the mountains gradually fell away and soon changed into rolling hills, beyond which we again approached flatter regions and reached the fortified Orenburg line. Since our journey took us from west to east, we had the Russian empire to our left and to our right an endless wilderness which in the south borders on Persia and East India and which extends to the Chinese Wall in the east; this desolate country is inhabited by various peoples, among whom there are primarily the Kirghiz,[45] who rove over the northern sections of the wilderness. These parts border on Russia herself and extend from the Caspian Sea to the Kalmyk Sea Nor Saysan. By their incessant inroads the Kirghiz cause great damage in the neighbouring provinces of the empire, in that they carry away not only personal belongings, horses, and cattle, but also drag human beings into slavery. They were particularly successful with such raids in the time of the internal disorders in the Russian empire, during which the Kirghiz enjoyed the proverbial "good fishing in troubled waters". At the time we did not find the border line in the best possible condition. All that Pugachev had destroyed had not yet been rebuilt, with the only exception of the fortress of Upper-Uralsk, which we reached late in the evening of the fourteenth.

The local commanding officer, Colonel Stupishin, seems to be sincere in his efforts to get the local district into better order. With the exception of him, however, the local commanding officers of this lonely outpost, having no important business outside of their small commands and enjoying no human company outside of themselves, prefer to devote themselves to the brandy bottle in an effort to pass away the time. These brandy bottles stand on their tables day and night and fascinate them to such an extent that they know nothing either about themselves or about the travellers who pass their post. Here one might indeed say: If the master does not guard the town, the guard guards for nothing.

The closer we came to the Siberian border the longer lasted the winter this year in these regions. Presnoyor

Kofsky is the first fortification on the Siberian line, and it is under the command of a Spanish Major de Gariga. The local captain of the dragoons, Areshkov, showed us many favours, and we had to thank his wife, who stems from the exiled house of Menchikov,[46] for the enjoyment of a deliciously prepared breakfast, which tasted all the better since we had had nothing warm in our stomachs for the last trip of 140 hours distance. Further on we came to the fortress of Petri-Pauli.[47] This is one of the most important spots along the Siberian line—and the best fortress which I have yet seen on the entire line. All together the commanders of the Siberian districts put much more work into keeping their posts in good condition than those of the Orenburg line, where, to be sure, Pugachev had caused such devastation. But he could never have caused all the damage, had they been more watchful, more often sober, and more careful of good order. Raids by the Kirghiz on the Siberian line are much rarer, since it is much more strongly guarded, and patrols ride from one border outpost to the next, and in addition travellers are given men as escorts in order to safeguard their journey. Thus, as long as we continued our journey along this line, we were constantly accompanied by five dragoons and five Cossacks on horseback, armed with swords and muskets. And nowhere did we proceed on our journey as rapidly as we did in this region, because we could not stop at any place for even a minute, except where we ourselves had specifically requested it. Horses are always ready; one has only to change them and immediately continue one's journey.

Of course, things are a bit difficult with the wild Khirgiz horses, which are used here both for riding and for draying purposes. As long as they are not attached to the carriage, ready to draw it, they kick most terribly, wild animals that they are, and a driver seldom gets away without injury, while frequently the cart or sleigh is smashed to pieces. As soon as they have been put into harness with the expedient of covering their eyes and stroking and caressing them, the traveller must be all ready, sitting in the carriage, for they will not stand still for one moment; and the driver himself can hardly swing himself rapidly enough onto his place. Without giving one a chance to hold them back the horses run in full fury until they are entirely out of breath.

Then they remain standing still on the spot until they have completely recuperated. Nothing is more dangerous than to travel with such horses along mountainous, unlevelled or poor roads. Lest one risk one's life, there is no alternative but to jump quickly out of the cart as soon as the horses run away. For this reason it is not advisable in this country to travel either in covered waggons or in one's own carriage. For one cannot easily make one's way out of a covered cart, and for lack of blacksmiths and wagoners one cannot find many places to have one's own wagon repaired when, as often happens, it is crushed to pieces. Such a misfortune befell me on the road to the fortress of Petri Pauli. Since I had fallen fast asleep in the sleigh, the horses suddenly became wild. The sleigh turned over on a hilly spot and the horses dragged me underneath the sleigh for more than a half of a quarter of an hour. If the snow had not made this road smooth, this day would have been the last of my life.

The commanding officer of Petri Pauli was an old Brigadier, one Sumarokov; and the commanding officer of the Siberian chasseur batallion stationed here was a Major Welikopolsky, whom we knew through our army contacts. In addition I met here a Lieutenant Fischer, who at one time had been a Prussian captain, but who, because of a mistake made by the War College in Petersburg, had although innocent, been sent to Siberia. He lives in a most pitiable fashion with his worthy wife and is constantly exposed to the persecutions of a godless major under whose command he serves. In fact, the most honest and upright people, who attend to their business conscientiously, are seldom left unmolested, especially hereabouts. If one walks from Petri Pauli across the great desert directly towards the south, one reaches East India, a distance of not more than 400 hours.

On the twenty-second of March we reached Omsk, the principal fortress and the headquarters of the general staff of the Siberian line. Immediately after our arrival we reported there to the Commanding General Skolon, and I cannot possibly tell you with what politeness and what demonstrations of friendliness we were received by this old and excellent gentleman, and how many good things we enjoyed through him and through his family as long and as often as we were in Omsk.[48] Here we began with the levying of Siberian troops. I faithfully aided the major in this work and gave physical examinations to all the men whom he had selected, in order to determine whether they were healthy or subject to bodily handicaps, and to see if those who pretended to be ill, were really ill. I had to investigate the type of their illness and whether I could possibly restore them to health. This was a business in the course of which many a colleague of mine would become a rich man, though at the expense of his good conscience, and others, for all the wealth they gained, would make themselves unhappy for the rest of their lives.

When our task was completed at the end of holy week, we were urged under any circumstances to spend the Easter holidays in Omsk. Here we met, in addition to General Skolon, the Senior Commander and Brigadier Claver, a Dr. Berens, and the minister, Rev. Luther, all men who received us exceedingly well and who successively were the best of hosts to us.[49] Since these were also learned men I had the good fortune of learning in their company much about the natural characteristics of the isolated Siberian regions, things of which I knew very little before. Hence, time flew and I could occupy myself during our stay in Omsk with things, the consideration of which coincided with my thirst for knowledge and enabled me to discover in this strange section of the world new wonders of nature and new proofs of the Almighty power of our Creator. Thus I was overjoyed when, in the study of Dr. Berens, I was surprised by the sight of animals, plants, and insects never before seen; or when, in the hall of the Chief Commandant, I saw on incomparably excellent maps and drawings the widely extending provinces of the Russian empire, a portion of which we had already visited and through more of which we were yet to travel. I could now form a definite concept of the location and character of the Siberian Asiatic region of the earth.

With so many pleasant occupations I hardly noticed the passage of time during the Easter holidays. Omsk itself is a neat fortress; even its location on the right bank of the Irtysh where the Om flows into it, is unforgettable, and the general staff makes this fortress even more impressive, for everything which is demanded by the rules of war and policy is given here the minutest attention. The newly built local stone church is so well constructed that as a masterpiece of architecture it could challenge for first place the most beautiful buildings even in splendid Petersburg. Among other excellent things which the deceased General Springer has introduced here[50] and which still continue to function for the benefit of the land, I ought to mention the local war school for children of soldiers, where the youths are instructed not only in speech and *belles lettres,* but where, as a sort of pastime besides their regular lessons, they also do normal military service. It gave us great pleasure on Easter Monday to see these youthful troops mount the guard and inspect arms. Officers' widows who have been left behind and orphans of German blood are excellently cared for here. A beautiful hospital is under construction and a pharmacy is being built, which will be the second one in all of Siberia. Before it there existed only a pharmacy in Tobolsk.

Before we could continue our journey into the distant regions of Siberia we had to return to the fortresses of Petri-Pauli and Presnogorkowski in order to continue there our task of drafting Siberian dragoons. Thus we travelled on the seventh of April from Omsk to Petri Pauli, [a journey of] 53 hours, and on the twelfth from Petri Pauli to to Presnogorkowski, [a journey of] 44 hours. At both places we chose the best men out of the dragoon squadrons who were stationed there, and, together with those chosen in Omsk, we dispatched them to Skobliny, the nearest market town in the Orenburg district. The ensign was placed in charge of this unit. We, however, returned to Omsk on the twenty-seventh of April and arrived there on the twenty-ninth.[51]

From the fortress of Presnogorkowski to Omsk, 97 hours or 70 miles, or 485 versts.

During the last days of the month of April the winter here came to an end. On the twentieth the river Ishym began to thaw near Petri Pauli and on the twenty-ninth the Irtysh near Omsk. On the first of May we were invited to a feast which the general had prepared for all the society of Omsk. I can only say that this was one of the greatest revelries which I have ever attended in my entire life. We enjoyed the first joys of spring on the first day of

May in a forest not far from Omsk. Because of its pleasant location I should like to compare it to our own old Sihl Grove. You can easily imagine, dearest parents, what a pleasure it must have been for me to see and enjoy in so strange and, to me, hitherto so unknown a region, of which I had expected only the worst, so much that was good, to have encountered so pleasant a company of upright German countrymen, and to find in them at the same time so many people anxious to render me a service.[52]

Next, we were to inspect those Siberian troops which had been transferred to the border posts along the Chinese Mongolian frontier, on the other side of Lake Baikal. We were shown two possible routes leading there, both of which were, however, dangerous at the time. The first one runs across the great Sayan mountains which extend from west to east between Russia and China,[53] the other and shorter one along the ordinary Siberian highway towards Tomsk, Krasnajarsk [Krasnoyarsk] and Irkuzky [Irkutsk] which, however, could hardly be travelled on in consideration of its swampy regions that were covered with water. Nevertheless, the major chose the latter road in preference to the other, for it was the shorter one, and fixed the date of our departure for the fourth of May. Meanwhile we were richly provided by our friends in Omsk with enough supplies of food, particularly with cold meat.

1776 May			hours	minutes
		From Omsk across the Baraba desert		
the 4th	To the village	Serebezkaja	5	–
4th	,, ,,	Ignatiowa	4	24
4th	,, ,,	Krasnojara	4	–
5th	,, ,,	Lukotinsky	8	–
5th	,, ,,	Unter Omsk [Lower Omsk]	5	–
5th	To the market town	Nicolskoy	5	12
6th	To the village	Ustarskoy	4	24
6th	,, ,,	Ober Omsk [Upper Omsk]	3	24
	From Upper Omsk			
6th	To the market town Wosdwyschensky [Vognensk]		4	24
	It is here that the two great Siberian highways from Tobolsk and Omsk meet.			
7th	To the village	Tartass	4	–
7th	,, ,,	Turunku	4	–
7th	To the market town Pokrowskaja [Pokrovsk]		3	12
7th	To the village Antoskynaja [Antoshkina]		4	24

JAKOB FRIES'S JOURNEY, 1774—1776   107

7th			Ballotowaja [Bulatova]	6	24
7th	To the fortified market town (in Russian				
	Ostrog Kaynskoy [Kainsk]			3	36
	One crosses here the Om river.				
8th	To the village Osinoy Kolkow				
			[Ossinowy Kolley]	6	24
8th	,,	,,	Kalmuskowoy		
			[Kolmazkoi Sim]	6	36
8th	,,	,,	Ubuy	6	24
8th	,,	,,	Karagalsky	5	36
9th	,,	,,	Karagazky [Kargatskoi]	5	36
9th	,,	,,	Dubrowa Kargazkowa	5	24
10th	,,	,,	Itkulsky [Itkul]	4	24
10th	,,	,,	Iektinsky [Sektinsk]	5	24
10th	,,	,,	Aftschinikowa	3	36
10th	,,	,,	Krutix-Loschkow [Kroutija]	5	24
11th	To the market town Tscheuskoy on the river				
	Tscheus			9	36
12th	To the village Orskagoboru [Orskoi Bor] on				
	the Ob river			4	36
12th	,,	,,	Dubrowina	4	12
12th	,,	,,	Tascharinsky [Tascherinskoi		
			Stanetz; Taschera]	3	24
12th	,,	,,	Ajaschansky		
			[Agasch Ojaschskaja]	4	36
13th	,,	,,	Korasiwoy	5	36
13th	,,	,,	Tschernoy [Outchernoi retchin;		
			Tschernaja;		
			Tschernoretschinskaja]	6	48
13th	,,	,,	Warichinoy	7	–
14th	To the city Tomsk on the right bank of the				
	Tom river[54]			8	–

From Omsk to Tomsk, 178 hours or 128 miles or 890 versts.

Unpleasant as the time of year was in which we travelled through the far-away regions of Siberia, we also had a great many difficulties and dangers to go through, which we could have avoided had we followed the advice of General Skolon and stayed longer at Omsk in order to await an advantageous time for our trip. All the rivers rose to an unheard-of level above their banks and set the whole stretch of land between the mighty rivers Irtysh and Ob under water. And since the whole region is anyhow very low and swampy, it was almost impossible to continue our trip without the greatest danger to our lives. Nevertheless, we dared to venture further and further. Thus, we had to go straight through the middle of swamps which at times stretched over five hours and more. At such places, because of the level of the water which came all the way up into our wagon, our precious *port-manteaux* got all wet and thus our clothes were immediately ruined. To add to our misfortune we often completely lost the trail in the midst of these swamps so that we neither knew whether to go forwards or backwards, nor what to do and how to help ourselves. Thus we remained stuck in swamps through whole nights not knowing whether we would freeze to death from the terrible night frosts or drown in the swelling flood.

Sometimes we had to cross forest streams where once we came so close to being swept over a fall across lime-rock and washed-out earth that we were in the greatest danger of life and could only wait until, upon our screams for help, people from the nearest village came to aid us. With the help of ropes which they threw us they pulled us to shore and thus we were saved from the most terrible death. The forest waters which originated through a terrific increase of the water level in the great Lake Tschana [Chany], not far from the fortified place of Kainskoy [Kainsk], will remain for me a lifelong horrible memory.

Hardly had we sweated out these frightening experiences when we again plunged from one great danger into another. I did everything I could to persuade my Major Riedel to postpone the trip at least until the waters had somewhat gone down; but it was all in vain since anyone who is on such a trip as that through Siberia and does not hurry, can travel for days and years before he is back again at his point of departure. The above mentioned place Tschewskoy, which had just been devastated by the flood, is only one hour away from the mighty river Ob, along which the Siberian road runs for twelve hours from Tscheuskoy, but which was now entirely under water. Therefore, if we did not wish to stay put in Tscheuskoy, we had to continue these twelve hours of our trip by water. Since all boats and vehicles had been washed away, we chose for this two barges, or rather hollowed-out trees, which had floated there in the water and which we tied together. Thus, in calm weather to which we certainly owed our lives, we went down one of the greatest rivers of the world and within six hours happily reached the village of Tacharinsky at a normal distance of twelve hours from the village Tscheuskoy. This river excursion on the Ob, risky as it might have been, was nevertheless very gay for us. I counted at least fifty islands which we passed, upon which the number of foxes, hares and beavers was so great that one often saw them coming to the water; and not far from Tascharinsky we had the pleasure of seeing a female bear and four young ones taking a walk along the banks of the river. In general we enjoyed many other manifestations of beautiful nature which make this foreign stretch of land the most pleasant and inhabitable place. No matter how marshy this Barabinsk [Baraba] plain may be, yet the soil of the same is extremely fertile. Therefore one sees so many beautiful villages here along the banks of the rivers and lakes and so many cultivated fields and pastures. Birches are especially numerous here, and it was here in the steppe or plain of Barabinsk that for the first time I have had occasion to drink the wonderful sap of these trees. On the shores of the lakes which are not inhabited one finds, just as on the lakes along the line, such an enormous quantity of swans, cranes, pelicans, wild and other geese, besides many kinds of wild and especially red ducks, that one might well think these animals have their common meeting place here. The swamps are full of bittern and snipe and the woods of grouse, mountain cock, and other fowl. In one word, the mass of winged game is so great here that they could hardly be found in greater numbers in any spot on earth, anywhere in the whole world. After sundown these manifold armies of winged creatures made such a terrific clamour that we could not even hear our own words.[55]

After enduring many misfortunes to which travellers in Russia are exposed, we reached the city of Tomsk on the other side of the Ob, after we had previously set across the swift and great Tom river. We went directly to the commandant of this place, Colonel de Villeneuve, born in Montpelier, with the intention of seeing to it that we could continue our journey without hindrance; for we suspected that we would again be long delayed, as in Omsk. This would have been just as agreeable to me and it would have been advantageous for all of us, because it was quite necessary to have our clothes restored, which were almost entirely rotted. But far from it; here too I was unable to achieve my wishes, for already the major was irritated that he was not allowed to continue at once, but that he was forced to delay his journey for at least a day and stay as a foreign visitor. For it does not happen very often that people from Russia travel to these distant regions, and therefore one receives the arriving stranger as a rare guest, with a kind of courtesy and hospitality that is unmatched. Much as we yearned for the rest which we would have gladly preferred to the most excellent entertainment, they were so happy about our arrival that there was nevertheless no possibility now to fortify our weary bodies again by enjoying some rest. We were dragged, so to speak, from one house to another, with the well-meant intention of entertaining us, while we were only weakened so much the more by this abundant hospitality. Since one isn't far from the Chinese border here, everyone received us according to good Chinese custom and treated us to many kinds of tea-water without milk and to Chinese confections, which consisted of preserved or candied fruits such as pomegranates, peaches and other types of fruit unknown to me. However, as regards customs and mode of living, I have found nothing extraordinary in the inhabitants of this place, nor generally throughout the whole of Siberia, and noticed nothing varying from the customary Russian humdrum way. Merchants, in particular, seem to be much more esteemed here. For while they are regarded as nothing in Russia, where everyone is judged according to military rank like cloth is measured by the yard, they are valued in Siberia all the more as there are here fewer people of military station and of rank, and one sees people esteemed more according to the size of their real estate and capital than according to their character, rank and title.[56]

Among others we were at the home of one of the wealthiest merchants of Tomsk, who had an excellent wife, five amiable children, and whose fortune amounted to 2,000,000 roubles. He journeyed to Peking once a year and, moreover, possessed so much breeding and virtue that his equal can be found rarely or scarcely ever in Russia; yet all his life he has seen no famous cities other than Irkutsk and Peking. The wife of this wealthy man found it especially strange that I spoke so little Russian. She deduced from this that my home was far from Russia, and she asked me therefore in a rather compassionate fashion, as if she took great interest in me, if I still had parents or brothers and sisters living and how I could have risked travelling so far, and so on. Upon my answering her questions, the worthy old woman was so moved that out of tenderness for me she began to weep. She got three Chinese scarves from her cupboard which she gave to me with the hope that I would divide them among my brothers and sisters if I should ever return home again. Whereas her husband made a present of two Chinese silk shirts to me as well as to the Major, the type which is worn here as well as in China, and which has the advantages, first, of being very soft, second of entirely absorbing the perspiration from the body so that one's coat never suffers, not even beneath the shoulders, and third, of saving cuffed shirts and money for their laundry.

The major of the garrison of Tomsk, a young and courteous man by the name of Bagdonov, led me around through the principal streets, and there I saw nothing other than what one finds or sees in most old Russian cities. Nothing but wooden houses, narrow irregular alleys covered with bridges of wooden planks. It is for this reason that in this enormously large Siberian trading city so many conflagrations originate which occasionally consume several hundred houses and more. During the last fire, in 1773, half of the city, which consisted of two thousand houses, was reduced to ashes. Debauchery and slothfulness, to be sure vices that hold sway everywhere in the Russian empire, are to be found here to the highest degree.[57] I shall hardly be believed when I say that one must wait an entire year before a tailor makes one a garment, or a cobbler a pair of shoes, unless one requests the commandant of the city to put the workman under guard until the work is done. We were very often compelled to try this means, but most unfortunately did not accomplish much with it, for I saw one of the cobblers, who was compelled by us to make our shoes, intoxicated with that very soldier who was to have guarded him. Venereal disease is so common among the people that I may well swear to it that from the Volga to the river Selenga I have not found a single home that was free of it.

A SIBERIAN JOURNEY

We left the city of Tomsk on the afternoon of the fifteenth and pursued our course to the city of Krasnoiarsk.

1776 May	From Tomsk			hours	minutes
the 15th	To the village	Semiluschkowa [Semiluschnoe; Semiltchinoe]		6	–
15th	„ „	Kaldeowa		2	48
15th	„ „	Turunteiowa		4	48
15th	„ „	Klyonaja [Kolljon; Klyon]		9	–
15th	„ „	Pilekul [Berekul]		10	–
16th	„ „	Kia [Kiiskoe] on the Kia [Kiya; Ki] river and across it near the ferry		11	–
17th	„ „	Saslowa [Suslovo; Souslovskoi]		5	–
18th	„ „	Deschinskaja [Teschinskaja]		5	48
19th	„ „	Itat [Kitatskaja]		6	48
20th	To the market town Bugatolsky [Bogotolskoi]			7	–
20th	To the village Krasnaretzakaja [Krasnoretchinsky] on the Tschulim river			6	–
20th	To the Ostrog Atschinskoy [Atchinsk] Here one crosses the Tschulim			5	48
21st	To the village Schernoy Reka [Chornaretsk; Tschernoretchichnoi]			6	36
21st	„ „	Gross Kemsch [Bolshoi Kemsch]		7	48
21st	„ „	Klein Kemsch [Malokemtchoutska; Kemtchoug]		7	–
22nd	„ „	Seldeowa [Zeledeyeva]		7	12
23rd	To the city Krasnoyarsk on the left bank of the Yenisei river			5	12

From Tomsk to Krasnoyarsk, 111 hours or 79 miles or 55 versts.

Even up to here, various obstacles which we could not avoid hampered the fortunate progress of our journey. In nearly all of the places indicated above live people transplanted here from Russia, and among them are many exiled malefactors who at the time were pressed by the most extreme want. They live in swampy places, in the middle of the deepest forests, where neither the fruits of the field nor even hay will grow and thrive.[58]

Because of the weather, which had become most unfavourable with rain and snow, the roads, which in any case are wretchedly poor, became now so bad that in the course of four days of journeying day and night we could scarcely travel thirty hours' distance, and we had to put up with spending the night here and there right in the morass. Another unendurable torture was caused us by the frightful quantity of bugs and vermin which made the homes of the people of these regions into literal hells. It is impossible to describe how loathsome the rooms appear in which all the walls swarm with these small monsters. I cannot at all understand how it is possible for bugs to implant themselves at places where, not more than four years ago, man had just begun to live and wither the colonists have come a distance of 500 German miles. Nevertheless, these vermin, so harmful to the repose of the people, are already so numerous that one does not know where to escape from them. The cockroaches, which are called *Tarakans* in Russian, make up the other sort of bugs in the houses here. They are divided into two types, namely the large ones, which are blackish-red, and the small ones, which look whitish. Both species increase in numbers unheard of, so that not only the floors, sockets, and walls, but also all the chests, cupboards, cooking and drinking utensils are filled with them. They don't bite like the bed bugs, but still they swarm around you when you lay yourself anywhere to rest; and when one wants to eat, his appetite is already satisfied by the disgusting sight of witnessing thousands of them fall into the bowls and plates as the result of the ascending smoke of the dishes on the table. In these disagreeable regions I would have soon been seized by homesickness had not the hope encouraged me that we did not need to be long on our pilgrimage. This thought was truly the only one which helped to ease our arduous journey.

Once, after we had passed over the Kia river and had endured a very bad road, we had some coffee prepared for us in a village, for which the lady of the house in which we were staying brought the cream. She had already heard from our servants that we wanted to drink coffee and therefore came very boldly to the major with the request to give her a cup of it. As it seemed strange to us that a peasant woman in Siberia should ask for coffee, the Major asked if she had ever drunk the like of it in her life. "Oh, yes," she replied; and because she noticed that we spoke French, she continued, "J'ai l'honneur à vous dire Monsieur Mayor, que je suis la Femme du malheureux Lapuchin, qu'on a envoyé en Sibérie." She said this and thereupon told us the entire course of her destiny—how she had been sent to Siberia with her husband (Lapuchin, an eminent Russian nobleman), how they had remained captive there for a long time, how her husband had finally died, still under the fetters of chains, and how she had decided to marry a peasant (he had just gone out on a bear-hunt) with whom she lived now very happily.[59]

At another place, when we were just planning to retire, our attention was called through pitiful exclamations to some well dressed women who entered our room. These unfortunates, who had noticed that we still had some cold roast and ham remaining, begged the Major for a bit of food for their journey. The good people could only whisper to us and tell us, while their distressed hearts were sobbing, that their husbands were to be sent by special post to the Nerchinsk mines and that they were condemned there to lifelong labour. This was what their pitiable wives told us. The greatest feeling of pity here overcame my Major, who presented them with everything that we still had on hand and, moveover, gave them ten roubles in silver for their sad journey. They did not allow us to see the two unhappy men who were in the covered and strongly guarded wagons, and much less were we able to learn who they were, whence they came, and why they had become so unfortunate. Their afflicted, pitiable wives, who voluntarily accompanied them with their children, thanked the Major with tears for his charity—and disappeared without our being able to learn anything of them afterwards.

Not far from Krasnoiarsk we encountered a transport which was plentifully laden with the blessing of nature from the Nerchinsk mines. It consisted of sixty wagons, each of which was laden with five longish chests and protected by five infantry-men from the Chasseur batallions. The captain in command, who with his stuff will assuredly have been most welcome to the empress of Russia, showed by his statements that he was conveying 920 pounds of pure molten gold and 5277 pounds of silver with this transport to Petersburg.[60]

The prospect in the vicinity of Krasnoiarsk is possibly the finest of all those that up to then I had seen in the vast Russian empire. One must just imagine how pleasant it must seem when one suddenly comes from dark, swampy forests, sometimes fifty hours and more in length, onto a place where everything is to be found that beautiful Nature brings forth both for the enjoyment and the use of man. Thus we proceeded now, before we reached Krasnoiarsk, through the pleasantest valleys in which the bloom of spring smiled at me. Innumerable herds of cattle from the nearest villages went to pasture here, and everywhere we saw joyful folk from the towns, who passed the Whitsun holidays here with all sorts of joyful festivities.

Krasnoiarsk lies on a plain through which the mighty Enesei flows and which heaven-ascending mountains encircle. In this basin the Krasnoiarsk citizens plant their corn, which they always harvest with bountiful blessing. This overabundance of grain, together with the incomparable summer and winter feed for the stock, makes the region of Krasnoiarsk one of the most blissful on the entire globe. Everywhere it appeared to me as if we had come into an entirely different region and climate, and even though we had already passed over a great part of Asia, I still had not felt that I was truly in Asia until now that I discovered a great quantity of plants, shrubs, and trees which I had never seen in Europe and which are indeed the special property of Asia.

In Krasnoiarsk we stopped at the home of the Tartar Prince Bielumsky, who holds here the place of a vice-governor. The man appeared to have much intelligence and the Major was very much obliged to him for the good instructions which he received from him with regard to our further journey. Among other things, the prince told me a great deal concerning the happy condition of his district on the Enesei river, and I must confess that I have never heard of anything so fantastic in my life. No place in the world can be found, I believe, where food is so abundant and so cheap as it is here in the year 1776. On the twenty-third of May one hundred weight of rye flour cost in our presence five kopecks, approximately three and one-half shillings according to Zurich coin; wheat flour costs six kopecks; one hundred weight of beef cost sixty-five kopecks or about fifty shillings. A whole steer costs one and one half roubles or approximately three *Gulden;* cows, one rouble; horses, two roubles; sheep or hogs from fifty to sixty kopecks each[61]. Could there be happier people in the world than the citizens of Krasnoiarsk if, through diligence and industry, through virtue and good usage, they would show themselves worthy of the use of these blessings of heaven instead of so greatly dishonouring benevolent nature by their revelry, idleness, and debauchery.

We left the town of Krasnoiarsk, in which we found nothing beautiful and in which we had stopped no longer than three hours, and close-by crossed the Enisei, which is frightfully swift here and over a half hour's distance wide. In the middle of the river an unusual sight was revealed to us, a view of the mountains which stretch the length of the river on its right bank and which belong to the great Sajan mountain chain. Among others there appeared before our eyes a lofty mountain whose peaks were divided into many tall masses of rock and cliffs of varied shape and size, like a city provided with a castle and many towers. Upon admiring this singularly beautiful prospect I was reminded of my brother and of Herrn Horner in the Augustiner Gasse, because I indeed know what they would have done had they, like me, seen this marvel of nature. Had I only learned to draw better from our town-clerk, Herrn Fuessli, L would have taken down many a fine view!

On the other side of the Enisei we continued our trip to Irkutsky [Irkutsk]. The road there leads to a large extent through very long mountains in which now broad and now narrow fruitful valleys alternated with woods of firs, cedars and ordinary leaf-bearing trees. One beautiful view after another appeared everywhere before my eyes. Sometimes we travelled for hours through long avenues under the shade of magnificent cedar trees and then again through fruitful dales irrigated by swift, clear rivers; and we were able to deduce from the beautiful and clean villages the diligence of the inhabitants. To be sure, a large part of the way was difficult and painful enough; but since we were already used to it, we did not concern ourselves much about it. Rather, we cheered ourselves with the

JAKOB FRIES'S JOURNEY, 1774—1776

hope of soon reaching the goal of our journey. In the Irkutsk government we found still better roads and far more beautiful villages than we had seen in the Tobolsk government. We then went ever farther into the Siberian Alps, and after we had caught glimpses of the first heathen people along the beautiful Occa, Kitay, and Angara rivers, we reached the city of Irkutsk on the Angara in [for?] one of the most pleasurable times of my life.

1776 May	From Krasnoiarsk	hours	minutes
the 23rd	To the village Botoy [Botanskoi]	5	12
23rd	,, ,, Kuskun [Kouskounskoi]	5	–
24th	,, ,, Baleyskowa [Balanskoi; Selo Balai]	6	36
24th	To the market town Ribna [Rybinskoi; Rybanskaja] on the Ribna river	10	24
24th	To the village Urinsky	10	48
24th	To the Ostrog Kanskoy [Kansk] on the Kan river[62] and close by the ferry	5	12
25th	To the village Ilansky [Illan; Ilinskoe]	5	36
25th	,, ,, Pojam	6	48
25th	To the farm Klutschy [Kljutschi; Kljutscheffskois; Koklyoutcheuskoi]	9	36
25th	To the village Jalowsky [Jelofskoie]	6	12
25th	To the market town Beresowa [Biryousov; Birjussinskaja] on the Beresewa [Birjussa] river and close by the ferry	2	24
26th	To the village Bajaranowka [Baranovskoi]	4	–
27th	,, ,, Alsaminsky [Alsamai]	9	–
27th	,, ,, Tamsorsky [Mzarskoi; Samsor]	6	36
27th	,, ,, Ukowsky	7	12
28th	To the Ostrog Udinsky [Nijnei Udinsk] on the Uda, and across the river close by the ferry	5	12
28th	To the village Tyngulsky [Chunguiskoi]	6	48
28th	,, ,, Schabordinsky [Schabartulskoi]	9	–
28th	To the market town Tulun on the Jayi [Iya] and across the river close by the ferry	9	48
28th	To the village Schyrogulsky [Charagousskoi; Scheragul]	5	24
29th	,, ,, Kyutunsky [Kuntui]	8	24
29th	,, ,, Kulmiteowa [Kameltia]	8	–
29th	,, ,, Timinskowa [Siminskoi; Zimanskoi] on the Occa and across the river close by the ferry	6	12

| 29th | ,, | ,, | Solorizkowa [Salari; Zalarinskoi] | 9 | 48 |

From Salorizkowa

30th	To the village Tscherumkowa [Tcheremnova]	6	12
30th	,, ,, Kululizkowa		5	48
30th	,, ,, Tatuskowa [Tautourskoi; Taiturskaja] on the Biola [Bielaja] river close by the ferry	8	–
30th	,, ,, Kitayzkoy [Kitoiskaja] on the Kitay river, close by the ferry	7	24
30th	To the city Irkutsk on the right bank of the Angara	9	24

From Krasnoiarsk to Irkutsk, 205 hours or 146 miles or 1025 versts.

Immediately upon our arrival in Irkutsk we had an audience with the deputy governor, Brigadier Nemzow.[63] The Major arranged some matters with him in view of our further journey and put the business in order, which lay before us at the Chinese border which was not far distant from here. Irkutsk is pleasantly and beautifully situated on the swift Angara river where it takes in the Irkut river coming from a south-westerly direction. The city itself is well built and provided with a few stone churches and other public and private buildings, is paved with stone, and is, all told, the best city in all of Siberia. The garden of the governor looked especially gay; together with the dwelling, it is laid out on the side of the river where it flows roaring past the city. One sees here very many summer houses built according to the Chinese way, which are, as well known, adorned with many galleries. Among the many wild animals running about in the courtyard, I was shown a small Kamchadalian [Kamtchatka] elk whose horns were, however, so terribly large and broad that I could not understand how this little animal was able to carry such a terrible weight of antlers on its head. We were welcomed in the chamber of the governor by a Chinese jackdaw [Dolle] which uttered several Chinese and Russian words as perfectly as a human being. The governor had the kindness to lead us to a place where two savage people from America, one of each sex, who had been captured not so long ago on the farthest northern coast of Siberia, lay sick with small-pox. As they were destined for the Russian empress in Petersburg, they were treated very carefully. Thus, we could not view them as closely and attentively as we would have liked to. This much did I see, nevertheless, that these dark brown savages had strangely formed faces with all sorts of figures tattooed on the forehead, cheeks and nose, and that they had pierced noses and lips as well as pierced ears, hung with small round rings. Since they were lying on Russian beds, I could not see how their clothes, which hung at the wall, suited them. These consisted of various small pieces of fur, of different types and sewn together and hemmed at the edges with all kinds of coral pieces and shells. They had the appearance of narrow cowls and may very well be closely related to our Zurich "bear's skin". Otherwise, this savage American couple supposedly has much in common with the inhabitants of the outermost parts of Siberia. Thus, even their speech, their mode of life and their clothing are believed to be in most parts the same as those of the others.

The short stay in the city of Irkutsk did not allow me to inspect a thousand other curiosities. For this is, indeed, my greatest complaint, that on our very hasty trip I was only able to view the surface of all the beautiful and unusual things that each place had to offer, and to survey them only fleetingly. My Major Riedel was the best man in the world, perhaps also the best soldier and most loyal officer of his empress. But that, then, was all. No majestic view of nature moved him, no forest full of mighty cedars, no strange creature, which he had formerly never seen in Europe. The soldiers' drill determined the entire history of his temperament. And since I had to be around and with him day and night, he never had anything but the same conversations with me, about which he understood much but I only little. Thus I was constantly deprived of the time and opportunity to derive a certain amount of advantage, for the sake of my knowledge and curiosity, from the rarities seen in such a distant and alien land. We travelled day and night almost continuously, and at the most stopped only one or two days in the cities, of which there are anyhow very few in Siberia. Whenever I wished to absent myself here and there from my fellow-traveller and master in order to see something new, I necessarily became terribly weary from the journey. And since, on account of weariness, I no longer felt the aches of my bruised bones, I slept so deeply even on the hard benches that I awoke sometimes only after eight to ten hours, provided I was allowed to sleep that long, and thus missed the time during which I might have observed something unusual and noteworthy.

In Irkutsk we otherwise became acquainted with the Vice-Governor Juny, with the chief commander of the place, and with various merchants. The foreign clergyman here, Pastor Lange from Hamburg, has no-one but himself to whom to preach the word of the gospel in German, for even the few German Christians who stay here are so indifferent toward everything that religion commands that it is hardly worth the trouble to maintain a clergyman at all.[64] I have noticed this shameful negligence of the German Christians in their public worship generally throughout all of Russia. Among very few have I come upon bibles, and Pastor Lange has assured me that he had not seen a bible with any one of his congregation and that no one had even desired one. The worthy man bewailed his distress to me with weeping eyes.[65] He would gladly leave behind all his property if he could only get away from here again. But, alas, who in Petersburg concerns himself with those who must spend all the days of their lives dissatisfied in distant Siberia? It is remarkable that here in Irkutsk I would never have heard anything at all of a pastor residing here, if I hadn't caught sight of the worthy man at a window while I was accidentally passing by and recognized his clerical office by his wig. In this manner I thereupon satisfied my curiosity and visited the pastor. I can say that he was just as happy as I was to meet him and he admitted to me without flattery that my presence was most agreeable to him. He knew of no greater favour for me than to take me to his only good friend in Irkutsk, and that was the Russian archbishop of this place.[66] I shall be thankful to Pastor Lange all the days of my life for the acquaintance with this worthy and able old Russian clergyman. Had only time allowed me then to stop longer than a quarter of an hour with this honest gentleman! He had just received a packet of letters from the Russian abbot in Peking with the extremely pleasant news that the emperor of China had now bestowed upon the Russian aliens in Peking the long requested privileges of residing free and unhampered in a suburb of Peking, of trading and pursuing their businesses, of building a church, and of maintaining a public Latin grammar school. Thereupon the archbishop sent a courier to the Petersburg Synod with this weighty news and entertained us with some extraordinarily delicate tea which he had also just received as a gift from Peking.[67]

Very early in the morning of the first of June we left the city of Irkutsk[68] and travelled in a very narrow valley between high mountains through which the Angara river rushes, until we reached the Baskowa farm. From there we went to the market town of Nikolsky, where the Angara flows from the Baikal, which is among the largest lakes in the world and which we had to cross in order to reach the Chinese frontier regions occupied by regular troops. On a hill above Nikolsk I viewed with extraordinary pleasure a prospect of the Baikal at the very same spot where, between two frightfully steep cliffs, as through a door which nature has pierced here, the Baikal finds an opening through which to flow and give the Angara river its origin. One hour's distance from this noteworthy spot, close by the shore of the Baikal, lies the rambling Lischwinischowa Inn, which is the place where one generally is taken across the lake and where a galleon regularly lies at anchor. Meanwhile, since we had to wait for favourable winds, curiosity impelled me to climb the high mountain here, which rises up directly from the shore of the lake. I reached its summit after having rested probably more than twenty times and had so exhausted myself from climbing that I could scarcely recover. In return for my troubles, though, I had a new, incomparable view of the south-western half of the Baikal. With indescribable pleasure I viewed the immeasurably long range of snow-capped mountains which border the south-eastern horizon of the lake and which constitute the same partition for Russia and China which nature has created between Italy and Switzerland by means of the Alps. On all my journeys I have never recalled my fatherland so vividly as now upon the sight of this view of the Baikal and of the snow-covered Chinese mountains. I again remembered what in my younger years I had seen on the Albis mountain, whenever I went over to visit my cousin, Pastor Horner.[69] Where

I overlooked it, the lake was sixty versts or a twelve hours' distance wide. Thus, I would not have been able to see the snow-capped mountains on the other side had the weather not been fine. I became almost giddy when I turned my eyes away from the distance and toward the abyss in which I could scarcely make out our galleon as a little boat.[70] The vertical cliffside, on whose edge I was overcome with an awful terror so that I dared look into the depth for only a moment, must be six hundred fathoms high, as the helmsman assured me. It was not without danger to my life that I again crept down from this terribly high rock, which is only sparsely overgrown with firs and small shrubs, but whose cliffs are much more adorned with strange flowers.

After I had received a rather pointed reprimand from the Major for my short mountain trip, I asked the helmsman for a closer description of the Baikal, which I received together with a new map thereof. Later I had the pleasure of sending the same to the Councillor of State [Collegen-Rath], Professor Euler in Petersburg. One hundred and eighty small and three large streams plunge into the lake from all of the lofty mountains that surround the Baikal, which appears as nothing else than an enormous gap between the same; whereas the Angara alone flows from the Baikal. Not only the shores of the Baikal, but also the bottom of it is, for the most part, stony and the water thereof is so clear and fresh that it is in no way inferior to the purest and sweetest spring water. Just as the steep cliffs rise up several hundred fathoms from the edge of the lake, so also do they go uninterruptedly and just as steeply down into the depth of the lake. The sounding-line of five hundred fathoms length which the helmsman had cast over to satisfy my curiosity could not reach the bottom, even though we were at less than one hundred fathoms' distance from the shore. According to the very latest observations, the length of the Baikal amounts to one hundred German miles, the width, though, to fifteen. The lake abounds in fish, and the inhabitants of the country make much of a type of fish which the Mongolians call *Omuly* and which in form is not unlike the herring. The larger part of the inhabitants of the neighbouring provinces get their chief nourishment from the fish of the Baikal.

On the second of June our company was augmented by

the suite of a Mongolian ambassador, whom the Chinese government had sent to the governor of Irkutsk to settle boundary affairs and who, after the receipt of his dispatch from the governor, was already on his return trip. The ambassador had the rank of a Mongolian colonel and his retinue consisted by degrees of officers of lesser rank, subaltern officers, and soldiers. The entire train of the ambassador with its followers was not quite as splendid as one would otherwise expect of the pompous and proud court of his chief.[71] The gentlemen had nothing on their bodies besides long blue gowns of Chinese cotton cloth, cut out according to their custom with wide belts, and considerably rusted side arms of long sabres, and on their heads they wore round but pointed caps with large red stones like the knob on a tower. The crystal knob on the cap adorned with peacocks' feathers constituted the only outward distinguishing mark of the ambassador, with whom I had on repeated occasions the honour of drinking tea. On the other hand, my proud Major Riedel did not even wish to speak with him, though it was by no means sure which one of the two was, or would have liked to have been considered, of superior rank. At eight o'clock in the morning of the third of June we set sail with a rainy north-west wind and on the fourth at the break of day we reached the south-eastern shore of the Baikal close to the Posolsky Monastery. The entire crossing of the Baikal, which is calculated at ninety-six versts or a bit over fourteen German miles, lasted thus not more than ten hours [sic]. Henceforth we pursued our course up the Selenga stream which flows into the Baikal not far from the Posolsky Monastery, and reached the city of Selenginsky on the sixth of June, after we had been set down across the Selenga close by the same.

What I said earlier about the surroundings of Krasnoiarsk is valid here also and it seems as if the Baikal as well as the Enesei separates two entirely different worlds from each other. As otherwise in Siberia, we passed regions unequalled in beauty along the Selenga river. Thus, the peasants here too are wealthy people, with so much breeding and order that their like is found perhaps nowhere else. They live in large well built and well furnished houses. One therefore need not be astonished to see the chests in their white rooms decked out with Chinese porcelain and silver table utensils. It is remarkable that one does not come upon house vermin as frequently in these clean and trim rooms as in the less clean and soiled peasant chambers. The governor of Selenginsk district, a Major Wlason, entertained us fatigued travellers so splendidly that we shall remain indebted to him for the rest of our lives.

On the seventh of June we left Irkutsk [sic. Selenginsk?] in order to bring our affairs at the boundary of the empire to a close. We made our way thither across the Selenginsk sand mountains and spent the night of the same day in a lonely but pleasant dale on the Perieschnaja stream. We had a good cup of coffee, of which we always had some on hand, prepared for us while our drivers boiled the *Kinpitschney,* or brick tea with salt and butter, which is customary in this region. This kind of tea which consists not of singly dried leaves, but rather of coarse pressed tea plants and is sold in shapes like bricks, constitutes the principal nourishment of the common man in this region and is supposedly quite satisfying when cooked with bread and butter and salt.[72] On the eighth we stopped at the village of Beregowoy and on the ninth we came to the camp of the Baikal division in the Chilgontin plain on the Tschikoy river at the Chinese border, having passed the following places from Irkutsk:

1776 Juny		From Irkutsk	hours	minutes
the	1st	To the farm Baskowa [Paschkowa]	6	—
	1st	To the village Nikolsky at the source of the Angara	5	48
	1st	To the inn Liswinischneja [Listwanischnoie Simowie] on the south-western shore of the Baikal	1	—
	3rd	To the Posolsky Monastery on the south-eastern shore of the Baikal	19	12
	4th	To the village Stepnaja	4	12
	4th	To the Ostrog Kabanskoy	5	24
	4th	To the village Tarakanowa [Tarakonova; Tarakanofskaja]	4	48
	5th	To the Ostrog Eliynskoy [Il'inskoi; Ilimskoi]	4	48
	5th	To the custom station Polowinnowa [Polavina; Polowinnaja Sastawa]	4	12
	5th	To the village Iwulga	6	36

JAKOB FRIES'S JOURNEY, 1774—1776

5th	,,	,,	Rangoy [Orongoi]	8	12
6th	,,	,,	Abukuy	4	36
6th	To the city Selenginsky [Selenginsk] on the right bank of the Selenga73			8	36
7th	To the stream Perieschnaja			8	12
8th	To the village Beregowoy on the Tschikoy river			8	12
9th	To the Mongolian idol temple in the Chilgontin plain			1	–
9th	To the camp of the Irkutsk division on the Tschikoy river across from the Chinese border			1	36

From Irkutsk to the Tschikoy river on the north-eastern border of the Russian empire	102	–

On the tenth we attended to our duties, selecting forty men for the Nizhni-Novgorod regiment from the Siberian squadron of dragoons encamped here and dispatching them directly to the village of Berogowoy. Meanwhile we gathered here in the camp new energies after a journey in which we had travelled a distance of 1184 hours or 854 German miles and which had lasted from the twenty-eighth of February to the tenth of June. The Baikal division encamped here consisted of the Ekatherinenburg Field Batallion, a squadron of dragoons, and several companies of Don and Mongol Cossacks, their overall command being in the hands of a Major Gagrin. My Major Riedel watched the review of troops for a time while from a close-by hill I overlooked the entire vast Chilgontin plain which derives its Mongol name from the abundantly growing brush which is greatly sought by the Mongolian cattle. Little had I previously in my life imagined that I would come to countries so far distant from my fatherland. On my knees I now thanked my Creator for so much favour shown me and for the marvellous guidance of His Almighty Will, whilst my soul was entirely engrossed with the joy of seeing and being permitted to wonder, throughout the greater part of Asia, at the greatness of the work of the Lord. The camels which belonged to Mongolian heathen who dwelled under felt tents and which were drinking in adjacent rivers, the herds of strange species of sheep and goats which I had never seen before, the lowing of hornless black steers (a species entirely peculiar to this region), various birds and insects unknown to me which flew around me — all this aroused in me just as many changes [sic] of joy and wonder to extol a new creation in a foreign land.

I continued to make my observations about many unexpected objects on the plain of Chilgontin when the Major again had me called to him in order to travel back to Beregowoy. The route there led through a valley covered with bare sand dunes and little woods on the side of the Chilgontin plain, which is renowned because of the great Mongolian idol temple found here. We stopped for an hour in that very place in order to see this important spot and visited the supreme head of the lama priesthood here, upon whom the Mongolian title of *Bandidi chambo Lama* is conferred. First the old idolator invited us to a cup of tea which he himself proferred to us with great pleasure in his tent. After that he showed us the entire splendour of his idol temple, which consisted of six small ones and one large temple, still entirely new and not completely finished. Everything beautiful that the Chinese architectural style exhibits seemed to have been lavishly put into effect in this large and extensive building. The old priest had in his younger days studied lama idolatry in the service of the famous Dalai Lama, and now he had this new Mongolian temple erected by Russian carpenters after the style of the great temple of the Dalai Lama. It is strange that in Russia one takes so many pains to spread the doctrine of the gospel among the heathen in some places whilst in another place new idol temples are erected. On the outside as well as on the inside of the temple we found a large number of horrible idols, partly hewed out of wood and partly painted onto the walls. The priests, whom one calls lamas here and who numbered more than one hundred, performed various leaps, bows, and other things with strangely twisted faces and grimaces, not so much for our pleasure but rather for that of the heaten present, and they called this behaviour worshipping the gods. Meanwhile, upon a signal given in the outer galleries of the temple by a type of large broad drum, the sacrifices brought for the idols by the people, consisting of candied fruits, roasted lambs and the like and prepared in the temple kitchen, were carried to the temple and placed before the idols by the light of many wax candles.

The entire idol worship lasted not more than three

quarters of an hour, during which time the heathen people for the most part lay on the earth before the idols with their faces covered. After its conclusion we set out for Beregowoy and were overtaken by a terrible thunderstorm and became dripping wet. In Beregowoy we had several things to settle with our new detachment of dragoons, who were dispatched by the Major to Selenginsk. He travelled with me, however, to the famous Russian and Chinese trading place of Kiaechta [Kiakhta], eight hours distant from here, where we arrived at daybreak on the twelfth of June. My curiosity to see this noteworthy border village and the Chinese living here was so great that I was full of unrest and impatience and could scarcely await the day.

In Kiakhta we put up at the house of Commander Nalabradie,[74] for whom we had a written order from the governor of Irkutsk to show us all that Kiakhta possessed in noteworthy features. In itself Kiakhta is not an especially favourable and good place in that it lies on a sandy desert where the inhabitants of the city cannot get enough water. A wooden church, a house for the commander, a rhubarb storehouse, a garrison of a company of soldiers, a detachment of dragoons and Cossacks, and a few fine houses of wealthy merchants or agents of Moscow merchants living here—that is all that is to be seen in Kiakhta and can be said for it.[75] Approximately sixty fathoms from the south side of Kiakhta, which is surrounded by a rampart and moat and *chevaux de frise,* lies the first Chinese city, Maimatschin, whither we went accompanied by Major Nalabradin [sic] and Pharmacist Brand of this place. Between these two border places, on an entirely dry plain, stood a boundary post adorned with two neat inscriptions. On one of these, which was in Russian, stood, "Here ends the Russian domain". Whereas on the other was written in Mongolian, "Here begins the Chinese empire".

Scarcely had the Chinese chief, or *Sargutschey* in their tongue, heard about our approach that he sent a messenger to meet us, through whom he invited us to his home. We had to go through the entire little town of Maymatschin on the way to this curteous Chinese, who lived at the southern end of it. Maymatschin is nicely built. It consists of two main streets which bisect each other in the middle and two others which run parallel to one of them from north to

128 A SIBERIAN JOURNEY

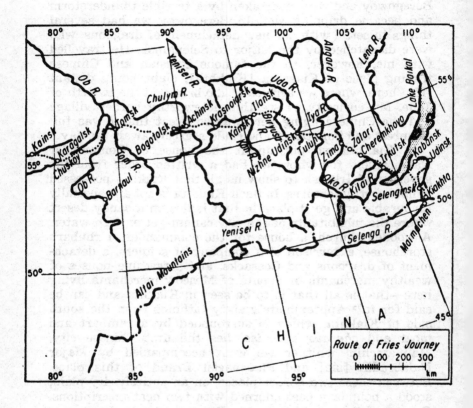

3 Fries's journey through Central Siberia from Kainsk to the Chinese border at Kiakhta and back to Kainsk, 1776 (for continuation, see Map 2).

south. They are unpaved, strewn with sand, provided with a trench in the middle, and are kept very clean. The buildings of the Chinese here are very uniform, not more than two fathoms high, built of bamboo and spread over with sizing. Their roofs are flat, projecting towards the street and propped up with pillars.

Each house has a large yard with a portal and consists of a living room, a shop, a storeroom, and a kitchen. One must pass through the portal to get into the house. The chambers, which never overlook the street, have large painted paper windows provided with a type of grating made of small, very delicately chased rods. Their walls are covered with coloured paper, and the benches form a panelling all around the room and are wide enough to eat from and to sit and sleep upon. The lime floor is clay-covered, and the stove consists of built-up rectangular bricks and is seldom higher than the bench, which, I imagine, has much in common with the divan of the Turks and Persians. Even though tea water is boiled continually on these stoves, still one does not discover any smoke in the rooms for everything is drawn away downward through a pipe which passes under the benches and into a smoke stack built onto the street. Also, the Chinese know how to burn coal so well that one does not perceive the slightest discomfort from the smoke, although a coal fire is permanently maintained because of the habit of smoking tobacco.

Aside from the usual tea utensils of porcelain, the Chinese pay little attention to other implements which Europeans otherwise expose lavishly to decorate their rooms. A finely finished chest for the house deity, who is painted with colours on paper, with a delicate ash container on it for the remainders of the incense candles and adorned with a silk hanging—that constitutes the only decoration of the rooms of the Chinese here. The distinguished Chinese also have flower pots for their enjoyment. It appears to be just as clean in the kitchen, in which in addition to the low stove that serves as a symbol [Zeichen] are to be found two or three secondary stoves with built-in iron kettles [drawers?; Kesteln]. Among other kitchen implements a bowl seemed especially strange to me in which the Chinese cooks always first chop up the unroasted boiled meat by means of large, broad rectangular knives, before they bring it to the table.

The old Chinese chief, or *Sargutsey,* was a man of noble Chinese origin, and we were told privately that he had been one of the foremost ministers or mandarins of the emperor, but that he had had the misfortune to have been removed to the Russian border because of a political crime.[76] Be that as it may, we were very much pleased with him. He entertained us according to good Chinese fashion with tea, Chinese confections, tobacco, dried sausages of mutton, and with somewhat sweetish wine. The interpreter, who must be around him constantly whenever a foreigner is with him, had to question us about everything—who we were, whence we came, and what our business was here at the border. Everything that we answered thereupon was repeated to him in Chinese, and then he made known by his friendly smiles that he was greatly pleased with us.

Meanwhile, I admired the extreme cleanliness of his living room. I saw many books lying on the table, which I was told were Chinese calendars, historical and geographical accounts and judicial journals with which the *Sargutchey* was in the habit of occupying himself. I also saw very finely executed hand-drawn maps and among others a fairly accurate drawing of a general map of Europe. Time alone was lacking for me to satisfy my curiosity as to the present amount of information the Chinese possess in these sciences. To my extreme regret Major Riedel did not want to stop too long with the Chinese. He requested the favour of inspecting the idol temples, which the Sargutschey not only granted us, but where he also accompanied us himself. One of these temples stands in the middle of the town at the very place where the two main streets intersect. It looks like a tower which is adorned with a portal and which gives a fine perspective to the street. This tower consists of two stories and as many galleries. The lower portion has a roof with four corners, the upper one had eight, which jut far forward and are hung with little iron bells in such a manner that they create a pleasing tinkle at the slightest breath of wind. Upon the lower portion is set up the image of the true god, Tien, who is regarded by the Chinese as their highest blessing and who is deemed a sovereign of thirty-two heavens. He sits with bared head covered with hair and surrounded by the glow of a light, approximately as one portrays the head of the Saviour. One hand of the idol rests in his lap; the other, or left hand, though, is lifted as if representing the act of benediction. At his side stand a young girl and a very old man.

The more magnificent and vaster temple, surrounded by *chevaux de frise,* is situated near the south gate of Kiakhta. One approaches it through beautiful portals and outer courts decorated with many columns, in which are to be found several small buildings in which things are stored pertaining to the worship of the idols, such as banners, candlesticks, escutcheons, shields, and so forth. The entrance hall of the temple as well as the temple itself is adorned with many lacquered columns of special types, with much gilded wood-carving, a pretty roof hung with many small iron bells, and a gallery whose walls are painted with the miracles and heroic deeds of the deities. The interior of the temple itself is extraordinarily well decorated, and here sit the idols who are fashioned from clay, gigantic in size, and portrayed in such horrible forms that at my first look I was so terrified that I was overcome with a secret shudder. It was impossible for me to examine closely these wonderful creations of the human power of imagination, for the leisure and the learned falcon eye of a Palles [S. Pallas] are required for that.[77] I could occupy myself only with the things on the surface. The bearded goldly-gleaming face and crowned head of the chief deity, which exceeds the stature of a man more than four-fold, his magnificent Chinese garments made of silk cloth, his aspect more of a peacable than a wrathful prince and judge, the altar standing before him, the lesser and servant gods set around this altar, their armour-like forms and figures with four to eight eyes, hands and feet and with frightful reddish-brown faces and corpulent bellies, the ugly forms of other idols set up in the temple, the war god, the gold and silver god, the fire god, the ox god, and so on—this was just all that I was able to impress upon my memory in the short time of half an hour which we spent in the temple, and what attention I could give I directed principally toward those things.

From the temple we were invited, besides, as guests to the homes of various Chinese. And there we were everywhere entertained with extraordinary courtesy, but also treated to so much tea-water drinking that I soon feared to contract dropsy. In regard to clothing the Chinese look to cleanliness just as much as they generally do with everything with which they come in contact. Thus one sees sooner a patched garment on their bodies than a soiled one. Their favourite colour is black, their most somber one, though, is white. Therefore, their mourning garments are white; therefore, also, they depict the devil as white. The clothing of the common person consists of cotton cloth, while, on the other hand, that of the gentle people consists of silk stuff. Likewise, their shoes are covered either with cotton or silk material. Their soles, however, consist of many pieces of pasteboard nailed one on top of the other; they have no heels and are probably three fingers thick, so that they are supposed, therefore, to last for several consecutive years. The summer hats with which the Chinese cover their heads are woven of straw like ours in Switzerland, but are fashioned completely like a folk costume hat. A knob, which is wound with silk thread when they are not in mourning, is fixed to the top of the hat.

The Chinese drive in wagons with high wheels and these revolve with the axle. Only the most eminent are allowed to drive with four wheels. The inferior ones make use of the so-called one-wheeled drays [*Einkarren*]. They ride on oxen just as readily as on horses. A ring is put through the pierced nose of the ox, and through this ring is put a cord by means of which the ox is held just like a horse is held at bridle. All Chinese have black hair, which they cut off except for the top tress, which they always wear braided like girls. The Chinese grow only sparse beards, and these they do not grow before they reach mature years. Their razor blades are very short but therefore so much the broader, and their barbers know how to use these with far greater dexterity than the Europeans. One recognizes the barbers' houses by small hoisted flags. The Chinese never cut their finger-nails but let them grow long as an adornment. The Chinese are great lovers of garden fruits. This is probably the cause of their fine healthy bodies, which they seldom ruin by intemperance in eating and drinking. Tea is their common beverage. They drink it weak and sweetened with sugar candy. They smoke tobacco heavily and they constantly carry their pipes around with them, together with their pouches which are tied fast to their hips. The Sargutschey keeps very good order among them, and people who must be punished are disciplined, regardless of person, according to their crimes.

Major Riedel must have been greatly pleased by the shops of these Chinese, for he stopped there longer than anywhere else. Truly, these shops were so nicely decked out that it was a pleasure to look around in them. Most unfamiliar to me was the variety of China inks which are sold here. Also, I was astounded by the many types of tea which they offered us for sale. They wanted to sell the Major a bale of good black Bou tea[78] or sixty pounds worth of tea, for twenty roubles, while fifteen pounds of the best available tea here could be bought for ten roubles. Here we would have gladly turned our money into tea and China ink had there been a possibility of transporting these things back undamaged for so far a distance as we had travelled. Most of the goods which are traded for Russian merchandise here come from Peking. This is calculated at a distance of two hundred and fifty hours or, according to the Chinese way, a twelve days' journey. On the other hand, the distance to the great wall supposedly amounts to little more than one hundred and fifty hours. But because one has to cross the great Mongolian desert on the journey, the trip is also filled with many hardships. In our presence the Chinese cremated two bodies whose ashes they preserved in porcelain vessels which they sent to Peking to the friends left behind by the deceased.[79]

We now returned again from the Chinese Maymatchin to Kiakhta where we spent the entire evening at the home of the pharmacist, Herrn Brand, who had been ordered here by the Imperial Russian Medical Council on account of the rhubarb.[80] Herr Brand led me through the vast rhubarb storehouse and showed me how this costly medicine is dried, rasped [*gerastelt*] and divided into superior and inferior types after it has been acquired from the Chinese through barter.[81] In Herrn Brand's chamber I saw a handsome collection of Chinese handicraft, and among these some true masterpieces of embossed porcelain. Later several Chinese merchants came to Herrn Brand's house—purely on our account, as we afterwards learned, and simply because they are not able to get their fill of the sight of foreigners. Our company played cards and they watched very eagerly. Some women seemed to be especially friendly toward the Chinese and, to be sure, I noticed that these gentlemen make nothing of an illicit connection with persons of the other sex, even though they are very jealous of their own wives.[82] As a whole, the Chinese treat people in the homes where they are only guests as if they themselves belonged to the household there. They sit down and smoke tobacco as they please; they leave and return without considering whether one is glad to see them or not.[83] As soon as retreat has been sounded and the gate-bell in Maymatchin has been rung, they all withdraw, as do also the Russians who returned from there. For it is a strict order that no Chinese shall stay in Kiakhta over night and also that no Russian shall remain behind in Maymatschin after retreat.

During the time that we were still staying at the home of Herrn Brand a heavy cloudburst occurred which lasted longer than five minutes and swelled the otherwise totally dry Kiakhta brook to three fathoms. We spent the night from the twelfth to the thirteenth of June at the house of the Commandant Nalabradin and early on the thirteenth prepared ourselves for the return trip to Russia. With indescribable satisfaction I withdrew for a few minutes into myself and considered myself far more fortunate now that I had seen and come to know the Chinese than previously. I purchased a few trifles, some cotton cloth, tea and China ink, in order to maintain so much the stronger the memory, at least, of having been at the Chinese border. How gladly would I have brought along from here something for you, too, my dearest parents and brother and sister, if only I could have been assured of being able to devise a safe and easy way of forwarding it to you. But I was more than one thousand German miles distant from you and, therefore, did not know how I should go about sharing with you the enjoyment of the things which good fortune had bestowed upon me. But I consoled myself, and satisfied my desire, with the hope that on another happy occasion I might enjoy the pleasure of giving through better proofs clear evidence of my filial obedience and my truest thanks which I owe you as long as blood runs through my veins.

On the thirteenth of June at eight o'clock in the morning we left the Russian boundary line and, in the name of Him who had so mercifully aided us up to here, set out on our return journey to the regiment.

June	Return trip from the Chinese border	hours	minutes
the 13th	To the fortress Troitskoi where the customs station is for the Chinese goods traded-in in Kiakhta	–	36
	To the farm Lipowschiwa	3	48
	,, ,, Kalischnowa	5	24
	,, ,, Klutchey	5	48
	To the upper ferry across the Selenga river	2	24
	To the lower ferry and to the city Selenginsk	2	–
	From Kiakhta to Selenginsk, 90 versts or 18 hours.		

In Selenginsk I saw nothing either beautiful or noteworthy. In itself, the place is not badly situated on the right bank of the Selenga river, but it is poorly built and surrounded by many sand-hills. It seems to me to be still lonelier here than in Kiakhta where one at least comes upon people of various degrees and where in addition one has connections with the Chinese. The rain which had started on the evening of the twelfth still persisted, and we and our detachment had therefore a very unpleasant journey by water on the Selenga.

June		hours	minutes
the 15th	To the winter station Gensurina	12	–
16th	To the city Udinsk	12	–
	From Selenginsk to Udinsk, 120 versts or 24 hours.		

Like Selenginsk, Udinsk is situated on the right bank of the Selenga, but it has a pleasanter location and is better built, too. Until today it continued to rain continuously and very severely.

We left Udinsk the same day and travelled overland.

Here we boarded our galleon again, but had to wait

June				hours	minutes
the 16th	To the village	Luky		–	24
	,, ,,	Soltikowa [Sotnikowa]		1	–
	,, ,,	Poselskoy		1	–
	,, ,,	Daschinsky [Taischichina]		1	24
	To the inspection house Polowinoy [Polowinnoie]			–	36
	To the Ostrog Ilynskoy			4	36
	To the village Tarekanowa			4	36
	To the Ostrog Kabanskoy			4	24
17th	To the village Stepnoy			5	24
	To the Posolskoy Monastery			4	–

until the twenty-third for favourable winds for crossing the Baikal. And then we were not so fortunate as to reach the opposite shore at the proper place. On the twenty-third we came to the winter-house of Golonsna. With unspeakable toil the galleon had to be towed from here to Liewinischow for forty versts along the rocky and, in many places, inaccessible shore. On the twenty-fifth of June we journeyed from there down the Angara to Irkutsk in a flat-bottom vessel, a distance of sixty versts or twelve hours which we covered within three hours.

From Kiakhta to Irkutsk, 100 hours or 150 versts.[84]

In Irkutsk we only took care of a few necessities, crossed the Angara on the twenty-seventh of June, and pursued our course.

June				hours	minutes
the 28th	To the village	Kitoyskoy on the Kitoy river		9	24
	,, ,,	Tatulskowa on the Riala		7	12
29th	,, ,,	Siminskowa on the Occa		29	48
30th	,, ,,	Tulunskowa on the Jayi		27	48

The Irkutsk government extends up to here. In these provinces we have generally come upon large and wealthy villages and country towns. The major part of the inhabitants of these provinces is made up of *Buraett* [Buriats] heathen who live along the rivers in this government, make—like the Kalmyks—their living chiefly by hunting and raising cattle and, like these, dwell in felt tents upon the open land. They are particularly rich in cattle, and

God blesses them as he formerly blessed the patriarchs with many thousand head of camels, oxen, cows, sheep, and goats and so forth. The Russian missionaries as well as the lama idolator-priests take great pains to convert this still savage people and, praise God, the light of the gospel is being spread among them and progresses more auspiciously than the lama beliefs. Many converted Buriats have already begun to live in the society of the Christians.[85] Our trip continued.

	hours	minutes
the 1st to the 3rd of July		
To the Ostrog Udinsk on the Uda river	25	12
from the 4th to the 6th		
To the market town Beresowa on the Beresa	32	24
On account of the rain that had set in we had here a day of rest on the seventh of July.		
From the 8th to the 10th of July		
To the Ostrog Kansk on the Kan	30	48

Along this route, which goes for several hundred versts through enormous and uninterrupted fir and cedar forests, we were plagued by the frightful gnats and horse-flies [*Brämen*], which propagate here in such great quantities that they darken the air and make it impossible for the people to breathe freely. Everyone here wears delicate nets woven of horsehair over his face, high boots, and leather gloves. Young foals are killed by these little monsters. Horned cattle and horses hide themselves during the day in the corners of the barns and stables and people can't be too careful about these noxious insects when they have to attend to the necessaries of life. I myself was stung so severely by a horse-fly upon this occasion that for three days I didn't know where to turn on account of pain, and I had the greatest trouble to prevent the setting in of gangrene [*Sphacelus, kalter Brand*] at this delicate portion of my privy parts infected by the sting. I noticed that these insects ran about the least at the midday hour, all the more abundantly, though, from four to seven o'clock in the afternoon. From midnight until dawn one had peace from them. It is then that one lets the cattle graze, too. They are most abundant and most dangerous in July, especially when great heat and dry air set in after long rainy weather.[86]

In this region there are also very many bears who cause the traveller many delays and inconveniences, because they upset the bridges with which the roads through the marshy forest are covered. It is unknown to me whether the beasts do this to hide from the gnats under the cast-up boards and beams, or to hunt a variety of ants which collects in heaps under the bridges. Near Kansk we had to pass four places where we first had to put in their previous order the beams which had been uncovered and thrown on top of each other by the bears, before we could proceed across the bridge. After this annoying work we saw the culprit sitting in a large cedar tree not far from the highway. He was now breaking off entire branches of cedar cones from the tree and, as we also observed, since we stopped for a while to watch the comedy, these were carried away by two other bears. The inhabitants of the nearby villages told me, however, that numerous as the bears here are, the people seldom suffer harm from them. Only occasionally, when the cedars bear little fruit, are the bears dangerous and go after the cattle. For this reason an adequate escort is sent along with single persons and travellers, as well as with the mail, from one station to another. There are rare examples of people who perish in the claws of the bears. Only one peasant told me that several years previous a bear had killed his son and sucked out his skull.

We travelled from the Ostrog Kansk	hours	minutes
from the 11th to the 14th of July		
To the city Krasnoiarsk on the Enisei	43	12
from the 14th to the 16th		
To the Ostrog Atchinsk on the Tschulim river	31	48
the 17th To Bugatol	11	48
18th To Kia on the Kia river	24	36
19th To Ischymskowa on the Jayl	25	24
20th Via Masalowa on the Kitat to Turnateiowa	4	36
21st To the city Tomsk, on the Tom river	13	36
From Kiakhta to Tomsk, 420 hours or 2093 versts.		

At Tomsk we had to halt for a few days on account of a lack of guides. A large district of the province of Tomsk belongs to the Barnaul mines which are located in the mountains only four hundred versts away from Tomsk.[87] Thus we had to await the command of General Irrmann[88] in order to obtain horses through his territory. Then we travelled

	hours	minutes
from the 25th to the 29th of July		
To Tascharinsky on the Ob river	33	36
from the 30th of July to the 1st of August		
Across the Ob to Tscheuskoy Ostrog	12	–
from the 1st to the 3rd of August		
To Karkanzky	39	24
the 4th To the Ostrog Kainsk on the Om	25	–
5th Across the Om to Wosnisensky	25	24
from the 6th to the 10th of August		
To the fortress Omsk on the Irtysh	43	48
From Tomsk to Omsk, 180 hours or 897 versts.		

During the time that my Major Riedel was occupied by affairs pertaining to his command, I often visited my dear friend Pastor Luther and his worthy family. Together with the Major, I visited the houses of General Skolon and Brigadier Claver. So we were able at least to rest ourselves a bit. But since the Major still intended to return to the regiment before winter, this joy was also shortlived.

We left Omsk on the boundary line and from the twelfth to the the twentieth of August we went to the fortress of Peter Paul on the Irsym—fifty-three hours. From here the Major sent me once again back to Omsk in order to receive there medicine for the sick members of our command. I arrived there on the twenty-fourth of August and also had the good fortune of speaking once more to Doctor Beres, who had just returned from a trip into the Sajany Mountains. Since Omsk had already become so very dear to me, as if I were at home there, It was really difficult for me to leave this place. After receiving my medicines I took leave of all my inestimable Omsk patrons and friends and hurried to catch up with my command.

From the 27th to the 29th of August
    From Omsk via Petri Pauli to the fortress
    Presnogorkowsky   100 hours or 510 versts

From the 30th August to the 2nd of September
To Skablinoy in Isetsk province of
the Orenburg government   28 hours 24 minutes

We joined here our Irkutsk dragoons with the detachments previously raised in Omsk, Petri Pauli [Petropawlofskaja], and Presnogorkowsky and now sought a comfortable and direct route by which to come to our regiment. The regions here are also among the most wealthy and most fortunate that I have come upon far and wide in Russia. The soil is so fertile in this province that the neighbouring villages, fortresses and mines are always able to obtain their proper provisions from the superabundance of grain. The wealthy peasantry lives in fairly large and well built houses, full of order and cleanliness—something that generally is not customary among the common folk.[89] We now continued our route.

		hours	minutes
the 3rd to the 13th of September			
To the fortress Upper Uralsk on the Ural river		72	–

From here we chose the mountain road across the Ural Mountains and came

September		hours	minutes
the 14th	To the river Igak	3	–
15th	To the river Myndak	5	–
16th	To the Twerdaschow iron works Biela Retskaja[90] [Bielorietsk]	4	–
18th	To the Demidov[91] iron works Umtschuk	4	–
19th	To the Baskir village Tukuy on the Biela river	3	–
20th	To the Demidov iron works Kuktur	5	–
21st	To the Demidov ironworks Absem [Awsano, Awsaeno]	5	–
22nd	To the farm Dmitrophanowa	7	–
23rd	„ „ Salarizkowa	5	36
24th	To the Twerdaschow copper works Bogohawlensky [Bogojabienskoi; Bogoyavlensk]	5	48
25th	To the city Tabinsk on the Biela river	1	48

This route over the Ural Mountains, which amounts to more than fifty hours, was so wretched and difficult that I can truly say that I have never had to endure so much in my life as here.[92] It snowed and rained without interruption from the sixteenth to the twenty-third of September. Nevertheless we had to put up on several occasions with damp and snowy night-quarters on the bare ground. Except for Bogohowlenskaja all the mines which we had to pass were destroyed.[93] Bieloretskaja was beginning again to be rebuilt while we were there. The carpenter employed for the construction was a common and unlearned peasant, but such an excellent mechanical genius that I came upon the most incomparable sawmill already completed by this outwardly simple man. The mountains over which we had to climb with the greatest effort were terribly steep and high. Nevertheless, I saw little snow lying on them. Until about the middle of our course from Werch, or Upper, Uralsk to Tabinsk I came upon nothing but firs and deciduous trees in the mountains. All at once, though, nature seemed to produce a change. For nearer to Tabinsk I found many oaks and other types of trees which nowhere up to here had I ever formerly come upon throughout the whole of Siberia. This has also caused the more recent scientists to regard the Ural mountains as the barrier between Asia and Europe. Everywhere on the mountains the air is very unhealthy. Infection of the eyes and scurvy are prevailing ills here. I tried to drink a cup of distilled horse's milk among the Baskian Tartars who inhabit this region,[94] and I became unexpectedly a little tipsy from it and was greatly indisposed and ill for three consecutive days.[95] The nausea which accompanied my curiosity was lost through repeated vomiting, while Major Riedel made the same experiment— and experienced nothing.

Our command took the direct route from the city of Tabinsk to the Volga. But on account of business the Major took me with him to Orenburg. Near Tabinsk we passed a forest stream, the Biala, and reached Orenburg on the twenty-ninth of September. From Tabinsk to Orenburg, fifty hours. On the route which cuts through the Ufim desert we came upon many wealthy Tartar and *Tschaewasch* villages.[96] On the plain, though, we now and then saw a great many blackish snakes of the thickness of an arm and possibly five or six feet in length. Whilst Major Riedel concerned himself on behalf of his affairs at the chancery of General Mansurow in Orenburg, I had the pleasure of becoming closer acquainted with Doctor

Roeslein.[97] I also visited my dear Pastor Huebner from Memmingen and in the company of these worthy men thus turned the short stay in Orenburg to good advantage. Regarding the present position of the town, its trade and other weighty subjects concerning the province of Orenburg, I have gathered accounts given to me by various friends and, God willing, I shall send these at another opportune time to the Friends of Geography and Natural History in Zurich.

The inspection of the squadrons of Orenburg dragoons still remained. Therefore, we made our way to the province of Bugulma where they had already set up winter quarters; from the second to the seventh of October from Orenburg to Bogoroslan on the Kinel river, 68 hours. Here we chose from four squadrons of dragoons those who pleased us best and united all the men selected for our regiment in Siberia and in Orenburg at the city of Sergiewsky [Sergievsk] on the Sok river, thirteen hours from Bogoroslan. And since nothing more remained for us to do we continued on our journey to the regiment as speedily as possible. We came

the 22nd of October
    To Chrischttschowka on the Volga—32 hours from Sargiowsky

Here we crossed the mightiest river of Europe and after having passed through the provinces of Kazan, Nizhni Novgorod and Voronets we finally reached the town of Tambow on the nineteenth of November, 107 hours distance from the Volga. We now handed our detachments over to the Nizhni Novgorod Dragoon Regiment which had been transferred here from Balachna while we were on our travels through northern Asia. We rested now from a journey in which we had travelled 12,588 versts or 2520 hours within 36 weeks and 4 days and during which we had suffered the loss of everything we possessed and had wasted the strength of our bodies. Major Riedel received the deepest thanks from the staff of our regiment for the trouble he had had and for the loyal service he had given. I also experienced the good fortune of being received with the same approbation by our present commander, Brigadier Schicharev.[98] Thus, after all the hardships I had endured, I had at least gained this—that I need not reproach myself for having eaten imperial Russian bread without due return. I never lost sight of the great duties of man: "Verrichte Deine Stands Geschaefte, und Nutze Deine Lebens Zeit". Providence always watched over me and my destiny; my heart felt this so strongly, as it also remembered the favours bestowed on me by heaven. I have become closer acquainted with the world and have taken a delight and become enriched by a thousand new subjects in observing the greatness of the works of the Lord. In a word, I now consider myself fortunate for life that in biding my time I was able to attain so much the sooner my aim of becoming a useful member of human society. I now lived contentedly with my new regimental army surgeon and through his friendship was admitted to advantages which I amply enjoyed among the Tambow nobility. Now and then I treated people in the Voronets government with various cures and I had free access to the great houses of the Sukotine, the Pushkins, the Achlebishins, the Hannibals, the Chicherins, Vorontsov, the Tambow archbishop, and of others, among whom, however, the home of my Brigadier, whom it would be impossible to esteem too highly, was ever the most valued.

Meanwhile it had pleased fate to send me once again into regions on the other side of the eastern European border, whence I had just returned a short while ago. The dragoon regiment of Nizhni Novgorod had received orders to be ready to start for Orenburg. The decampment took place on the sixteenth of August, 1777, and we marched

from the 17th of August to the 10th of September	
From Tambow to Pense [Penza]	60 hours
from the 14th of September to the 1st of October	
To Samara in the Orenburg government	also 60 hours

The staff of our regiment established here its quarters while the squadrons were moved to the Kinel and Sok rivers in the Stavropol province. Brigadier Schicharew proposed to me that in addition to my otherwise not very frequent duties at the time in the regimental hospital I take care of his children with whom I had already been acquainted for three years. Apart from the homes of the Brigadier and of my regimental field-surgeon I frequented most often and with special preference the homes of bandmaster Werner and belt-maker Heimann, both of whom I am unable to value highly enough because of their good manners and noble-minded disposition. With both of them I made many useful observations in the region of Samara. For, how could I spend the time better at one of the most excellent places on earth than by contemplating what creation has produced for the advantage and pleasure of mankind.

The city of Samara lies close by the Volga river where it receives the Samara river. The city is thus enclosed on two sides by rivers which give it a very pleasant location. From a hill near Samara I repeatedly surveyed the so-called Samara Arc which the Volga makes here over a distance of ten hours. The other side of the mighty river with the mountainous estates of the Counts of Orlov which stretch far along the banks, gives to the eye a majestic view. On the other hand, the flat regions along the Samara river possess such an abundance of hay, garden fruits, honey and all sorts of game for the sustenance and pleasure of the inhabitants that they could make the people happy enough if they only knew how to use these favours of nature.

The inhabitants of Samara support themselves altogether by catching fish, which costs them very little labour and which constitutes their entire trade. The Volga river near the city of Samara is over a quarter of an hour's distance wide and five to six fathoms deep. Nevertheless, when the river is covered with ice, they know how to build a fence diagonally across it which goes from one bank to the other and reaches the bottom of the river. In the middle of the stream the fishermen leave an opening through which the fish must necessarily pass when they go upstream, as they customarily do in the winter. Now as soon as they cross the opening they find themselves enclosed in a rectangular space likewise fenced in. On the bottom of this rectangular enclosure is spread out a stout net to which a row of threads is fastened which in turn are tied fast to a pole laid diagonally across the surface of the ice. As soon as these threads stretch apart, for which someone must constantly keep watch, it is a sure sign that a fish has gone through the opening of the fence under the ice. The net is drawn up immediately by means of a windlass and as soon as the caught fish is taken out, it is again lowered. On the place where the fish are caught a hut with a fireplace is built, where even in the most terrible cold the fishermen patiently await their catch in the greatest comfort. We often watched this way of fishing with much pleasure and on the fourth of February, 1778, we witnessed a catch of a quantity of fish[99] which was one hundred and twenty-six English inches long and 1,800 pounds in weight. From this selfsame fish the fishermen prepared a delicate fish soup for our Brigadier who happened to be present with the entire staff, and treated us to the fresh roe, which alone weighed three hundred and twenty pounds, seasoned with onions, salt and pepper— a delicacy which is considered the greatest of all in Russia. This fishery on the Volga, together with that of vastly greater importance along the shores of the Caspian Sea and in the mouth of the Ural river, mean the same for Russia what the herring fisheries constitute for Holland.[100]

After a moderate winter, which came in this area to an end at the beginning of April, I turned my attention toward the breaking up of the ice on the Volga and toward the swelling of the river which acts the master in Europe. It stood still for one hundred and ten days during this winter and the ice attained a thickness of thirty English inches. On the third of April the ice began to break up, and this lasted until the seventeenth of April. Until the twelfth of May the water of the Volga increased and rose to a height of ten Russian fathoms or eight hundred and forty English inches, whereby the flat land along the river was put under water for a distance of one mile from the banks. The water remained at its peak until the sixteenth of May and after that gradually sank down to a level of twelve fathoms on the eighth of August. While it was at its highest point an innumerable quantity of large and small vessels sailed down the Volga to Astrakhan, just as many returned again from Astrakhan when the water receded. The inundated level fields bordering the Volga and Samara thereafter became so fertile that the inhabitants were able to gain the most excellent harvest of hay at the very places where in spring we had sailed about in boats for pleasure. With unbelievable rapidity garden fruits also ripened in the formerly flooded parts, and I found the saying demonstrated that through its overflowing the Volga, like the Nile in Egypt, bestows fertility and blessing upon the land. I made no less important observations in regard to the weather, about which I shall mention here only the following: since Samara borders in the south and in the east on the immeasurably great desert which extends between the Russian empire, China, India, and Persia, and since this desert is full of salt lakes, Samara has naturally much to endure from the winds which blow so often across this frightful desert and fill the air with salt and sand which they carry from there. On the fifteenth of June, 1778, such a terrible sand storm blew from south-east that as I stood with our Brigadier on the high south bank of the Volga we could not endure to turn our faces toward the wind even for a moment unless we wished to run the risk of suffocating. Moreover, the wind was as hot as if it came from a red-hot stove. Infection of the eye, which generally prevails here, is also attributed to this wind.

Our regiment was encamped an hour's distance from the town, toward which I took a pleasant walk along the Volga twice a day, in the morning and in the evening. I corresponded often with Herrn Roder in Kazan and with Pastor Huebner of Orenburg. During that time I also enjoyed the pleasure of the society of various fine officers in the regiment and was able to derive many advantages from my relations with our Brigadier. At the beginning of the present year, 1779, my Brigadier sent me to the winter quarters of the regiment in order to visit various invalids. The squadrons were posted on the Tscherumshan [Tcheremchan] and Kinel rivers and drew a cordon of more than one hundred German miles. I began my regimental inspection on the eighth of January and first travelled to the squadrons along the Tcheremchan river. I found these quartered sufficiently scattered in well-to-do villages. The inhabitants of these are Chuvashian tribes and Mordva,[101] a type of recently converted Tartars who previously adhered to the heathen religion, but for forty years now have, to outward appearances, joined the public worship of the Russian church even though they have not yet forgotten their previous heathen customs and manners, but rather are still greatly attached to them in secret. They are nevertheless honest people thoroughly devoted to farming, cattle raising and bee keeping and are extraordinarily fond of hunting, where they especially pursue the great enemies of beehives—the bears. I myself had the pleasure of seeing a bear roused from his den and shot. Aside from a large number of foxes, wolves, martens, and ermines which are caught here, I have also come, among others, upon coal-black wolves, snow-white martens and, here and there, beavers.

From the first to the twentieth of January the weather was continuously stormy from the northeast with terrible snow storms and intense cold. The oldest men here in the country were unable to recall having experienced such a frightful winter. Where the wind could not touch and sweep away the snow I found it a full fathom high, and many engulfed and frozen people, entire companies, indeed, of peasants who had come from Orenburg with grain, were lost underneath. Sometimes the storm, and with it the snow blizzard, was so great that it was impossible to see without becoming right away a pillar of snow and freezing to death unless one knew a place to take immediate refuge. I was unable to understand how the Kalmyks who still wander frequently across these regions were able to manage to keep alive in this frightful weather, in their felt tents on the open plain, and how their poor cattle, bound to the tents, were able to endure it uncovered under the open sky, without freezing to death. Yet, he who has been born under the open sky and has been reared there from the time of his youth is obviously able to live without once in his life entering a warm room. These Kalmyks, too, are generally baptized Christians, but unfortunately they know nothing more of the religion of the Saviour than to cross themselves with the Russians when the priest babbles forth ten times in one breath the *"Hospodipomilui"* or the "Lord have mercy upon us". Likewise one cannot break the Kalmyks of their wretchedly poor ways of life. Their most delicious dish still consists of the filthy entrails of dead horses. No Christian soul is able to endure without disgust to stop for even a moment in their unclean tents, which smell of all sorts of carrion.[102] Another bread of filthy people are the *Kusulbaschen,* who were probably driven out of Persia and whom the Russians took under protection. As the Bokharans maintain, they are descended from the same lineage as the gypsies. They are greatly addicted to slothfulness and therefore live so wretchedly in these regions that they would have long since perished had not their Christian neighbours supported them out of pity.

I had scarcely travelled through all the squadrons of our regiment during this most severe cold of January when I was very unexpectedly summoned to Orenburg, where the command of the Orenburg division had just been transferred from Lieutenant General Mansurow to our Brigadier. Consequently, I got ready to start for there immediately and, because I was already used to riding with the post, I presently arrived at Orenburg, on the third day. Astonished as I was that the Brigadier demanded my presence here in such haste, I was even more pleased to receive directly upon my arrival in Orenburg the command from the Brigadier to accompany General Mansurow to Plescau [Pskov], where the empress had made him governor. The way to my future success was prepared by this opportunity. May my heart never forget the Brigadier Schicharow, and may my most genuine thanks go to this righteous man who was the principal and immediate cause of my good fortune. The Brigadier introduced me now to General Mansurow and thus I immediately received the order from His Excellency to prepare for the journey and to take along the medicines necessary for whatever emergency might arise. After that I attended also to a few other matters, but did not forget either to visit my Orenburg friends as often as the small span of time allowed and as often as was possible for me. Pastor Huebner had become particularly dear to me. I observed incomparable traits of character as well in the two physicians here, Doctors Roeslein and Sanden. On the twenty-ninth of January I was still present at the last reception of the governor, von Reinsdorf—just as a Catholic clergyman from the German colonies on the Volga, Father Johannes of Bavaria, was brought back to Orenburg. He had been captured by the Kirgizh in the year 1774 and had been sold into slavery in Buchara [Bokhara]; but through the praiseworthy arrangements of General Mansurow he was rescued from Bokhara and ransomed for four hundred roubles.[103]

On the thirtieth of January the Brigadier sent me ahead

to Samara in order to await the general there and meanwhile to receive my release from the regiment. I left Orenburg on the afternoon of the thirtieth and reached the city of Samara in the forenoon of the first of February at eight o'clock. From Orenburg to Samara, 425 versts, or 85 hours. I chose the customary road on the Samara line, along the Samara river. The stormy weather continued in the meantime. The roads became entirely unusable and every day one heard one sad case after another of people who had perished through accidents. We also experienced very unusual air phenomena [meteors] here. The snow throughout the forests was three fathoms deep and for that reason the largest trees now looked like young shrubs. On the twenty-third of January there was a severe thunderstorm in Samara, and yet the cold was so extreme that the faces of most of the dragoons standing watch were frostbitten. On the fourth of February our Brigadier came to Samara and on the tenth Lieutenant General Mansurow arrived. On the twelfth I received my dismissal from the regiment and obtained the Brigadier's permission to journey to Petersburg after I had arrived in Plescau with the general. In Petersburg I was to apply to the College of Medicine for my examination for which I was provided with the necessary certificates by the divisional doctor, Roeslein, and by my regimental surgeon Ponts, and by the regiment itself.

On the seventeenth of February I left the regiment to which I had belonged for more than five years and journeyed with the general directly to his governorship in Plescau. We passed through the towns of Stawrapol [Stavropol], 16 hours; Sarabsk [Saransk], 64; Krasnostobodskoy [Krasnoslobodsk], 20; Temnikow, 9; Casimow [Kasimov], on the Occa, 25; Pereslaw Resansky, 23 hours. The general rested here for a few days at the house of the governor von Kretschetnikow.[104] Then we continued our journey via Sareysky [Zaraisk], 13; Kaschyr [Kashira], 10; Serpuchowlo [Serpukov], Kaluga, 10 hours. Not far from Kaluga the general visited his estate and his already grown-up daughters who stayed there and in whom I observed a good education and fine virtues. The library was the choicest of all that I have ever seen in Russia. After a ten days' stay at this estate and after many kindnesses which I enjoyed here, I continued the journey to Moscow with His Excellency. From Kaluga, 24 hours. The general stopped here for only a day because a courier from the court had just come to the general with the order of the empress to hasten his trip to Pskov. Therefore I had only a moment to speak to Pastor Brunner[106] and other friends, whom I met, however, gathered in church, because it was Good Friday and communion was being given. On the thirty-first of March, on Holy Easter Sunday, we arrived in Tver where my general had to discuss affairs of government with the governor of this place, Herrn Sievers.[106] Circumstances required that we delay in Tver for two weeks, during which time I had the good fortune to become acquainted with Governor Sievers.[107] In his library I saw for the first time Lavater's *Physionomische Fragmente*.[108] On the fifteenth of April the general left Tver and, after we had passed the towns of Torschok, Wischnewolotschok [Vishni Volotchok], and Novgorod, arrived in Pskov on the twenty-third of April. Owing to an indisposition I stayed here with the general for a few more days. On the twenty-ninth of April he gave me leave, and so I left the gentleman in whose company I had passed the best days in the world and who had taken care of me like his own child. Finally, after I had travelled through the city of Narva and Jamburg I reached St. Petersburg on the third of May.

> Iamque hoc immensum spatiis confecimus aequor
> Et iam tempus aequum fumantia solvere colla.

Since the beginning of the present year I had again travelled a distance of six hundred hours and therefore experienced a weakness in my exhausted body which I again relieved by enjoying some rest and through health-giving medicine. The Medical Board admitted me to the Sea Admiralty Hospital of St. Petersburg, and here, God willing, I shall be promoted to a surgeon in the examinations of next autumn, after having already served the Russian empress for eight years and after having sweated for my salary with much painful labour. Be therefore content, dearest parents, with that which you now know of me. Would God that soon I should also have news of you, as you have read, by this time, what has befallen me since and how wonderfully a merciful Providence has preserved me. If you let anyone read my letter, let it be read by those who have always meant me well. The Secretary of the Council, Herr Fuessli, may well be the first of these upright ones.[109] You see indeed that I have allowed no more room to be able to speak further with you. I shall save this for another opportunity, and now I commend you to the protection of the Almighty—you, father, mother, brother, and sister, all my dearest relatives. I am completely convinced, though, that you all will grant my request and no longer let me wait for news from you. Farewell, ever farewell, and do not forget that I remain your most obedient and loyal son, brother and cousin.

JACOB FRIES
Assistant-surgeon in the Admiralty Hospital

August 1, 1779   at St. Petersburg.

P.S. Wherever my brother may be, I beg of you, father, to share my letter with him. Herr Rentgen in Neuwied has indeed gained much honour through his works of art both with the queen of France and with the entire world. Did not my brother perchance assist with them? I am almost certain of it. And then surely Herr Rentgen must share the honour with him. May the young Herr Werdmueller at Ochsen, who by now is probably already on the Council, be thanked a thousand times for delivering your letter to me so well in the year 1774. His father, of blessed memory, read my first letter at that time. Now you may well give this one to read also to his worthy son. I only request of all those into whose hands these pages may possibly fall that they be so kind as to pardon the mistakes and carelessness in them. I have had neither the time nor the patience to rewrite and correct my letter, since I am now concerned with weightier affairs. But when I have achieved the goal toward which I am now hastening, I shall take the greatest pleasure in imparting to you in better order additional observations that I have made abroad. In the meantime I am awaiting accounts of things that have befallen you for the past few years. Do write me as much news as you know and are able to write. Only don't write about anything concerning the poisoning of the Lord's Supper, for I don't wish to hear anything about that. Zurich is still much too devout for such a presumptuous outrage to be committed among you. Even in the remote regions of Russia people have been shocked by this and have asked me how it is possible for such a terrible sin to occur in Switzerland, which until now has always been one of the best countries, in which virtue and religion, justice and human love govern the hearts of the inhabitants.

My loved ones, I thought that I would not finish my letter soon enough. Therefore I have so greatly hurried toward the end of it and therefore, too, I have forgotten much, which I would otherwise have cited. First, I wanted to send it to you through the *Glarner* [Glarus] merchants, but these departed too early for me. Then I requested the director of the posts here for a proper transmission of the letter. Since, however, transmission to Nuremberg was promised me, even without having to pay any postage, I would have risked entrusting my packet to the mail had I not suspected that the Zurich post-officer might perhaps demand from you the entire postage amount for it. Therefore, I have preferred to follow the good counsel of Herrn Fuessli, to hand him the letter to have it enclosed with his, and thereby freed myself of all fears that the letter might perhaps be lost. Soon I shall again inform you about how I have fared with my future examination and what kind Providence has further decided for me. Now I employ my time entirely and solely with studying and when at any time I have an hour left over for pleasure I find amusement enough in our botanical garden, in the Academy of Arts, or at the Imperial Art Cabinet. Also, the house of the Euler family is always open to me, and likewise that of Doctor Goeldenstaedt, the collections of a Professor Palles, or Lepechin, and the friendly home of our good Herrn Fuessli, from which I am separated only by the gently flowing Neva. I can say that the enjoyment of the friendship that Herr Fuessli has shown me since my arrival in Petersburg contributes much to the peace of my soul and also much to my future happiness. The Imperial Summer Garden is also the nearest place in magnificent Petersburg that I sometimes visit on Sundays, and there I enjoy the pleasure of seeing the great monarch of the Russian empire, which has become so well known to me, now going for a walk. Even the hospital in which I live furnishes me with pleasure and pastime enough when I do not wish to go out after I have visited my patients, dressed their wounds, and completed my other duties. I go into the anatomical museum and look at the masterpieces of the Creator in all parts of the human body. Then I fancy in my thoughts that I see before me the preparations of our Zurich Winslow, Surgeon Burkhardt.[110] Out of a window of my room on the Neva side I see everything beautiful that nature and art combined exhibit in one of the finest cities in the world. From another window I have the Petersburg common before me, where I see the shells of the gunners fly just as high as if they had been thrown by my father or Herr Bakofen in the Kuttelgass. Is that not so, my dear father, I still remember everything? Yes, to be sure, and it has now become customary with me, whenever I see something unfamiliar in the world, to call to mind similar things in my fatherland. And I am so obstinate in this that I always prefer the things of Zurich to what is foreign. Thus, a walk in the Imperial Summer Garden does not please me nearly as much as a paradisical promenades along the murmring Limmat under the shady linden trees, and the magnificent Peterhof of the empress I consider not as beautiful as the country estate of Councillor Hirzel near the Harfe on the Viking Mountain. No water, regardless of how many places in Europe and Asia I have tried it, tastes as sweet as the water of my fatherland. Nowhere, it seems to me, is the air so pure, and nowhere does the wind blow so gently as around our beloved Zurich.

But if I continue in this way, I shall soon become homesick. I shall not object to staying willingly wherever Heaven commands. The works of the Lord are great everywhere, and one can find a roof and nourishment everywhere, and live everywhere as pleasantly as the conditions of the time and the circumstances of each person demand. How ungrateful I would be, would I want to be better off than I am at present, and what great cause do I not have to thank Providence for so much grace as it has always shown to me. Thus, at present I lack nothing except solely and simply the knowledge of what you, my dearest parents, sister and brother, and relations are doing. So long as I have no news of you, I cannot be completely peaceful and content. Accordingly I am expecting much from you, really much. God grant that everything corresponds to my [expectations]. In this expectation I commend you once again to the assistance of Heaven and recommend myself to your paternal love and protection and remain your most obedient

JACOB FRIES

Petersburg, August 16, 1779.

Notes to Part II

1. Field surgeons and field pharmacists were introduced in the Russian army as early as 1615. Richter, II, 155.
2. Soltikov (Saltykov), 1730-1805, became governor of Vladimir and Kostroma, then of Kiev, and of Moscow. Later, he became field marshall, inspector of the cavalry and commander of the Ukrainian army. In 1795 he fell out with Rumiantsev and for a time was in retirement.
3. In 1773, General Suvorov had twice attacked Tutukey (Turtukey or Turtukaia) in order to cut the Turkish lines of communication along the Danube. Cf. N. M. Korobkov, *Generalissimus Suvorov*. *Sbornik*, 1947, Nos. 33-40. Fries describes here the three-day battle between the Russians under Saltykov and the Turks, who once more had occupied Tutukey. Saltykov sought to cross the Danube and to force the Turks to retreat in the direction of Rushchuk.
4. Rumiantsev had distinguished himself in the Seven Years War. He became field marshall and, as successor of Prince Golitsyn, commander-in-chief in the Turkish campaign. He excelled as tactician rather than as strategist.
5. The following three and a half pages of the letter are devoted to news related in the father's letter, to a discussion of family affairs, and to inquiries about brother and sister and other relatives and friends. They contain nothing of historical interest. At the end of page 6, Fries resumes the story of his travels.
6. Fries's description of the wealth of Wallachia perhaps helped to pave the way for other descriptions of these Rumanian areas—descriptions that were composed around 1820 in order to induce Swiss people to emigrate there and to Russian Bessarabia. Cultivators of vineyards were foremost among those attracted. But it turned out that the hopes of the emigrants were only partially fulfilled. Cf Jakob Etterlin, *Russland Schweizer* . . . , Leipzig-Zürich, 1938. Also Walther Kirchner, "Emigration to Russia", *American Historical Review*, XV (1950), 561. Many Swiss emigrated via Southern Germany, where they were joined by Germans. But numbers of them later returned, deeply disappointed, and mocking verses greeted them, such as:
   Sie zogen nach Russland mit Blumen und Sträuss
   Und kamen von daher mit Lumpen und Läus.
Historical literature on their fate is abundant; according to private information I received, additional interesting material

7. Rushchuk constituted the key to the Turkish defence in the Danube area. It bravely held out until peace was concluded at Kuchuk-Kainardji on July 10, 1774.
8. Prince Alexis Meshchersky had served under Suvorov during the campaign and had participated in the battles for Tutukey.
9. Since the peace was concluded on July 10 (21), Fries obviously refers to the date when the news reached his army contingents.
10. Wallachia and Moldavia, parts of Rumania, were at the time under Turkish sovereignty. Known to be fertile, they attracted many immigrants, including members of various Protestant sects. Shortly after the conclusion of the peace, many Swiss emigrated there and settled as agriculturists. Others founded a clock industry.
11. Stanislas II Augustus ruled from 1764 to 1795.
12. Petr Abramovich Tekeli (1720-1793) came from a Serbian family and had entered Russian service in 1747.
13. See Richter, *passim*.
14. Field Marshall Rumiantsev had been in command of the expedition. The Cossacks were utterly taken by surprise. Their leaders were seized and banished to monasteries; their land was distributed among the Russian gentry; part of the people were drafted for military service under Potemkin, others fled across the Danube and settled in Turkey. Cf. Boris Nolde, *La formation de l'Empire russe*, 2 vols., Paris, 1952-53, II, 108 ff.
15. See below, p. 166, note 105.
16. The iron industry of Tula was started early in the seventeenth century during the reign of Shuisky. At Tula, the Dutchman Vinius founded, with the help of foreign master craftsmen, the first gun factory in 1632. The raw material came from nearby iron works. In 1712, Peter the Great founded the great state armament factory.
17. Fries apparently refers here to Adolph (Fedor Petrovich) Burmann, who had distinguished himself during the Turkish war.
18. Two brothers, Peter and Egor Fedorovich Baron Asch, both doctors, were Germans who had entered the Russian service. Under Catherine II both became members of the Imperial Medical College. The Baron von Asch here mentioned was Egor Fedorovich (Georg Thomas). See also Kirchner, "Zur Geschichte der Pest".
19. Krementchug, founded in 1571, saw, from 1765 to 1789, a short period of flourishing as capital of New Russia. Situated where the Dnieper becomes navigable, it developed into an important trade centre, of importance mainly to the White Russian and Polish hinterland.
20. Ivan Alekseevich Potapov, whose military career had begun in 1737.

NOTES TO PART II

21. The government took a special interest in the growth of Voronets and in making it a centre of shipbuilding.
22. The Arsamasian province, half way between Moscow and Kazan and south of Nizhni Novgorod, belonged to the most prosperous regions of Russia. As well as for its potatoes, hemp, and rye, it is even today famous for its geese (in the areas along the Oka), in addition to its forged tools.
23. Petr Borisovich Sheremetev (1713-1788) came from an old boiar family. He was the son of Peter the Great's famous field marshall and was known for the luxury he displayed and for his extravagance.
24. Mikhail Fedotovich Kamensky (1738-1809) had participated in the war against the Turks under Rumiantsev and Saltykov. Later he became governor general of Riazan and Tambov and participated in further wars. Having retired from the service for some time, he became, under Paul I, field marshall and fought also against the French.
25. Fries has made an error with regard to the last two dates.
26. Alexis Alekseevich Stupishin (died 1786) was also governor of Kostroma and Viatka.
27. Not until July 1774, when the rebellion neared its end was Kazan taken by Pugashev and burned down, except for the fortress. Pugachev could not hold it long; in August he was decisively beaten by the army under General Michelson.
28. (1713-1799). Meshchersky was governor of Little Russia until 1775. Later he became governor of Kazan, Simbirsk, Viatka, etc. and finally governor general of Kazan.
29. Roder had formerly been an officer and engineer in Prussian and in Portuguese service. He taught mathematics in Kazan. v. Schulthess, p. 40.
30. Cf. Pushkin's story, *The Captain's Daughter*.
31. Ivan Ivanovich Michelson (1740-1807). He came from an English family, which, by way of Denmark, had emigrated to Sweden and later, like many Swedish noble families, had settled in Estonia. He was only a premier-major, but it was owing to his ability that Pugachev's rebellion was checked after Pugachev had taken Kazan. The rebels were decisively defeated. Michelson later became a general of the cavalry.
32. Fries's information does not agree with that which we derive from other reports. In 1773, the Lutheran community had been allowed to erect a house of worship, but it burned down in 1774. Its pastor, A. Chr. Wittneben, was taken prisoner by Pugachev, but seems to have later escaped. *Zentral Kommite der Unterstützungskasse für evangelisch-lutherische Gemeinden in Russland*, St. Petersburg, 1909, part 2, p. 26.
33. The Kazan Cathedral was built by Ivan the Terrible after the capture of the city in 1552.
34. Alexander Ilich Bibikov (1729-1774). He had participated in the Seven Years War and, in 1771, in the campaign in Poland. Owing to poor health and exhaustion, he died not long after beginning the campaign against Pugachev, which he conducted

with energy and circumspection. He had recognized that the rising was not merely the rebellion of an ambitious Cossack but that it was a great movement which was based on deep general dissatisfaction. A brief factual non-Soviet account of the rising in: A. Gaissinovitch, *La révolte de Pougatchev*, Paris, 1938.

35. Pallas (I, 235) refers to Reinsdorp. Ivan Andreevich Reinsdorp had entered Russian service in 1746 and had directed the defence of Orenburg during the rising. He died in 1782.
36. Pavel Dmitrevich Mansurov belonged to a noble family which derived its line from Tartars who had immigrated in the fourteenth century. He became Lieutenant General and later Senator.
37. Orenburg fortress had originally been built at another place, and only in 1734 was it rebuilt at the spot which Fries describes. See above, p. 58, note 89.
38. The belt or line of fortresses from Orenburg to the Upper Irtysh had been established in 1752. Originally it consisted of two fortresses and thirty-three redoubts. Two thousand Cossacks were settled in the region. Later the number of fortresses was increased. Pallas refers to the line in vol. II, p. 405.
39. As a matter of fact, the Kirghiz belonged to the most dreaded native populations. They were the ones who in Fries's time contributed most to the disaster that overtook the Kalmyks (see below, p. 166, note 102). Originally heathen, they were during Catherine's reign converted by Orthodox Russians to Mohammedanism owing to an error, since the government built Mohammedan temples for them on the assumption that they already had adopted the Mohammedan faith. Cf. Andre Lobanov-Rostovsky, *Russia and Asia,* New York, 1933, 90 f.
40. The "irregular" forces were composed of Bashkirs, Kalmyks, and other Tartar peoples who, like the regular Cossacks, attended as mounted troops to war and guard duties. They received a solde. Otherwise, they were allowed to govern themselves, elect a hetman, and enjoy the protection of a special constitution of their own.
41. In 1772, a wooden house was erected in Orenburg which could serve as church and as living quarters for the pastor. Only 3 months after Fries's visit in Orenburg was a regular church, St. Catherine's Church, inaugurated there, namely on July 24, 1776. *Zentral Kom.*, part 2, 33. Pastor Huebner had come to Russia in 1767. He had had some adverse experiences at the famous Franke Orphanage in Halle, and his countryman Jacob von Stählin had helped him with his emigration. Unable to find a good position in Petersburg, he went to Orenburg, and he later married there. Karl Stählin, *Aus den Papieren Jacob von Stählins,* Leipzig 1927, 371-373.
42. One can follow the first part of the trip on the map of Pallas (III, 574) as well on that of Erdmann (II, v). The various distances between Wosnesenskaja and Tanalyk do not seem

NOTES TO PART II

to be quite correct, but the total distance is.

43. Called Verchiaizkaia in Gmelin's time (Gmelin, IV, 337 ff.).
44. The route which Fries took was not commonly used. Speransky, in his later recommendation to Hansteen, described it as the most interesting one leading into Siberia. Hansteen, p. 17. For a description of the region between Orenburg and Upper Uralsk, cf. Falck, I, 187-192.
45. Formally the Kirghiz were subjects of the Russian empress, but they also had taken an oath of allegiance to the Chinese emperor. They belonged to the most 'disturbing neighbours of Russia, and only ten years after Fries's journey was a policy of quieting them initiated, and schools were founded in their land.
46. Alexander Danilovich Menshikov, the famous general and minister of Peter the Great and the lover of Catherine I, had been banished to Siberia, together with wife and daughter, after Catherine's death in 1727. He died there in 1729. Cf. Walther Kirchner, "The Death of Catherine I of Russia", *American Historical Review*, LI (1946).
47. Petropavlovsk had been founded in 1752. It assumed importance not only as a fortress but also as a trading centre. Cf. R. M. Kabo, *Goroda zapadnoi Sibiri*, Moskva, 1949, 175.
48. General Skalon came from a Huguenot family which after the revocation of the Edict of Nantes had come to Russia via Sweden. In contrast to his predecessor's lack of amiability, about which Pallas (II, 448) complained, Skalon was most amiable.
49. Regarding Dr. Berens, see p. 139 (Pallas, who stayed a few days in Omsk, does not mention him). As to Pastor Luther, this was, no doubt, the German Lutheran Pastor G. Luther, who had been installed in his office at Tobolsk in 1768 and who also took care of the Omsk community. It is not known when the Omsk parish was founded, but we know that in the 1760s a pastor was tending to the community there. A Lutheran church was not built until 1792. Also later, Omsk and Tomsk formed repeatedly one single diocese. *Zentral Kom.*, part 2, pp. 89, 92.
50. Pallas mentions General Springer with praise, II, 448, 450, but the general had already died.
51. When Pallas came to Omsk, just a few years before Fries, he found the old and the new parts of the city just in the process of reconstruction after a number of great fires that had occurred. Pallas, I, 450 ff. Consequently, Omsk was not a large city, nor did it grow rapidly, for even fifty years later the population amounted to no more than 7500. Schools, however, seem to have been both numerous and good. Cochrane, p. 135. For further statistics, cf. Erdmann, II, 103.
52. A rather extensive literature exists dealing with German immigration, especially into Southern Russia. E.g., cf. F. P. Schiller, *Literatur zur Geschichte und Volkskunde der deutschen Kolonien in der Sowjet Union ..., 1764-1926*, Pokrovsk, 1927.

But a comprehensive description of immigration into Siberia is still missing. It is difficult to give such a description because most of the Germans as well as the citizens of other nations came to Siberia individually, following a personal spirit of enterprise or being sent there in the service of the government; they did not come in large, organized groups, as to Southern Russia. Cf. also Gregory Pisarevsky, *Iz istorii inostrannoi kolonizatsii v Rossii v XVIII v. Zapiski Moskovskago Archeologicheskago Instituta*, V (1909).

53. This route—which Fries did not take—had been used by another German-Russian military doctor, the surgeon Thiele, who in 1763 had travelled by it to Ust-Kamenogorsk. Laxmann, p. 67.

54. Cahen (p. 396) figures the distance Kainsk-Tomsk at 524 versts; Gmelin (IV, 88) and Pallas (III, 461 ff.) likewise figure the distance at less than the 542½ versts given by Fries. To be sure, the route of Pallas differed from that of Fries.

55. The Baraba or Barabinsk steppe (desert, plain) extends from the Irtysh to the Ob. Its southern parts yielded no crops; the centre part through which Fries travelled is cultivable, fruitful, and rich in birch trees; the north is largely covered by swamps. Cf. Fischer, p. 280; Falck, I, 284. Human habitations were scarce; even on the main road, in many parts, no houses were met with for a hundred or one hundred and fifty versts. Cf. Wagner, p. 149.

56. After abolishing the old *mestnichestvo* and introducing, for his officials, new tables of rank, which corresponded to the ranks in the military service, Peter the Great had sought to raise also the status of the merchant. Catherine II tried the same, at least during the early part of her reign. The efforts came more or less to naught—perhaps less for reasons of pride of status than for practical reasons. For in Russia, the nobility was much interested in trade, carried it on at their own expense and risk, and naturally tried to prevent the emergence of competition. For similar reasons, even the peasants opposed the granting of privileges to merchants. But in Siberia, the nobility was largely restricted to the performance of administrative duties; *pomestie* estates and serfdom hardly existed, and peasants lacked markets for their produce. As a result, the merchant class could develop more freely.

57. Despite its excellent location and role as a trading centre, Tomsk is described also by Pallas as filthy and unattractive. Pallas, II, 657 ff. Gmelin speaks of the laziness of the inhabitants. Gmelin, I, 308 ff; IV, 1 ff. As a result, and because of frequent fires, Tomsk—founded in 1604—failed to grow as it otherwise might have. Fries's figure of 2000 houses before the fire in 1773 compares with Sauer's figure of 1500 houses in 1786, Davydov's 5000 inhabitants in 1802, and Cochrane's 9000 inhabitants another twenty years later. The whole province was supposed to have, at that time, 500,000 inhabitants. Unlike Fries, Sauer describes the people of Tomsk as more hospitable,

healthy, clean, and industrious than elsewhere in Russia.

58. Punishment by exile to Siberia goes back to the time of Boris Godunov (1598-1605). The code of 1648 legalized an'd codified this type of punishment. In the course of the eighteenth century, economic considerations concerning the colonization of Siberia contributed primarily to the increase of penalty by exile. This led to a situation where many other types of punishment were converted into punishment by exile.

59. Natalie Lopuchin, whose beauty provoked the jealousy of Empress Elizabeth, offended the empress still more by copying her dresses. As a result, her husband, General Lopuchin, was accused in 1743 of having conspired with the Austrians and thus having shown disloyalty to the empress. Both husband an'd wife were tortured, publicly knouted, and banished to Siberia. In 1762, as soon as Elizabeth had died, her successor Peter III pardoned Mme. Lopuchin. Possibly, internal political considerations had played a role, since Stephen Lopuchin was a relative of the first wife of Peter the Great. But whatever the story, Fries seems to have been deceived, for after being pardoned, Mme. Lopuchin had returned to Russia, where she died in 1763.

60. Since time immemorial, it was known that silver could be foun'd in the surroundings of Nerchinsk. But the Russian government did not establish mines there until 1700. After 1772, peasants who were settled in the region and criminals who were sent from Europe had to serve as mine workers. Cf. George Kennan, *Siberia and the Exile System*, 2 vols., New York, 1891, II, 279 f.

61. Pallas, who had visited Krasnoiarsk a few years before Fries, gives the following prices: Rye flour: 5 to 6 kopecks a *pud* (ca. 40 lbs.); beef: 15-25 kopecks; cows: 1 rouble a piece; horses: 2 to 3 roubles; sheep: 30 to 50 kopecks; and pigs: "a little more". Pallas, III, 5. As to general conditions, Pallas states that Krasnoiarsk has made but little progress since the time of Gmelin, owing to the lack of industriousness and to the love of luxury of the inhabitants. Even fifty years later, by the time Cochrane visited Krasnoiarsk, the town had no more than 3,000 inhabitants despite its favourable location. Seventy of these were wealthy Jews. Cochrane, p. 174.

62. Kansk was foun'ded in 1640. Fischer, p. 512. The Kan river was called, according to Cochrane, the "Styx" of the convicts who, once beyond it, seldom returned. Cochrane, p. 175.

63. Fedor Glebovich Nemtsev was governor of Irkutsk from 1775 to 1778.

64. An ukaze of 1767 established the first Lutheran diocese in Irkutsk. I. K. W. Gabriel, the first pastor, started on his duties in 1768. He had to minister to the whole area, including Eniseisk and Transbaikalia. *Zentral Kom.*, part 2, p. 97.

65. In his *Geschichte der reformirten Kirche in Russland*, Gotha, 1865, p. 67, Hermann Dalton likewise notes that there was little vigour in the life of the Church in Russia during the

last decades of the eighteenth century. The Enlightenment had shaken many foundations of the Church and real piety was seldom found.
66. Michael Mitkevich was at the time archbishop of Irkutsk. He had been inaugurated on March 17, 1773. The episcopate there had been founded in 1724. *Irkutskaia Letopis. Trudi Vostochno-Sibirskago otd. Imp. Russ. Geogr. Obshchestvo,* No. 5, Irkutsk, 1911.
67. Russian Church services in Peking were an object of constant discussion, strife, and negotiation. Even before 1695, Orthodox Church services were held in Peking in a former pagoda, which the Chinese emperor had put at the disposal of the Russians. Cahen, *Histoire des relations* . . . ,pp. 245 ff. The treaty of Kiakhta of 1727, at a time when the Chinese just took measures against the Catholic Church, stipulated Russian privileges anew. Paul E. Eckel, *The Far East since 1500,* New York, 1947, 76 ff. Foust, pp. 50-51. In 1730, an earthquake destroyed the first Russian church building, but a new one was erected in 1732.
68. Early in the eighteenth century Irkutsk had, according to Bell, about 2000 houses, but Gmelin, more than a decade later, gives a figure of only 939. Gmelin, II, 159. Sauer states that in 1786 there were 2,500 houses, 12 stone churches, a cathedral, two monasteries, and about 20,000 inhabitants. Davydov gives the population in 1802 at 25,000. When Cochrane travelled in the Irkutsk region the whole government general had, according to him, 650,000 inhabitants. This figure included, however, the governments of Iakutsk, Okhotsk, and Kamchatka. The development of Irkutsk was rapid and impressive. Cf. Cochrane, p. 512.
69. At the same spot, Erman is also reminded of a Swiss scene, although he speaks of the bay of Alpnach on Lake Lucerne rather than of the Albis. The view itself is world famous; Bell says: "One cannot imagine a more beautiful prospect of nature, than is seen from the top of these mountains". Bell, I, 260. Cf. Georgi, I, *passim.*
70. Pallas writes that at the time of his visit in 1772, only one vessel fit to sail Lake Baikal existed, the galleon *Boris und Gleb.*
71. The overbearance of the Chinese court under the Manchu dynasty was well known, but it had lessened after the death of the K'ang hsi Emperor (d. 1722), who had still demanded the kow tow from all ambassadors. His grandson, the Yung cheng Emperor, had deigned to send a first embassy to Russia as a sign of politeness. Cf. Nikolas Nikolaevich Bantysh-Kamensky, *Diplomaticheskoe sobranie del mezhdu Rossiiskim i Kitaiskim gosudarstvami, s 1619 po 1792 god.,* Kazan, 1882, 165. Thereafter, more normal relations developed. At the time of Fries, the same Yung cheng Emperor still ruled.
72. In Russian: *kirpichnyi chai,* or brick tea. It is made by pressing into brick-like shape what is left over from good quality teas.

73. In Pallas's time (III, 105), Selenginsk had about 200 houses, 1000 inhabitants and as many soldiers. It had just suffered greatly from two fires. Cochrane writes later that it was "a miserable, decayed place".
74. Commander Nalabradie was, no doubt, Second Major Kalina Nalabardin, who had been sent to the Chinese border in order to settle disputes over the border with the Chinese and who later became governor of Irkutsk. *Sbornik Imp. Russk. Ist. Obshch.*, LXII, 53.
75. The period when Fries happened to be in Kiakhta was not favourable for the growth and development of the town. During the thirty-five years before the reign of Catherine II, only six Russian caravans had reached Peking, and during the following thirty years trade with China was interrupted for almost half the time, owing to Chinese trade prohibitions. Yet, when Catherine had come to the throne, in 1762, she had issued a manifesto and, in order to strengthen trade relations with China, had abolished the existing government trade monopoly for the direct trade with Peking. Regarding the period 1762 to 1768, cf. Bantysh-Kamensky, *loc. cit.*, and Foust, 262-278, *passim*. The new negotiations which the Russian envoy Kropotov led in 1768 brought no more than temporary improvements. Interestingly, it was then that for the first time reciprocal extra territorial rights were stipulated in a treaty with China. Cf. Hosea B. Morse, *The Trade and Administration of the Chinese Empire*, New York, 1908, 181. Also: Michel N. Pavlovsky, *Chinese-Russian Relations*, New York, 1949, 23. Despite the treaty, relations thereafter remained unsatisfactory. The Russians exchanged mainly furs, imported textiles, and industrial products against cotton goods, tea, rhubarb and porcelain from China, but the strict supervision and regulation of all trade by the Chinese government constituted a persistent hindrance to its growth. The Chinese went so far as to demand that their merchants learn the Russian language, whereas for the sake of preserving trade secrets, the Russians were prohibited from being taught Chinese.
76. Maimachen (Mai-mai-ch'eng) often served as place of exile for high Chinese administrative officers, who had fallen in disgrace.
77. Fries refers here to the description which Pallas (III, 118 ff.) gave of Maimachen.
78. Named after a mountain in China from where this type of tea comes. Larousse, *Grand Dictionnaire universel du XIXe siècle*, II, 1042.
79. Maimachen was famous among travellers. Pallas, to whom Fries referred above, has given an extensive account of the temple, of the Chinese inhabitants, and of their trade. Pallas, III, pt. 1, 115 ff. An etching of the town may be found in Coxe, whose description is based on that of Pallas but who adds notes on the commerce between China and Russia. Coxe,

pp. 221 ff., 231. ff. Cochrane is reminded of a Moorish town in southern Spain. He comments on its cleanliness but with his urge to make disparaging remarks he goes on to say: "Of all the celebrated places I have seen and which have nothing to support their celebrity, Maimatchin is the most eminent." Cochrane, p. 501. His snobbish statement is belied by Fries's interesting description as well as by those of Pallas, Coxe, and others, among whom Erman, who just a few years after Cochrane's travels participated at a festival in Maimachen and gave a long description of the town.

80. Brand (or Brandt) had previously lived in Kolyvan where he was acquainted with Laxmann. p. 90.

81. Rhubarb was one of the most valuable and coveted products, and the Russians tried for a long time to break the Chinese monopoly on it. Cf. Coxe, pp 332-344. About the rhubarb trade which—sometimes in private hands, sometimes in those of the government—was very lucrative, cf. Richter, II, 136 ff; III, 232 note. Foust, pp. 164-185.

82. Women were not permitted into Maimachen. Also in Kiakhta, residence was from time to time prohibited for women. Eckel, p. 78.

83. Cf. Pallas, III, pt. 1, 131.

84. Fries has made here a mistake when converting the distance from hours into versts.

85. Eventually, the Russian attempts at converting the Buriat Mongols failed after all. Most of them became or remained Buddhist, under a Lama, and continued to live as nomads. The Russian government occasionally drafted them for service in war, somewhat in the way it was handled with the Cossacks. Regarding the efforts at baptizing the Buriats, cf. Procofii Gromov, *Nachalo christianstva v Irkutske*, Irkutsk, 1868, 231 ff.

86. Hardly a single summer traveller in Siberia has failed to mention the terrible gnats and horse-flies, although the majority seem to have suffered more in regions farther west and particularly in the Baraba steppe. Gmelin speaks of an "unendurable torment" which deprived him of all sleep. Gmelin, IV, 74 ff. He also mentions the region Fries refers to, not far from Kansk, and describes the kind of sieves which the inhabitants wear over their faces. III, 389. Bell, Chappe d'Auteroche, Davydov, Holman, Erman are among others who comment on the plague. Kotzebue states, p. 124, that even in the city of Tobolsk he was pestered by the gnats.

87. Demidov founded here the first metal works in 1739. It was in Barnaul that Polzunov (died 1766), probably without being acquainted with the preliminary work done in Western Europe, introduced the first steam engine. From 1766 on, it was used to pump water out of the mines. James Watt's English patent dates from 1769. About Polzunov, Cf. V. V. Danilevsky, *I. I. Polzunov, Trudi i zhizhn,* Moscow, 1940, with many

illustrations. Also I. Ia. Konfederatov, *Ivan Ivanovich Polzunov*, Moscow, 1951.
88. Major General Andrei Avraamovich Ritter von Ihrmann had entered the Russian service in 1742.
89. Speaking of the European side of the Urals, Cochrane states that "he was charmed with the beauty of the surrounding scenery. And if I might judge of the number of its inhabitants by the quantity of cultivated land, I should say it was one of the most populous, as well as finest spots I had ever seen." p. 101.
90. Ivan Borisovich Tverdishev, a Moscow merchant (died 1773), founded iron furnaces in the middle of the eighteenth century. Cf. Roger Portal, *L'Oural au XVIIIe siècle*, Paris, 1950, pp. 146, 148 f., 161 f.
91. Alexander Grigorevich Demidov. The family fortune goes back to Nikita Demidov and Akinfei Nikitich Demidov, founders of many iron works in the early part of the eighteenth century. Though the iron industry in the Urals was started around 1623, the Demidovs were the ones who were responsible for its vast growth, which is illustrated by the following figures: Works founded between 1699 and 1719: 11; between 1719 and 1739: 35 between 1739 and 1782: 119. Most of them were located on the Asiatic side. Erdmann, II, 67. At about the time of Fries's visit, there existed 70 forges and 532 large hammers, all of which were working. Tooke, III, 300. The holdings of the Demidov family gradually diminished. In the early nineteenth century they possessed, according to Erdmann, only 13 iron works out of a total of 90, 24 of which belonged to the crown. Erdmann, II, 248 ff.
92. The deplorable state of the roads in the southern parts of the Urals is also attested by others. Gmelin, who like Fries travelled in the neighbourhood of Upper Uralsk, speaks of the great hardships he had to endure, increased, in his time, by dangers from unfriendly bands of roaming natives. Gmelin, IV, 265. Neither does Chappe d'Auteroche, who came to the same region, fail to mention the bad roads. Chappe, IV, 265.
93. Portal (p. 172) enumerates the following mines destroyed by Pugachev: Absem (No. 6), Beloretskaia (No. 9), and Bogoiavlenskii (No. 14). On pp. 341 ff., he discusses the effect the Pugachev rising had upon the development of the mining industry.
94. The Baskian Tartars or Bashkirs are of Bulgarian, Finnish, and Turkish origin but strongly mixed with the blood of surrounding peoples. They were Mohammedans. See Nolde, I, 234 f.
95. Erdmann tells about the making of brandy out of horse's milk. I, 23.
96. The Chuvashian tribes were closely related to the Bashkirs. Besides Georgi, cf. also Werner Leimbach, *Die Sowjetunion*, Stuttgart, 1950, p. 191.
97. Probably the staff surgeon mentioned by A. W. Fechner,

Chronik der Evangelischen Gemeinden in Moskau, 1876, II, 16.

98. Fries refers here to Brigadier General Stepan Zhikharev. I wish to thank Prof. Erik Amburger, Giessen, for his help in identifying Schicharew as well as Peutling and for his information on Riedel. For further information, he calls attention to *Spisok voinskomu departamentu* . . . for the year 1776, available in the Library of the University of Göttingen.

99. Note in the original manuscript: "In the last line but one it was difficult to understand whether the name of the fish was 'Hausen' or whether it meant 'Haufen' ['a quantity'] of fish."

100. In view of the importance of the Russian fisheries, many travellers have reported about the various practices of Russian fishermen who, particularly on frozen rivers, seem to have made a great impression upon Western visitors. Thus, Bell speaks of the methods of catching fish in the Tom river, I, 213 f.; Gmelin refers to several different regions (for instance, I, 317 ff., II, 199); Wagner mentions fisheries on pp. 114 f.; Chappe d'Auteroche on I, 445 and *passim;* Lepekhin, who like Fries refers to the Volga, I, 152; Cochrane, p. 215; Erman, p. 79. The latter points out the decline of the fisheries on the Irtysh and Ob rivers; soon, he says, the abundance of fish will be known by hearsay only.

101. The Mordva (or Mordvines) are related to the Chuvashians and Bashkirs, but in Fries's time they lived on a somewhat higher cultural level than these.

102. The Kalmyks were divided into various tribes. Those settled in Russia proper had adopted Christianity in the middle of the eighteenth century, but some of them apostasized and returned to Lama-Buddhism. Philaret, *Geschichte der Kirche Russlands*, 2 vols., Frankfurt a.M., 1872, II, 185-188. In 1771, those Kalmyks who lived on the lower Volga suddenly left their lands in order to return to China whence they had come. But thousands of them perished during the winter on the march through the Kirghiz steppe. Lobanov, p. 90; Erdmann, I, 24.

103. Gottlieb Bauer has described the incursions of the Kirghiz into the German colonies, *Geschichte der deutschen Ansiedler an der Wolga*, Saratow, 1908. He mentions Pater Johannes. According to him, Pater Johannes was not captured until 1776 and was ransomed two and a half years later by sheep traders from Orenburg. They brought him back to the German colony at Mariental. From there he is supposed to have returned to his "Heimat Polen". Fries's report will help to rectify the errors in Bauer's account.

104. Presumably Michael Nikitov Krechetnikov (1729-1793), governor general of Tula.

105. Salomo Brunner (1732-1806) was pastor of the Reformed Church in Moscow. He came from Zürich, had arrived in Moscow in 1768 and for thirty-eight years attended faithfully to his ministry. His Reformed Protestant community existed in Moscow since 1669. Its members were largely Dutch and English. The first Swiss pastor of the community was appointed

in 1767. There was also a Reformed Church community in Petersburg, which existed there since 1723. As to Lutheran churches, there existed two in Moscow, St. Michael and St. Petri-Pauli. The Lutheran community was older and went back to the sixteenth century. The two Lutheran church buildings as well as that of the Reformed Church fell prey to the great fire of 1748. They were rebuilt, but a new Lutheran (Evangelical) pastor was not appointed until 1754. *Zentral Kom.*, part 2, p. 3.

106. Graf Jakob Johann Sievers (1731–1808) was one of the most capable governors and a special friend of Catherine II. He became known through the reforms he carried out in the provinces of Novgorod and Tver, through his proposals for a reform of the office of governor, and through his interest in building a net of canals. Later he was named ambassador in Poland and he became a senator.

107. Probably Fries was particularly interested in the Tver region also because there, Swiss cheese makers had started in 1771, not long before Fries's visit, a first, very successful production of Emmental-style cheese. This manufacture was established on an estate belonging to the above mentioned family Meshchersky. Joseph A. Malinowsky, *Die Planerkolonien am Asowschen Meer*, Stuttgart, 1928, p. 230. Sievers himself showed particular interest in the work of the Swiss, and Catherine was thinking of conferring upon him the task of bringing the population of a whole canton of Switzerland to Russia. M. Lavater Slomann, *Catharina II*, Zürich, 1941.

108. The work of Fries's famous countryman had just been published in 1775 to 1778.

109. Fries refers to Johann Kaspar Fuessli, who was Secretary of the City Council, but also a painter and writer, and who died in 1781.

110. Hans Heinrich Burkhard, director of the anatomical institute in Zürich.

Bibliography

Adelung, Friedrich von, *Kritisch-literarische Uebersicht der Reisenden in Russland bis 1700* . . ., 2 vols., St. Petersburg, 1846.
Adelung, Johann Christoph, *Geschichte der Schiffahrten und Versuche . . . zur Entdeckung des nordöstlichen Weges* . . .,Halle, 1768.
Alekseev, Mikhail P., *Sibir v izvestiiakh zapadno-evropeiskikh puteshestvennikov i pisatelei*, Irkutsk, 1941.
Der allerneueste Staat . . . nebst einer historischen Nachricht von . . . gefangenen Schweden, Nürnberg, 1720.
Andreev, Aleksandr I., *Ocherki po istochnikovedeniiu Sibiri . . . XVIII vek (pervaia polovina)*, "Nauka", Moscow-Leningrad, 1965.
The Antidote or an Enquiry into . . . A Journey into Siberia . . . by the Abbé Chappe d'Auteroche, a Lover of Truth, London, 1772.
Anzeiger der Post Stationen durch Russland und Sibirien, St. Petersburg, 1761.
Archiv gemeinnütziger physischer und medizinischer Kenntnisse, ed. by Johann Heinrich Rahn, II, pt. I (1789).
Bagrow, Leo, "Ivan Kirilov, Compiler of the First Russian Atlas, 1689–1737", *Imago Mundi*, II (1937).
Bakhrushin, Sergei V., *Ocherki po istorii kolonizatsii Sibiri v 16 i 17 vv.*, Moscow, 1928.
Bantysh-Kamenskii, Nikolai Nikolaevich, *Diplomaticheskoe sobranie del mezhdu Rossiiskim i Kitaiskim gosudarstvami s 1619 to 1792 god*, Kazan, 1882.
Beckmann, Johann B., *Münz-, Geld- und Bergwerks-Geschichte des russischen Kaiserthums, 1700–1789*, Göttingen, 1791.
Bell, John, *Travels from St. Petersburg in Russia to diverse parts of Asia*, 2 vols., Glasgow, 1763.
Bentham, Samuel: see Walther Kirchner.
Benyowski, Mauritius Augustus de, *Memoirs and Travels*, London, 1904.
Berg, L. S., *Ocherki po istorii russkikh geograficheskikh otkrytii*, Moscow, 1946.
Billings, Joseph, *Account of a geographical . . . Expedition to the Northern Parts of Russia. In the years 1785 to 1794*, ed. by Martin Sauer, London, 1802.
Bogdanov, Modest, *Uebersicht der Reisen und natur-historischen Untersuchungen im Aralo-Kaspi-Gebiet, . . . 1720 bis . . . 1784*, *Russische Revue*, VIII (1876).
Cahen, Gaston, *Les cartes de la Sibérie au XVIIIe siècle*, (*Nouvelles Archives des Missions scientifiques*, N.S.T.1), Paris, 1911.
──────, *Histoire des relations de la Russie avec la Chine 1689–1730*, Paris, 1941.

Chappe d'Auteroche, *A Journey into Siberia . . . in 1761*, London, 1770 (French edition: *Voyage en Sibérie . . . 1761*, 4 vols., Paris, 1768).
Chteniia v imperatorskom obshchestve istorii . . . pri Moskovskom Universitete, III (1866).
Cochrane, John D., *Narrative of a Pedestrian Journey through Russia and Siberian Tartary*, London, 1824.
Cook: *The Voyages of Captain James Cook round the World*, London, 1813.
Cox, Edward G., *A Reference Guide to the Literature of Travel*, 3 vols., Washington, 1935.
Coxe, William, *Account of the Russian Discoveries between Asia and America*, London, 1780.
Cross, Anthony G., "An Oxford Don in Catherine the Great's Russia", *Journal of European Studies*, X (1971).
Culin, Stewart, "Across Siberia in the Dragon Year of 1796", *Asia*, XX (1920).
Dalton, Hermann, *Geschichte der reformierten Kirche in Russland*, Gotha, 1865.
Danilevsky, Viktor V., *I. I. Polzunov, Trudy i zhizn*, Leningrad, 1940.
Davydov: *Reise der russ.-kaiserl. Flott Offiziere Chwostow und Dawydow von St. Petersburg durch Sibirien nach Amerika und zurück in den Jahren 1802, 1803 und 1804*, Berlin, 1816.
De l'Isle, Nicholas, *Explication de la carte des . . . découvertes au Nord de la Mer du Sud*, Paris, 1752.
Dictionnaire historique et biographique de la Suisse, III (Neuchatel, 1926).
Dobell, Peter, *Travels in Kamtchatka and Siberia*, 2 vols., London, 1830.
Du Halde, P., *The General History of China*, 4 vols., London, 1741.
D'Wolf, John, *A Voyage to the North Pacific and a Journey through Siberia*, Cambridge, 1861.
Eckel, Paul E., *The Far East since 1500*, New York, 1947.
Egli, J. J., "[Fries]", *Zeitschrift für wissenschaftliche Geographie*, III, pts. 3 and 4 (1882).
Engel, Samuel, *Mémoires et observations géographiques et critiques sur . . . pays septentrionaux*, Lausanne, 1765.
Erdmann, Johann Friedrich, *Reisen im Innern Russlands*, pts. 1-2, Leipzig, 1825-26.
Erman, Adolph, *Travels in Siberia*, 2 vols., Philadelphia, 1850.
Etterlin, Jakob, *Russlandschweizer und das Ende ihrer Wirksamkeit*, Zürich, Leipzig, 1938.
Fabry, Abbé de, *Mémoires de mon Emigration* (Société de l'histoire de France, No. 66), Paris, 1933.
Falk, Johann Peter, *Beyträge zur topographischen Kenntniss des russischen Reichs*, 3 vols., St. Petersburg, 1785-1786.
Fechner, A. W., *Chronik der evangelischen Gemeinden in Moskau*, 2 vols., Moscow, 1876.
Fischer, Johann Eberhard, *Sibirische Geschichte*, 2 vols., St. Petersburg, 1768.
Fisher, Raymond H., *The Russian Fur Trade* (University of California publications in history, XXXI), Berkeley, 1943.

Fick, Heinrich, "Unterthänigste Vorstellung . . . in Nord-Syberien . . . unterworffenen . . . völcker . . .", Tartu Uelikooli Toimetused [Dorpat University] ed., *Acta et Commentationes*, B Humaniora, XVII (1930).
Foust, Clifford M., *Muscovite and Mandarin, Russia's Trade with China* . . . *1727–1805*, Chapel Hill, 1969.
Gaissinovitch, A., *La révolte de Pougatchev*, Paris, 1938.
Georgi, Johann Gottlieb, *Beschreibung aller Nationen des russischen Reiches*, St. Petersburg, 1776–1780 (English edition: *Russia, a . . . Historical Account of all the Nations which comprise that Empire*, 4 vols., transl. by Wm. Tooke, London, 1780–83).
——————————, *Geographisch-physikalische und naturhistorische Beschreibung des russischen Reiches*, 3 vols. in 6, Königsberg, 1796–1802.
Gibson, James R., *Feeding the Russian Fur Trade* . . . *1639–1856*, Madison, 1969.
Gmelin, Johann Georg, *Reise durch Sibirien 1733–1743*, 4 vols., Göttingen, 1751–1752.
Golder, Frank A., *Russian Expansion on the Pacific*, Cleveland, 1914.
——————————, ed., *Bering's Voyages*, 2 vols., New York, 1922–1925.
Gromov, Prokopii, *Nachalo christianstva v Irkutske*, Irkutsk, 1868.
Gromyko, Marina M., *Zapadnaia Sibir v XVIII veke*, Novosibirsk, 1965.
Hämäläinen, Albert, "Nachrichten der nach Sibirien verschickten Offiziere Karls XII . . .", Suomalais-ugrilainen seura, *Aikakauskirja* (*Journal* de la Soc. finno-ugrienne), XLIX (1938).
Hansteen, Christoph, *Reise-Erinnerungen aus Sibirien*, Leipzig, 1854.
Harris, John, *A complete collection of Voyages and Travels*, 2 vols., London, 1744–1748.
Haven, Peter von, *Reise in Russland*, Copenhagen, 1745.
Hedenström, M., *Otryvki o Sibiri*, St. Petersburg, 1850.
Hennin, George W. von, *Opisanie Uralskikh i Sibirskikh Zavodov*, *1735*, ed. by M. A. Pavlov, Moscow, 1937.
Henning, Georg. *Die Reiseberichte über Sibirien von Herberstein bis Ides* (Mitteilungen des Vereins für Erdkunde zu Leipzig), Leipzig, 1905.
Holman, James, *Travels through Russia, Siberia, Poland, Austria, Saxony, Prussia, Hanover* . . . *1822, 1823 and 1824 while suffering from total blindness*, 2 vols., London, 1825.
Hug, A., [Fries], *Neue Zürcher Zeitung* (Feuilleton, Nos. 66–73), March 7–14, 1882.
Ides, E. Ysbrants, *Driejaarige Reize naar China*, Amsterdam, 1710 (English edition: *Three Years Travels from Moscow . . . to China*, London, 1706).
Istoriia Sibiri ed. by A. P. Okladnikov, V. I. Shunkov *et als.*, II (Leningrad, 1968).
Kabo, Rafail M., *Goroda zapadnoi Sibiri*, Moscow, 1949.
Kennan, George, *Siberia and the Exile System*, 2 vols., New York, 1891.
Kerner, Robert J., *Northeastern Asia*, 2 vols., Berkeley, 1939.
——————————, *Urge to the Sea*, Berkeley, 1946.

BIBLIOGRAPHY 171

Kirchner, Walther, "The Death of Catherine I of Russia", *American Historical Review*, LI (1946).
————, "Emigration to Russia", *American Historical Review*, LV (1950).
————, "Samuel Bentham and Siberia", *Slavonic and East European Review*, XXXVI (1958).
————, "Zur Geschichte der Pest in Europa: Ihr letztes Auftreten im russischen Heer", *Saeculum*, XX (1969); "The Black Death ... 18th Century ...", *Clinical Pediatrics*, VII (1968).
Kisak Tamai, *Karawanen-Reise in Sibirien*, Berlin, 1898.
Klaproth, Julius Heinrich von, *Reise durch Russland und Sibirien*, Tübingen, 1815.
Kopylov, A. N., *Kultura russkogo naseleniia Sibiri v XVII-XVIII vv.*, Novosibirsk, 1968.
Kotzebue, August von, *Das merkwürdigste Jahr meines Lebens*, 2 vols., 1801 (English edition, London, 1802).
Krasheninnikov, Stepan Petr, *Opisanie zemli Kamchatki*, St. Petersburg, 1755 (English edition: *History of Kamtchatka ...*, transl. by James Grieve, London, 1764).
Kubalski, N. A., *Voyages en Sibérie*, Tours, 1853.
[Lange, Laurent], ["Reise"], *Neue Nordische Beyträge*, II (St. Petersburg-Leipzig, 1781) (English translation by John Bell, *A Journal from St. Petersburg ... to Pekin ... 1719*, Glasgow, 1763).
Langsdorff, Georg von, *Voyages and Travels ..., 1803-1807*, Carlisle, 1817.
Lantzeff, George V., *Siberia in the seventeenth century*, (University of California publications in history, XXX), Berkeley, 1943.
Lavater Slomann, M., *Catharina II*, Zürich, 1941.
Laxmann, M. Erich, *Sibirische Briefe*, ed. by August Ludwig Schlözer, Göttingen-Gotha, 1769.
Lebedev, D. M., *Ocherki po istorii geografii v Rossii XVIII v.*, Moscow, 1957.
Leimbach, Werner, *Die Sowjetunion*, Stuttgart, 1950.
Lensen, George A., *The Russian Push toward Japan: Russo-Japanese Relations, 1697-1875*, Princeton, 1959.
Lepekhin, Ivan, *Tagebuch der Reise durch verschiedene Provinzen des russischen Reiches*, transl. by Chr. H. Hase, 3 vols., Altenburg, 1774-1783.
Lesseps, Jean Baptiste Barthélémy de, *Journal historique du voyage de M. de Lesseps*, 2 vols., Paris, 1790.
Lobanov-Rostovsky, Andre, *Russia and Asia*, New York, 1933.
Malinowsky, Joseph A., *Die Planerkolonien am Asowschen Meer*, Stuttgart, 1928.
Martynov, Andrei Efim., *Zhivopisnoe puteshestvie ot Moskvy do Kitaiskoi granitsy*, St. Petersburg, 1819.
Masterson, James R. and Helen Brower, *Bering's Successors, 1745-1780*, Washington, 1948.
[Messerschmidt] "Nachricht von D. G. Messerschmidts siebenjähriger Reise in Sibirien", *Neue Nordische Beyträge*, III (1782).
D. G. Messerschmidt: *Forschungsreise durch Sibirien, 1720-1727*

(Quellen und Studien zur Geschichte Osteuropas, VIII), ed. by Eduard Winter, N. A. Figurovsky, G. Jarosch *et als.*, 4 vols., Berlin, 1962–1968.

Meusel, Johann Georg, ed., "Beschreibung der Buräten", *Beyträge zur Erweiterung der Geschichtskunde,* 2 vols., Augsburg, I (1780–1781).

Mezhov, Vladimir I., *Sibirskaia bibliografiia,* 2 parts, St. Petersburg, 1891.

Mirsoev, V. G., *Istoriografiia Sibiri (XVIII v),* Kemerovskoe knizhnoe izd., 1963.

————, *Istoriografiia Sibiri, Pervaia polovina XIX veka,* 1965.

Modsalevsky, Boris L., *Spisok Chlenov Imp. Akad. Nauk, 1725–1907,* St. Petersburg, 1908.

Morse, Hosea B., *The Trade and Administration of the Chinese Empire,* New York, 1908.

[Mueller] "Akademiki Mueller i Fischer i opisanie Sibiri", *Chteniia v Imp. Obshchestve . . . pri Moskovskom universitete,* III (1866).

Müller, Gerhard Friedrich, *Sammlung russischer Geschichte,* 9 vols., St. Petersburg, 1732–1764.

————, *Voyages from Asia to America,* transl. by S. Müller, London, 1761.

[Müller, Johann Bernhard] *Johann Bernhard Müllers . . . Leben . . . der Ostiaken,* Berlin, 1720.

Munro, Wilfred H., *Tales of an old Sea Port,* Princeton, 1917.

Nerhood, Harry W., *To Russia and Return,* Ohio State University, 1968.

Neue Nordische Beyträge, 7 vols., St. Petersburg-Leipzig, 1781–1796.

Nolde, Boris, *La formation de l'Empire russe,* 2 vols., Paris, 1952–1953.

Okun, Semen B., *Rossiisko-amerikanskaia kompaniia,* Moscow, 1939 (English edition: *The Russian American Company,* Cambridge, 1951).

Pallas, Peter Simon, *Reise durch verschiedene Provinzen des russischen Reiches,* 3 vols.; St. Petersburg, 1773-1776.

Pamiatniki sibirskoi istorii 18 veka, 2 parts, St. Petersburg, 1882–1885.

Parkinson, John, *A Tour of Russia, Siberia and the Crimea, 1792–1794,* ed. by William Collier, Frank Cass, London, 1971.

Patrin, A. M., ["Reisebericht"], *Neue Nordische Beyträge,* IV (1783).

Pavlovsky, Michel N., *Chinese-Russian Relations,* New York, 1949.

Philaret, *Geschichte der Kirche Russlands,* 2 vols., Frankfurt a.M., 1872.

Pisarevsky, Grigory, "Iz istorii inostrannoi kolonizatsii v Rossii v 18 v.", *Zapiski Moskovskago Arkheologicheskago Instituta,* V (1909).

Poppe, Nicholas, "Renat's Kalmuck Maps", *Imago Mundi,* XII (1955).

Portal, Roger, *L'Oural au 18e siècle,* Paris, 1950.

Raeff, Marc, *Siberia and the Reforms of 1822,* Seattle, 1956.

Recueil de Voyages au Nord, Amsterdam, X (1836).

Richter, Wilhelm Michael, *Geschichte der Medizin in Russland*, 3 vols., Moscow, 1813–1819.
Russische Bibliothek, I (St. Petersburg, 1772).
Rychkov, Nikolai, *Tagebuch über seine Reise durch verschiedene Provinzen des russischen Reichs, 1769–1771*, transl. by Christian Heinrich Hase, Riga, 1774.
Rychkov, Petr Ivanovich, *Topografiia Orenburgskoi gubernii 1762*, Orenburg, 1887.
[Sarychev] *Gawrila Sarytschew's achtjährige Reise im nordöstlichen Sibirien*, transl. by Johann Heinrich Busse, Leipzig, 1805 (English edition: *Account of a Voyage of Discovery to the North East of Siberia*, 2 vols., London, 1806).
Scherer, Johann Benedikt, *Georg Wilhelm Stellers Beschreibung von dem Lande Kamtschatka*, Frankfurt-Leipzig, 1774.
Schulthess, Erica von, "Ein Züricher Chirurgus im Reiche Katharinas II", pt. 1, *Neujahrsblatt der Hülfsgesellschaft in Zürich* (1955).
Scurla, Herbert, *Jenseits des steinernen Tores, Entdeckungsreisen deutscher Forscher durch Sibirien . . .*, Berlin, 1963.
Semionov, Youri, *La conquête de la Sibérie*, Paris, 1938 (German edition: *Sibirien. Eroberung und Erschliessung der wirtschaftlichen Schatzkammer des Ostens*, Berlin, 1954).
Shangin, Petr Ivan, [Reisebericht], *Neue Nordische Beyträge*, VI (1793).
Sievers, Johann, *Briefe aus Sibirien an seine Lehrer*, St. Petersburg, 1796.
Sparks, Jared, *Life of John Ledyard*, Cambridge, 1829.
Stählin, Karl, *Aus den Papieren Jacob von Stählins*, Leipzig, 1927.
Stejneger, Leonhard, *Georg Wilhelm Steller*, Cambridge, 1936.
Strahlenberg, Philipp Johann von, *Das Nord- und Ostliche Theil von Europa und Asia*, Stockholm, 1730 (English edition: *An Historico-Geographical Description of the North and Eastern Parts of Europe and Asia*, London, 1736).
Tooke, William, *View of the Russian Empire*, 3 vols., London, 1800.
Unverzagt, Georg Johann, *Die Gesandschafft . . . von Gross-Russland an den Sinesischen Käyser . . . 1719*, Lübeck, 1725.
Vagin, V., *Istoricheskie svedeniia o deiatelnosti grafa M. M. Speranskago v Sibiri 1819–1822*, 2 parts, St. Petersburg, 1872.
Van Stone, James W., "An Early Account of the Russian Discoveries in the North Pacific", *Anthropological Papers of the University of Alaska*, VII (1959).
Voyages en Sibérie, 2 vols., Bern, 1791.
Vrangel, Ferdinand P. [Wrangel], *Putechestvie po Severnim beregam Sibiri, 1820–1824 g*, 1948 (English edition: *Narrative on an Expedition to the Polar Sea . . .*, New York, 1841).
Wagner, Johann Ludwig, *Mémoires*, transl. from the German, Bern, 1790.
Waxell, Sven, *The American Expedition*, London, 1952 (A German edition: *Brücke nach Amerika*, Olten-Freiburg, 1968).
Weber, Friedrich Christian, *Nouveaux Mémoires sur l'état présent de la Grande Russie ou Moscovie*, Paris, 1725.

Winter, Eduard, *Halle als Ausgangspunkt der deutschen Russlandkunde*, Berlin, 1953.
────────── *et als.* eds., *Die Berliner und die Petersburger Akademie der Wissenschaften im Briefwechsel Leonhard Eulers*, 2 vols., Berlin, 1959–1961.
────────── *et als.* eds., *Die deutsch-russische Begegnung und Leonhard Euler*, Berlin, 1958.
Wreech, Curt Friedrich von, *Wahrhaffte . . . Historie von denen Schwedischen Gefangenen in Russland und Sibirien . . . nach . . . Pultawa*, Sorau, 1728.
Yefimov, A. V. [Efimov], *Iz istorii russkikh ekspeditsii na Tikhom Okeane, pervaia polovina XVIII v.*, Moscow, 1948.
Zentral Kommite der Unterstützungskasse für evangelisch-lutherische Gemeinden in Russland, part 2 (St. Petersburg, 1909).
Zinner, Ervin P., *Sibir v izvestiiakh zapadno evropeiskikh puteshestvennikov i uchenikh XVIII v.*, Vostochno Sibirskoe knizhnoe izd., 1968.

INDEX

Absem, 140
Abukuy, 125
Academy of Sciences, St. Petersburg, 19, 20-22, 24, 25, 27, 30, 31, 37, 40, 42, 44, 50.
Achinsk (Atschinskoy), 112, 138
Achlebishin, family of, 143
Achmetowoy, 94
Admiralty Hospital, 49, 150, 151
Africa, 28
Aftschinikowa, 107
Agyschywoy, 87
Ajaschansky, 107
Alaska, 34, 42, 43.
Albeste, 71, 84.
Albis, 121.
Alexander I, emperor, 5.
Alexiewsky, 94.
Alpnach, 162 n. 69.
Alsaminsky, 117.
Altai Mountains, 27, 34, 37, 40, 44.
America, 19, 33, 38, 39, 43, 45.
Amur, river, 27.
Angara, river, 14, 20, 22, 25, 28, 117, 118, 121, 122, 124, 136.
Anna, empress, 17.
Antoskynaja, Antowkino Simovie, 106
Appenzell, 77.
Aral Sea, 8
Areschkow, captain, 102.
Argis, river, 68, 71, 84
Arsamasa province, 87.
Asch, Egor Fedorovich von, 83.
Astrakhan, 30-32, 87, 145.
Astrakhan Carabineer Regiment, 67, 68, 73, 79, 83-85, 88.
Asurowoy, 95.
Avacha Bay, 22
Awsano *see* Absem

Bagdonov, Major, 111.

Baikal, Lake, 12-14, 24, 31, 34, 36, 39, 40, 44, 46, 47, 52, 106, 121-124, 136.
Bakofen, 153
Balachna, 85, 87-90, 142.
Balagansk, 12
Balanskoi (Baleyskowa), 117.
Baltic Sea, 4, 11
Baltimore, USA, 28.
Baraba (Barabinskaia) steppe, 14, 21, 36, 42, 106, 109.
Barakan, 99
Baranovskoi, 117.
Barnaul, 7, 27, 37, 39, 40, 139.
Bashkirs, 100, 140, 141
Baskowa, 121, 124.
Beckmann, Johann B., 28, 57 n. 64.
Bekulowoy, 95
Belaia (Biela), river (Europe), 32, 140, 141.
Belaia (Bielaja, Biola), river (Siberia), 118.
Belgium, 41
Belgorod (Bielgorod), 86
Bell, John, 12, 13.
Belojarsk, 26
Beloretsk (Biela Retskaja), 140, 141.
Bentham, Samuel, 37
Benyowski, Mauritius Aug. de, 10, 28, 59 n. 94.
Berdea, 96
Beregowoy, 124-127.
Berekul (Pilekul), 112
Berenovsk, 28.
Berens, doctor, 104, 139.
Beresewa, river, 117, 137.
Beresnago, 82.
Beresowa, 16, 99, 137.
Bering, Vitus, 6, 8, 11, 13, 17-22, 24, 33, 35, 38, 52.
Berkhan, painter, 8.
Berlad (Berlat), 71, 84.

175

Berlin, 24, 44, 46, 49.
Bern, 89, 91
Bernoulli, Daniel, 62, n. 145.
Beswodna, 90.
Bibikov, Alexander Ilich, 95.
Bielogory, 94.
Bielowolsk, 90.
Bieltsi (Belsa), 83.
Bielumsky, prince, 115.
Billings, Joseph, 38, 39.
Birjussa, see Beresewat
Bogaky, 86.
Bogojavlenskoe (Bogohowlensky),140, 141.
Bogorodize, 86.
Bogoruslansk (Bogoroslan), 142.
Bogotol (Bugatolsky), 112, 138.
Bokharans, 147, 148.
Bolsharesk, 18.
Bolshoi Kemsch (Great Kemsch), 112.
Bolshoi Skuratova, 82.
Boris Godunov, 161 n. 58.
Borissowka (Barisowka), 86.
Botanskoi (Botoy, Botojska), 117.
Boytowyz, 83.
Brachow, province, 74.
Braclav (Bratislav), province, 85.
Brand, pharmacist, 127, 133, 134.
Branyzky, 75.
Braunschweig, 10, 73.
Brazil, 28.
Breslau, 73.
Brikmann, Lt. Colonel, 77.
Brill, von, Governor, 36.
Bristol, R. J., 43.
Brovary (Prowarow), 82.
Brunner, Pastor, 81, 150.
Buache, 10, 22, 58 n. 73.
Bucharest, 67, 68, 71, 84.
Bug (Bog) river, 79, 83.
Bugulma, 95, 142.
Bulatowa (Ballotowaja), 107.
Bulgaria, 68, 84.
Buriats, 18, 36, 136, 137.
Burkhard, Hans Heinrich, 153.
Burmann, Fedor Petrovich, 82.
Busch, Henrik, 17.

California, 27.
Candis, 95.
Carpathian Mountains, 67.
Caspian Sea, 8, 32, 98, 101, 145.
Catherine II, empress, 32, 33, 114, 119, 152, 160 n. 56, 163 n. 75, 167 n. 107.
Chany, Lake, 108.
Chappe d'Auteroche, 26, 63, n. 157.
Cheleowa, 86.
Chernigov (Tschernigow), 82.
Chicharev (Schicharew), Ignatius, 142-149.
Chicherin, family, 143.
Chilgontin, plains, 124-126.
China, Chinese, 11-13, 17, 20, 24, 28, 34, 37, 40, 43, 44, 47, 48, 51, 96, 98, 106, 109, 118, 120-125, 127, 129-135, 146.
Chirikov, Aleksei, 18, 22.
Chrischttschowka, 142.
Chulim (Chulym, Tschulim), river, 112, 138.
Chunguiskoi, see Tyngulsky
Chuvashians, 146, 165 n. 96
Chvastov (Chwestowa), 83
Claver, General, 104, 139
Cochrane, John D., 45, 46
Connecticut, 38
Cook, James, 38, 39
Copenhagen, 42
Cosleste, 84
Coslobsky, 75
Cossacks, 69, 92, 93, 102, 125, 127

Danube, 68, 70, 71, 84, 85
Danzig, 13, 14
Davydov, Gavrilo Ivanovich, 42
Delisle de la Croyère, Joseph N., 21
Delisle de la Croyère, Louis, 10, 20-22
Delisle de la Croyère, Nicholas, 21, 22
Dembowitsch, river, 71, 84
Demidov, family, 26, 37, 140
Demshinsk (Deschina), 86
Deschinskaja, 112
Dessna, river, 82
Djungaria, 17
Dmitrophanowa, 140
Dnieper, river, 32, 78, 82, 85
Dniester, river, 74, 83, 85
Dobell, Peter, 44
Dolgowsky, 99
Don, 86
Driasgy (Dresgy), 86
Dubrowa Kargazkowa, 107
Dubrowina, 107
Dusmetowoy, 95
D'Wolf, John, 43, 53

Dymskoy, 95

Egypt, 39, 146
Ehrenberg, Gottfried, 46
Ekaterinburg, 26, 27, 31, 32, 38, 39, 42-44, 46, 52
Ekaterinskaja, 86
Elisabeth, empress, 17, 52, 161 n. 59
Elisabeth, fortress, 77-79, 85, 87
Endabeste, 86
England, 28, 33, 37, 45
Enisei (Jenisei), river, 14, 21, 22, 27, 29, 36, 40, 112, 115, 116, 123, 138
Eniseisk, 12-14, 18-20, 24
Erdmann, Johann Friedr., 44
Ermann, Adolph, 46, 47, 53
Euler, Leonhard, 48, 49, 122, 152
Eversmann, E., 46
Ewanewsky, 99

Fabruy, Abbé, 41
Fakina, 90
Falck, Johann Peter, 6, 10, 29-31
Fick, Heinrick, 16
Fischer, Johann Eberhard, 6, 9, 10, 23, 25
Fischer, Lieutenant, 103
Fluri, 81
Fokshani, 71, 84
France, 33, 39, 41, 151
Franchoneste, 84
Francke, A. H., 16
Freiburg, 43
Füssli, Johann Kaspar, 116, 151
Füssli (beym Schäfli), 95, 152

Gabriel, I. K. W., 161 n.64
Gabrilowa, 87
Gagarin, Matvei Petrovich, 62 n.157
Gagariowa, 99
Gagrin (Gagarin), Major, 125
Gariga, Major, 102
Gensurina, 135
Georgi, Johann Gottlieb, 6, 9, 27, 30, 31, 40
Germany, 33, 41, 48, 50, 75
Glarus, 81
Glasowa, 86
Gluchov, 82
Gmelin, D. Samuel, 30, 32
Gmelin, Johann Georg, 6, 8, 10, 13, 20-27, 29, 30, 46, 51
Golonsna, 136

Golovin, Count, 43, 44
Golz, doctor, 75
Göttingen, 42
Grocholsky, Baron von, 75
Güldenstädt, doctor, 152
Güldenstädt, Johann Anton, 30, 32

Halle, 14, 16
Haller, Albrecht von, 21, 24
Hamburg, 16, 120
Hannibal, family, 143
Hansteen, Christoph, 46, 47
Haven, Peter von, 26
Hedenström, M., 46
Heidelberg, 42
Heimann, belt-maker, 73, 144
Hennin, Wilhelm de, 25
Herberstein, Sigismund von, 4, 53
Hirzel, Ratsherr, 153
Holberg, Ludwig, 26
Holland, 29, 145
Holman, James, 45, 46
Horner, Pastor, 116, 121
Huebner, Pastor, 98, 142, 146, 148
Humboldt, Alexander von, 46

Iakutsk, 12, 17-20, 23-25, 28, 36, 38, 39, 43
Ides, Ysbrant, 4, 51
Igak, river, 140
Ignatiowa, 106
Ihrmann, Andrei Avr. Ritter von, 139
Ija (Jayi) river, 117, 136
Ilanskii, 117
Ilimsk, 12, 13, 15, 18-20, 28
Ilinskoi (Eliynskoy), 124, 136
Ilyeskoi Pustina, 90
Imeninowa, 94
India, 96, 101, 103, 146
Ingul, river, 77, 85
Irkutsk, 12-15, 17, 18, 20, 23, 24, 29, 36-47, 52, 106, 110, 116-121, 123, 124, 136
Irsym, river, 139
Irtysh, river, 12, 14, 18, 20, 29, 40, 44, 100, 104, 105, 107, 139
Isawoy, 95
Isberde, 86
Isbylez, 87
Ischymskowa, 138
Isets, province, 22, 30, 140
Ishim, river, 42, 99, 105
Italy, 121

INDEX

Itat, 112
Itkulsky, 107
Iwulga, 124
Izmailov, Lev Vasilevich, 5, 12, 13, 44

Jablonowa, 86
Jaik (Ural), river, 52, 95, 96, 98, 100, 140
Jakupowoy, 95
Jalomiz, river, 84
Jamburg, 150
Japan, 11, 19, 41, 43
Jarkaja, 99
Jassy, 71, 83, 84
Jayl, river, 138
Jefferson, Thomas, 38
Jegoriewa, 94
Jeleza, 83
Jelofskoie (Jalowsky), 117
Jemanschelinskaja, 99
Jepantschina, 86
Jerikly, 94
Jerseowa, 86
Jews, 72, 77
Johannes, Pater, 148
Juny, governor, 120
Jurga, 28
Jurminsky, 99

Kabanja (Kabanaya), 99
Kabanov, 94
Kabanskoy, 124, 136
Kagnarow, 83
Kainsk (Kaynskoy), 42, 46, 107, 108, 139
Kaldeowa, 112
Kalischnowa, 135
Kalmyks, 17, 18, 30, 44, 136, 147
Kalmuskowoy (Kolmatskoi Sim), 107
Kaluga, 149, 150
Kama, river, 32, 94
Kamchatka, 8-10, 17-19, 24, 25, 28, 38, 39, 44, 46
Kameltia (Kulmiteowa), 117
Kamensky, Mikhail Fedotovich, 88
Kamynskaja, 99
Kan, river, 117, 137
Kansk, 47, 117, 137, 138
Karabasch, 95
Karagalsky, 107
Karagayskaga, 99
Karagaytugaya, 98

Karagazky (Karganzky), 107, 139
Kargala, 96
Kashyr, 149
Kasimov, 149
Kazan, 12, 30, 39, 42, 43, 87, 89-91, 93-96, 142, 146
Ket, river, 18
Khvostov, 42
Kiev, 82, 93
Kija (Kia), 112, 113, 138
Kija, river, 113, 138
Kinel, river, 142, 143, 146
Kirgizh, 18, 41, 98, 101, 102, 148
Kirgizh steppe, 32, 40, 96
Kisak Tamai, 41
Kitat, river, 138
Kitayzkoy, 118, 136
Kitoy (Kitay), river, 117, 118, 136
Kitschujewsk (Kutschuewsky), 94
Kjakhta (Kiakhta), 24, 27, 37, 40, 42, 44, 47, 52, 127, 131, 133-136, 138
Klaproth, Julius Heinrich von, 44
Klin, 81
Klutschy, 117, 135
Klyonaja, 112
Kodiak Islands, 39, 42
Kolokowky, 99
Kolyvan district, 6, 20, 27, 29, 30, 37, 39, 47
Königsberg, 46, 48
Kopec, Joseph, 10
Korasiwoy, 107
Korocha, 86
Korolevech (Krolewza), 82
Koseletz (Kaselza), 82
Kosmodemianski, 90
Kottuschinowa, 94
Kotzebue, August von, 28, 41
Koylskaja, 99
Koytskaja-Iatkulskaja, 99
Kozino (Kosina), 87, 89
Kozlow (Coslow), 86
Krasheninnikov, Stepan, 5, 9, 20, 23, 25, 26
Krasnaretzkaja, 112
Krasnojara, 106
Krasnojarsk (Krasnoiarsk), 14, 15, 20-24, 28, 29, 31, 37, 39, 40, 42-47, 52, 106, 112, 114-118, 123, 138
Krasnostobodskoy, 149
Krechetnikov, Mikhail Nikitov, 149
Kremenchug (Krimentschuk), 85, 87
Kromy (Kromach), 82

Kropotov, ambassador, 163 n.75
Krukow (Kriukov), 85
Krusenstern, Admiral, 41, 42
Krutik-Loschkow (Kroutija), 107
Kuktur, 140
Kululizkowa, 118
Kuntui (Kuytunsky), 117
Kurgan, 41
Kurganskoy, 100
Kurtamischewsky, 99
Kurtschawoy, 99
Kusankiny, 94
Kuskun, 117
Kusnikow, 90
Kusowlewe, 86
Kusulbaschen, 147
Kutlimetowoy, 95
Kutsnetsk, 14, 20

Lagschansky, 86
Lange, Lorenz, 13
Lange, Pastor, 120
Langsdorff, Georg von, 42, 43, 53
Lavater, Johann Kaspar, 150
Laxmann, Erik, 25, 27, 28
Lebjaschia (Lebeschuia), 100
Ledyard, John, 38, 39
Leipzig, 48
Lemke, farrier, 73
Lena, river, 14, 20, 28, 36, 38, 39, 42, 43, 152
Lepekhin, Ivan, 6, 8, 10, 30-32
Lepowky, 83
Lerche, State Councillor, 17
Lesseps, Jean Baptiste B. de, 39, 53
Lesunowa, 87
Lindenau, Jakob, 6, 25
Linnaeus, Karl von, 28, 30, 31
Lipovech (Lipowka), 83
Lipowschiwa, 135
Lischwinischowa (Liswinischneja), 121, 124, 136
Livonia, 16
Lomonosov, 9
London, 29
Lopasne Pachra, 81
Lopuchin, Natalie, 114
Losowoy, 100
Lukotinsky, 106
Luky, 136
Lürsenius, 8
Luther, G., 104, 139

Macao, 28
Madagaskar, 28
Maimatschin (Maymatschin), 47, 52, 127, 133, 134
Malokemtschug, 112
Mangazea, 27
Mansurov, Pavel Dimitrevich, 96, 141, 148-150
Mansurowa, 99
Martini, Alex Philipp, 25
Martiny (Taben), 70, 84
Martynov, Andrei Efimovich, 44
Masalowa, 138
Mechelmann (married Fries), 49
Medweschoy, 100
Meissner, saddler, 73
Melnischnoy, 100
Memmingen, 98
Menshikov, Alexander Danilovich, 102
Meshcherskii, Alexei, 70, 73, 79, 156, n.8, 167 n.107
Meshcherskii, Platon Stepanovich, 91, 93
Mesmer, Pastor, 77
Messerschmidt, Daniel Amadeus, 6, 8, 13-15, 24, 27
Michelson, Ivan Ivanovich, 93, 157 n.27
Minschoy Skuratova (Skuratow), 82
Mitkevich, Mikhail, Archbishop, 162 n.66
Mjena (Mony), 82
Moldavia, 71, 72, 74, 83
Mongolia, Mongols, 14, 18, 51, 122, 123, 125, 126, 133
Montpelier, 109
Mordva (Mordvinians), 146
Morosowsky, 83
Moscow, 13, 16, 20, 23, 30, 31, 36, 39, 43, 44, 46, 49, 50, 81, 84, 94, 150
Motowylowsky, 83
Müller, Gerhard Friedrich, 5, 6, 8-10, 17, 20, 22, 23, 25
Müller, Johann Bernhard, 16
Müller, Subchirurgus, 83
Mustasanoy, 95
Myndak, river, 140
Mzarskoi (Samsorsky), 117
Mzensk (Amtchemsky), 82

Nalabardin, Major, 127, 134
Narva, 150

INDEX

Narym, river, 12, 18, 24
Naryshkina, 87
Nayrasowoy, 95
Nemirov (Niemirow), 74, 83
Nemtsev, Fedor Glebovich, 118
Nerchinsk, 14, 20, 27, 37, 114
New Servia, 77, 85
Nicolskoy, 106
Nikitinskoy, 98
Nikolskaja, 100
Nikolsky, 121, 124
Nile, river, 39
Nilov, Governor, 28
Nizhni Novgorod (Nischynowograd), 79, 85, 90, 142
Nor Saysan, 101
Novgorod (Nowogorod), 51, 81, 150
Nürnberg, 72
Nygoste, monastery, 84
Nystad, peace of, 14-16

Ob, river, 12, 18, 35, 107-109, 139
Obolonaja, 82
Obrescha, 83
Obreskow, Colonel, 67, 83
Oeri, 87
Oka (Occa), river in European Russia, 81, 82, 87, 90, 149
Oka (Occa), Siberian river, 117, 136
Okhotsk, 8, 17-19, 25, 28, 36, 39, 43
Oluschewsky, 82
Olviopol (Olchakov), 79
Om, river, 28, 104, 107, 139
Omsk, 30, 44-46, 52, 98, 100, 103-107, 139, 140
Orel, 82
Orenburg, 25, 27, 30-32, 49, 52, 88, 94-96, 98-100, 105, 140-143, 146-149
Orenburg Line, 98, 101, 102
Orlov, family, 144
Orol, 82
Orongoi (Rangoy), 125
Orskogoboru (Orskoi Bor), 107
Osinoy (Ossinowi) Kolkow, 107
Ostiaks, 16, 18
Oxford, 40

Pallas, Simon, 6, 8-10, 26, 28-33, 37, 38, 40, 46, 51, 52, 131, 152
Paris, 38, 44
Parkinson, John, 40
Patrin, A. M., 37
Paul I, emperor, 41, 42, 62 n.148

Pavlovo (Pawlowa), 87
Pechora, 83
Peking, 12, 13, 43, 110, 120, 121, 133, 163 n.75
Penki (Penkowa), 87
Penza (Pense), 143
Pereslav Resansky, 149
Perieschnaja, 124
Perieschnaja, river, 125
Pérouse, Jean François Comte de la, 39
Perret, Major, 71
Perscherna, 86
Persia, 11, 96, 101, 146, 147
Peshchanoe (Peschtschanoy), 99
Peskowatny, 86
Peter I, emperor, 4, 5, 11, 13-16, 18, 33, 52, 62 n.157, 86, 156 n.16, 160 n.56, 161 n.59
Peterhof, 153
St. Petersburg, 13, 14, 16, 18-25, 29-31, 38-41, 43, 44, 49, 53, 81, 94, 105, 114, 120, 149, 150, 152
Petropavlovsk (Petri Pauli), 38, 99, 102, 103, 105, 139, 140
Peutling (Beutling), Lt. Col., 100
Philippines, 60 n.114
Pillau, 27
Pitgesky, 75
Plenisner, draftsman, 8
Ploskowoy, 100
Pojam, creek, 117
Pokrovka (Pokrowskaja), 100, 106
Poland, 74, 75-77, 83, 85
Poldynaja, 100
Polowinnowa, 124, 136
Poltava (Pultawa), 15, 16, 85, 86
Polzunov, I. I., 164 n.87
Pomerania, 31
Poniatowski, Count (Boniatowsky), 75
Ponts, surgeon, 149
Portugal, 42
Poselskoy, 136
Posolsky, monastery, 23, 124, 136
Potapov, Ivan Alekseevich, 86
Potemkin, Count Grigorij Alex., 156 n.14
Potsdam, 48
Presnogorkovsk, 99, 101, 105, 139, 140
Presnogorkowskaja, fortress, 99
Presno Ibanowoy, 99

INDEX

Presnowskaja, 99
Pretschistinskaja, 98
Priballotnoy, 99
Protoschynoy, 99
Prussia, 27, 103
Prut, river, 71, 83, 84
Pskov (Pleskau), 51, 149, 150
Ptyzowa, 99
Pugachev (Pugatschew), 91-93, 95, 96, 98, 100-102, 165 n.93
Pushkin, family, 143

Ragusinskii, Sava Vladislavich, 44, 56 n.47
Regnier, 36
Reinsdorp, Ivan Andreevich von, 96, 148
Renat, Johannes Gustav, 17, 55 n.27
Rentgen, 151
Retschkylowy, 99
Rezanov, Nicholas P. von, 43
Riala, river, 136
Riedel, Major, 49, 52, 53, 73, 79, 88, 89, 108, 119, 123, 125-127, 130, 133, 139, 141, 142
Riga, 32
Roder, teacher, and wife, 91-94, 146
Roeslein, doctor, 142, 148, 149
Romanov, 67, 81, 83
Romanowsky, 83
Rose, Gustav, 46
Rumiantsev, Count Peter Alex. (Zadunaiskii), 68, 82, 83, 155 n.2, 4, 14
Rushchuk (Rostik, Roschttschuk), 70, 71, 84, 85
Russian-American Company, 6, 34, 42
Rybinskoi (Ribna), 117
Rychkov, Nicolai, 8, 30, 32
Rychkov, Peter Ivanovich, 6, 27

Sakmara, 95, 96, 98
Sakmara, river, 52, 96, 98, 100
Sakretsky, Lt. Col., 73
Salairskaja (Salayskoy), 100
Salarizkowa, 140
Samara, town and river, 30, 143-145
Samoieds, 18
Sanden, doctor, 148
Sarabsk, 149
Saratov, 30, 31
Sareiow, 86

Sareysky (Zaraisk), 149
Sarmanowoy, 95
Sarona, 74
Sarychev, Gavriil Andreevich, 6, 39
Sassovo, 87
Sauer, Martin, 38
Sawode, 82
Sayan Mountains, 106, 116, 139
Schabordinsky, 117
Schaden, professor, 36
Schaffhausen, 83
von Schenk, Major, 73, 77
Scherer, Johann Benedikt, 10
Schiwotna, 86
Schlözer, August Ludwig, 17, 28, 57 n.64
Schmidt, surgeon, 73, 77
Schnitscher, Johann Christian, 17
Schober, Gottlob, 17
Scholta, 95
Schyrogulsky (Charagousskoi), 117
Sektinsky, 107
Selayr, river, 100
Selayrskaja (Salayskoy), 99
Seldeowa, 112
Selenga, river, 36, 111, 123, 125, 135
Selenginsk, 12, 13, 27, 37, 47, 52, 123-125, 127, 135
Semiluschkowa, 112
Semipolok, 82
Serebezkaia, 107
Sergievsk (Sargiowsky), 142
Sergiewsky, 82
Serpuchov, 81, 149
Serret, river, 84
Shadrinsk, 42
Shangin, 37
Shatsk, 87
Sheremetev, Peter Borisovich, 87
Sievers, Jakob Johann, 150
Sievers, Johann, 40, 44
Sievsk (Siewsky), 82
Simbirsk, 29, 31
Siminskoi, 117, 136
Sinjucha (Sinucha), river, 77, 85
Sinsarskoy, 99
Skalon (Skolon), general, 103, 107, 139
Skaminskoy, 98
Skelmersdale, Lord, 40
Skobliny (Skablinoy), 105, 140
Skopinoy, 99
Skorodea, 87
Skowsky, 117

Skvira (Skwyry), 83
Sok, river, 142, 143
Soksowa, 87
Solikamsk, 12, 16, 52
Solothurn, 71
Solowa, 82
Soltikov (Saltikov), Ivan Petrovich, 67, 68, 84, 155 n.2
Soroki (Sarocca), 83, 85
Sosnitsa (Sosniza), 82
Sotnikowa (Soltikowa), 136
Spanberg, 18, 19
Spener, Philipp, 16
Speransky, Mikhail Mikhailovich, 36, 47, 159 n.44
Spichiny (Spylschynez), 83
Springer, general, 105
Stachina, 90
Stadinez, 90
Stählin, Jacob von, 55 n.40, 158 n.41
Stanawaja, 99
Starago Okola (Staroi Oskol), 86
Stavropol, 149
Stavropol, province, 143
Steller, Georg, 5, 6, 10, 13, 19, 20, 22-25, 29
Stepnaja (Stepnoy), 124, 136
Stettin, 49
Strahlenberg, Philipp Johann von, 14, 15
Strassburg, 31
Stucha, 86, 87
Stupina, 86
Stupishin, A. A., Colonel, 90, 101
Suchaborsky, 99
Sukotin, family, 143
Sumarokov, general, 103
Sumka, 90
Suslowo (Saslowa), 112
Suvorov (Suvarov), general, 155 n.3
Suzdal, 51
Sviask, 90
Sweden, Swedes, 11, 15, 18, 19, 33, 86
Switzerland, Swiss, 48, 50, 75, 79, 121, 152

Tabbert *see* Strahlenberg
Tabor, 83
Tabynsk, 140, 141
Taischichina (Daschinsky), 136
Tambov, 142, 143
Tanalyk, 99
Taptilowa, 86

Tara, 12-14, 19, 24, 30, 37, 47
Tarakanowa, 124, 136
Targowice, 77, 85
Tartars (Tatars), 18, 51, 76, 93, 95, 96, 98, 141, 146
Tartas, 106
Tascharinsky, 107-109, 139
Tatuskowa (Tatulskowa), 117, 136
Tekeli (Teggeli), Peter Avramovich, 76
Temnikov, 149
Tengusowa, 87
Thiele, surgeon, 160 n.53
Thomaspol, 83
Tiumen, 12, 22, 26, 30, 32
Tobler, surgeon, 77
Tobol, river, 29, 98, 99
Tobolsk, 12-21, 23, 26-30, 37-47, 105-107, 117
Tom, river, 29, 107, 109, 138
Tomsk, 12-15, 19-22, 24, 28, 30, 31, 37-40, 42, 43, 45-47, 52, 106, 109-112, 138, 139
Torschok, 81, 150
Troitsa, 12
Troitskoy, 135
Tsaritsyn, 30, 31
Tschemera, 82
Tscherewatowa, 87
Tschernewa, 87
Tschernoy (Outchernoi retchin), 107
Tschernoy Reka, 112
Tscherumkowa, 118
Tscherumshan, river, 146
Tscheus, river, 107
Tscheuskoy, 107-109, 139
Tschikoy, 124, 125
Tschistoy, 100
Tschotowa, 87
Tschubachshary, 90
Tschulim *see* Chulim
Tschuwaschen, *see* Chuvashians
Tübingen, 10, 20, 21, 25
Tukuy, 140
Tula, 82
Tuligow, 82
Tulkischinowa, 94
Tulskoy Pachra, 81
Tulun, 117, 136
Tungus, 18
Turca Formasa, 83, 84
Turkey, Turks, 49, 51, 68-72, 74, 78, 84, 85
Turminsky, 99

INDEX

Turtukai (Tutukey), 68
Turunku, 106
Turunteiowa (Turnateiowa), 112, 138
Tver (Twer), 51, 81, 150
Tverdishev, Ivan Borisovich, 140
Twerdaschowa, 99
Tyngulsky, 117

Ubuy, 107
Uda, river, 117, 137
Udinsk, 45, 117, 135, 137
Ufim Desert, 141
Ui (Uj) river, 98
Ukowsky, 117
Ukraine, 82
Umtschuk, 140
Unkowski, Johann, 18
Unverzagt, Georg Johann, 12, 13
Ural river *see* Jaik
Urals, 12, 14, 16, 20-22, 25-27, 29, 32, 34, 39, 44, 48, 51, 52, 98, 100, 140, 141, 145
Urinsky, 117
Usmanowoy, 95
Ustarskoy, 106
Ustjug Velikii, 49
Ust-Kamenogorsk, 44
Ust-Kut, 19
Uyskaja (Uisk), 99

Vasilkov (Wasilkowa), 83
Velikopolsky, Major, 103
Verchne Omsk, 106
Verchne Uralsk, 52, 99, 101, 140, 141
Verkhoture, 12, 32, 52
Versailles, 39
Viatka, 12, 30
Vienna, 41
Villeneuve, de, Colonel, 109
Vioménil, de, 41

Vishny Volochok (Wischny Wolotschok), 81, 150
Volga, 29-32, 79, 85, 87, 90, 111, 141, 142, 144-146
Vologda, 18, 49, 50
Voronets (Worones), 86, 142, 143
Vorontsov, family, 143
Voznesenski (Vozdvizhensk), 52, 106, 139
Vrangel, F. P. (Wrangel), 46
Vynnycia (Winize), 74, 85

Wagner, Johann Ludwig, 27
Waldey (Valdai), 81
Wallachia, 67, 71, 72, 81, 84
Warichinoy, 107
Warlomoy, 99
Waxell, Sven, 19
Weimar, 41
Werdmüller, 151
Werner, Conductor, 144
Westphalia, 22
Windheim, 24
Wittneben, A. Chr., 157 n.32
Wlason (Vlason), Major, 124
Woltschiwoy, 100
Woronowitse, 85
Woschen, 82
Wosnesenskaja, 98
Wreech, Curt Friedrich von, 16
Wusley, 99

Zalari (Solorizkowa), 118
Zaporog (Soporoser) Cossacks, 49, 76, 79
Zebanka, 98
Zimanskowa *see* Siminskoi
Zubert, doctor, 84
Zuev (Sujef), Vassili Fedorovich, 6, 58 n.88
Zürich, 48, 50, 51, 87, 89, 142, 151-153